GOLDEN BOY

PAUL HORNUNG

As told to William F. Reed

SIMON & SCHUSTER

NEW YORK   LONDON   TORONTO   SYDNEY

SIMON & SCHUSTER
Rockefeller Center
1230 Avenue of the Americas
New York, NY 10020

For information about special discounts for bulk purchases,
please contact Simon & Schuster Special Sales at
1-800-456-6798 or business@simonandschuster.com

Designed by Julie Schroeder

Manufactured in the United States of America

2   4   6   8   10   9   7   5   3   1

Library of Congress control number 2004056520

ISBN 0-7432-6619-6

Contents

6007

To Dick Schaap, the all-time number one fan and
friend of Lombardi's Green Bay Packers

GOLDEN BOY

Foreword

Almost forty years after he played his final game for the Green
Bay Packers, Paul Hornung remains an American original, an
icon who's still recognized as the "Golden Boy" whenever the
legends of the game are discussed. He's still the only player to
win college football's Heisman Trophy while playing on a losing
team (Notre Dame, 1956) and he still owns the National Football League record for most points in a season (176 in 1960).

Beyond that, however, Hornung symbolizes a bygone era
when many athletes played as hard off the field as on it. He freely
admits that he and wide receiver Max McGee led the Packers,
and maybe the NFL, in chasing women, hanging out in bars and
nightclubs, and generally trying to circumvent the strict rules of
Vince Lombardi, the team's larger-than-life coach.

Their extracurricular exploits often went unreported, of
course, because the sports media of the 1950s and '60s adhered
to the philosophy that the personal life of an athlete or coach was

off-limits, unless it was so serious that addressing it was unavoidable. Such was Hornung's plight in 1963, when the NFL caught him gambling on the Packers to win and suspended him, along with Alex Karras of Detroit, for the entire season.

To this day, Hornung ranks as one of the most versatile players in NFL history, as well as one of the league's greatest clutch players. When the Packers got inside the opponents' twenty-yard line, they were in Hornung country. He could score by running, passing, or kicking a field goal.

It was inevitable that Hornung's life after football would revolve mainly around radio and television. He was the most glib and quotable of the Lombardi Packers, an outgoing sort who enjoyed dealing with the media instead of dreading it. Over the years, Hornung has earned far more from radio and TV, along with some shrewd business investments and commercial endorsements, than he ever made as a player.

But beyond the glitz and the glamour—Hornung hung out with the fast-lane crowd in Hollywood and once almost quit football to pursue a movie career—Hornung was, essentially, a football player. He's most at home with ex-teammates and opponents, talking about the game and sharing memories of what the Golden Boy calls the NFL's "golden era."

Mostly, he loves to talk about Lombardi.

On April 20, 2004, Hornung flew to Madison, Wisconsin, to pick the brains of three former teammates about material that he wanted to include in this book. His chartered jet stopped in Detroit to pick up Ron Kramer, the tight end who remains one of Hornung's closest pals. Or, as Hornung says, "It's the same now as it was then—to get to me, you've got to go through Ron Kramer."

Then it was on to Madison to hook up with Jerry Kramer (no

relation to Ron), the introspective offensive guard who teamed with writer Dick Schaap to produce *Instant Replay*, a national best-seller about the Packers' 1967 season. Kramer, who lives in his native Idaho, was in Madison to give a speech on behalf of Buckets for Hunger, a statewide charity in Wisconsin.

The fourth member of the group, Max McGee, flew in from Minneapolis, where he had bought an International House of Pancakes restaurant "just so he could have a place to have breakfast with his buddies," according to Hornung. During the Lombardi era, McGee was Hornung's alter ego, constant companion, and fellow hedonist.

Today they're all in their late sixties or early seventies, and their memories, like a lot of other things, aren't what they used to be. But McGee and Jerry Kramer still seem to be in good shape physically. Hornung weighs considerably more than his best playing weight of around 215 to 220 pounds, and Ron Kramer has been slowed by shoulder, hip, and knee replacements. Still, they have about them not only the bearing of once-great athletes, but of champions.

As the master of ceremonies, Hornung was in charge of operating the tape recorder. "Big, big mistake," McGee said. But once the tape started rolling, the stories and the laughter began flowing. Only a few of the stories were new to the participants, but it made no difference. They revel in yet another telling because it's their shared experiences that bonded them then and bonds them still today.

Since its inception in 1921, the NFL has produced only six real dynasties. The first was the Chicago Bears of 1940–46, who won four titles in seven years. Next came the Cleveland Browns, who were champions three times and runners-up three times from 1950 to 1955. They were followed by my personal favorite, the Lombardi Packers, who won five NFL titles (and the first two Super Bowls) from 1960 to 1968.

From Green Bay, the torch was passed to Pittsburgh, where the Steelers won four titles in the six-year period from 1975 through 1980. The 1980s were dominated by the San Francisco 49ers of Joe Montana and Jerry Rice, who won four titles in the nine-year period from 1982 to 1990.

Finally, and most recently, are the Dallas Cowboy squads that won three championships in four years from 1993 to 1996. The Cowboys probably could have won even more, but they weren't able to keep their coaching staff and squad together because of free agency, a concept that didn't exist in Hornung's playing days.

Of the six dynasties, the Packers arguably are the greatest. Besides dominating their opposition on the field for almost a decade, they became the epitome of teamwork, determination, and the quest for perfection, traits that Lombardi instilled in every one of them. Finally, they had a cast of players who both redefined the way their positions were played and who were interesting enough as individuals to become household names.

So now here were four of them, trying with limited success to articulate how Lombardi molded them into winners and turned them into the men they are today. Hornung talked about Lombardi's uncanny ability to understand how to get the most out of each player. Ron Kramer mentioned Lombardi's obsession with perfectionism. McGee brought up the fits Lombardi threw, and how difficult it was to tell which were real and which were shows.

To a man, they still believe in the Lombardi credo, "The Habit of Winning," which Hornung considers to be the coach's best speech.

"Winning is not a sometime thing," Lombardi said. "You don't win once in a while. You don't do things right once in a while. You do them right all the time. Winning is a habit. Unfortunately, so is losing. There is no room for second place. There is only one place in my game and that is first place. I have finished second twice in my time at Green Bay and I don't want to ever finish second again. It is, and always has been, an American zeal to be first in everything we do. The object—to win!

"Every time a football player goes out to play, he's got to play from the ground up. From the soles of his feet right to his head. Every inch of him has to play. Some guys play with their heads. That's OK; you've got to be smart to be No. 1 in any business. But in football, you've got to play with your heart. With every fiber of your body. If you are lucky enough to find a guy with a lot of head and a lot of heart, he's never going to come off the field second.

"Running a football team is no different from running any other kind of organization—an army, a political party, a business. The problems are the same. The objective is to win. To beat the other guy. Maybe that sounds hard or cruel. I don't think it is.

"It is a reality of life that men are competitive and the most competitive games draw the most competitive men. That's why they're there—to compete. They know the rules and the objectives when they get in the game. The objective is to win—fairly, squarely, decently, by the rules—but to win. And in truth, I have never known a man worth his salt who in the long run, deep down in his heart, did not appreciate the grind. The discipline. There is something in good men that yearns for—needs—discipline and the harsh reality of head-to-head combat.

"I don't say these things because I believe in the 'brute' nature of man, or that man must be brutalized to be in combat. I believe in God and I believe in human decency. But I firmly believe that any man's finest hour, his greatest fulfillment to all he holds dear, is the moment when he has worked his heart out in a good cause and lies exhausted on the field of battle victorious."

As Hornung pointed out to his teammates' agreement, the best sentence is the last one and the key word is *victorious*. Lombardi didn't believe that hard work is its own reward. He believed that hard work was meaningless if it didn't result in victory.

"I use that speech every time I talk to a corporate group anywhere in America," Hornung said.

The evening was going along well until Jerry Kramer began talking about how revered he and his teammates still are throughout Wisconsin and the entire football world. He mentioned a time when a fan thrust an old program at him to sign. When Kramer looked at it, he noticed the signature of Ray Nitschke, the Hall of Fame Packers linebacker who died in the late 1990s.

"I saw that and I went 'Uhhhhh,' " Kramer said. "It was almost like the wind was knocked out of me. It's still hard for me to believe he's gone, and I still miss him."

For a few moments, the room was silent. Then conversation quickly returned to safer ground. Another Lombardi story was told, and the laughter and memories overwhelmed the grim reality of the moment. Like most of us, legends don't like to confront their own mortality.

—Billy Reed
Louisville, Kentucky
April 21, 2004

Preface

I began work on this book in the spring of 2001, when I was in New York having dinner with Dick Schaap, the famed writer and host of ESPN's popular Sunday morning TV show, *The Sports Reporters*. I had gotten to know Dick in the 1960s, when he came to Green Bay to cover our championship teams. He wrote a little paperback about me in 1962 called *Paul Hornung—Golden Boy*, but he really hit it big when he collaborated with Jerry Kramer, our great offensive guard, on *Instant Replay*, a diary of our 1967 season that became a national best-seller and one of the most important sports books ever.

Dick was the best reporter I've ever known. For more than fifty years, his work appeared in newspapers, magazines, and on radio and TV. He wrote an incredible thirty-three books. His thirst for knowledge was too vast to be contained by the sports world, so he reviewed plays and covered big news stories such as the 1965 riots in the Watts section of Los Angeles, and the Son of

Sam murders in New York in 1976–77. I guess one reason I liked Dick was that he was sort of the journalistic equivalent of me as a football player—he could do it all!

On this particular night, we were having dinner at Rao's, which is one of the toughest reservations in New York. You must "own" a table one night every week. Dick had a table there every Monday night. Out of the blue, Dick said, "I think we should write a book." Without hesitation, I said, "I like the idea." I told him that since I wanted to tell my whole story, including the gambling and the womanizing, a lot of people probably would be nervous that they might be exposed. Instead of *Run to Day-light*, which had been the name of one of Vince Lombardi's books, I suggested we call it *Run for Cover*.

I'd been thinking about doing a book for a number of years, but didn't want to collaborate with someone who really didn't know me or my history. Dick knew too much. He loved covering the Packers and our guys enjoyed having him around. Dick was a great listener, he was trustworthy, and there was nothing phony about him. I doubt that Dick had very many enemies, which is remarkable when you consider all the big egos (present company excepted, of course) that he knew and covered.

Before I agreed to do the book, I told Dick I had to clear it with my wife, Angela. We began dating in 1976, and she has been my love and my life since we were married in 1979. From long before she met me, she had a background in pro football. From 1971 to 1976 she was secretary to Mike McCormick, the head coach of the Philadelphia Eagles. I needed to get her OK for the book because I intend to revisit some old times with various women from my past. Being aware from her past experience

about the lives of pro football players, she gave the project her
blessing.

Dick came to Louisville in December 2001 and spent four
days with me and Angela. He charmed her, as he did most people he met. I took him to see where I had grown up, where I had
lived and played, and what businesses I was in. He returned to
New York thinking he was going to get the process rolling. First,
however, he had to check into the hospital for hip-replacement
surgery. Much to my shock, he died in the hospital on December 21, 2001. The cause of death was listed as "complications
from hip-replacement surgery."

God, what a tremendous loss for his family, his friends, jour-
nalism, and the sports world.

When I got around to thinking about the book again, I knew
that nobody could adequately replace Dick. I met with various
talented writers who wanted to do the book with me, but they either didn't know me well enough or I didn't feel comfortable
with them. Just when I was about to give up and try to go it alone,
I remembered that there was a good writer who lived in my
neighborhood, less than a hundred yards from my home.

Billy Reed remembers getting autographs from me and my
friend, Sherrill Sipes, when we were playing basketball for
Flaget High in Louisville in the winter of 1951–52. He spent
twenty-nine years writing for *Sports Illustrated* under the byline
William F. Reed. He also campaigned hard for my induction
into the Pro Football Hall of Fame when he was sports editor of
the *Louisville Courier-Journal* in the early 1980s, and he testified
on my behalf in 1985 when I sued the NCAA for keeping me off
college football telecasts.

Besides that, Billy knew Dick Schaap very well. He once was a guest on Dick's TV show, and he had talked with Dick about Schaap's latest book only a few months before Dick died. When I contacted Billy, he said it would be an honor to fill in for Dick, whom he admired greatly, and a pleasure to work with me because of our long-standing friendship.

Writing this book with Billy has been the first real job I've ever had. I mean, *ever.* I provided the words and the stories, and Billy polished them for me. We pored through the scrapbooks that my mom had kept all those years (thanks, mom) and we went over the record books to make sure we had all the names and dates right. Of course if you find a mistake, it's Billy's fault. Let me know and I'll make him run up and down the hill between my house and his.

It was a labor of love, because I've been incredibly blessed to have made so many friends and had so many enjoyable experiences. I know that Billy joins me in dedicating this book to Dick Schaap, our friend and the all-time No. 1 fan and friend of Lombardi's Green Bay Packers.

1

MY LIFE ON
SCHOLARSHIP

Heading toward the fall of 1965, I was a twenty-eight-year-old bachelor in the prime of my football career with the Green Bay Packers. I had a well-deserved reputation as a ladies' man, as did Max McGee, my best buddy and partner in crime. Our coach, Vince Lombardi, had a rule that we thought was really unfair. After preseason exhibition games in Green Bay, the married players got to be with their wives at home or a hotel, but the single guys had an 11 P.M. curfew and were expected to spend the night at St. Norbert College, the little school just outside Green Bay that we used as our training camp.

After an exhibition game on a Saturday night, Max and I decided that we didn't want to spend the night in Sensenbrenner Hall, our dorm, so we booked a couple of rooms in the Northland Hotel in Green Bay and spent the night with a couple of girls. At about 5 A.M. Max finally chickened out and went back to the dorm. But when he was told that Lombardi wanted to see us together that morning, he came back to the hotel to pick me up.

Lombardi had the greatest spy network in the history of football. I don't know how he found out about it, but he did. The SOB *always* knew where we were and what we were doing. We found him at 10 A.M. Sunday, watching film of our opponent with his assistant coaches. Max was scared to death, but I wasn't in the mood to take any of Lombardi's crap.

When Lombardi saw us, he went wild, screaming and cursing and threatening. Finally, he shouted, "Hornung, do you want to be a player or a playboy?" That was it for me. "A playboy!" I screamed back. "See me at 4 o'clock," said Lombardi, "and I'll decide what I'm going to do with you."

Well, the hell with that, I thought. I was so pissed off that I was determined to leave camp, tell the story to *Sports Illustrated*, and force Lombardi to trade me to the Chicago Bears. My teammates knew how hot I was, and they chanted "Go, go, go" as I packed my suitcase in the dorm.

Somebody distracted me, and when I came back, I couldn't find my car keys or my suitcase. It turned out that Jerry Kramer had hidden them so I couldn't leave. By this time, my anger had pretty well burned out and so had Lombardi's.

When we met that afternoon, he apologized for screaming at me in front of the other coaches. But I still had to pay the $500 fine he slapped on me. Big deal. Every year, Max and I were fined more than the rest of the team put together. Hell, we could have financed a small Caribbean country with our fines.

And that was the way it went between Lombardi and me from 1959, his first season with the Packers, until 1967, when he reluctantly put me on the expansion list for the new team in

New Orleans, the Saints. They used their first draft pick on me in the hope that I had recovered from my injuries. But I hadn't, so I retired. I was never a Saint.

Our ill-tempered confrontations aside, I loved Lombardi. A lot of people could never understand our relationship. He was the ultimate disciplinarian and I was the ultimate coach's nightmare. In fact, his wife, Marie, liked to tell a story about the time the Lombardis got a 4 A.M. phone call during football season.

"Oh, my God," said Vince, "what's happened to Hornung now."

"Pick it up," said his wife.

"I'm afraid to," said Lombardi.

"Vince," said Marie, "it could be about your own son or daughter, you know. Yet all you think about is Hornung."

Lombardi and I understood each other perfectly. He wanted to win more than anybody I've ever known, and he once said I was the best clutch player he ever coached. He always knew that no matter where I'd been or what I'd done the night before, I'd be ready to play on Sunday.

After we had won our first championship in 1961, Lombardi told a reporter about how he handled Max and me.

"Those fellows have to blow off steam," he said. "Now I know just what Hornung does. Maybe he'll give you the idea that everything is a party, but don't believe it. When I have him out at practice, I take one look and can tell you what he's done the night before. It's nothing, believe me. Look what he's like in a game."

I never had the heart to tell Vince what I did the night before we played the Colts in Baltimore on Sunday, December 12, 1965. I didn't think I was going to play because I was having trouble with my left arm, which eventually forced me to retire. As it happened, the Redskins, who had acquired my buddy Rick Casares in a trade with Chicago, were playing in Washington that same Sunday. Like me, Rick didn't think he'd play because of an injury, so he arranged for us to meet a couple of girls at a restaurant halfway between the two cities.

We had such a good time that I went back to our hotel in Baltimore for bed check, then sneaked out again to meet Casares and the girls. I didn't get back in until about 8:30 the next morning, and the first thing I asked Max was if there had been a second bed check. "No, you lucky SOB," said Max, who might have been a bit jealous. "You got away with it." So Max and I immediately went downstairs to join our teammates for breakfast.

As we were eating, Lombardi came by with his tray.

"How are you feeling?" he asked me.

"Hell, I feel great," I lied.

"Good," said Lombardi, "because I'm going to start you today."

Max almost coughed up his breakfast, but he, of all people, should have known better. I had one of the best games of my career, scoring five touchdowns in a 42–27 win that sewed up the Western Division title for us.

I was feeling so good that the Colts' Lenny Lyles, once advertised as "the fastest man in football," chased me for eighty yards and couldn't catch me. Like me, Lenny's from Louisville, Kentucky, and today we're partners in a shopping center there. I still tease him about that time.

When I look back now, at the age of sixty-eight, I can hardly believe some of the stories myself. I was known as "The Golden Boy," a great nickname that created an image that was colorful, if not always accurate. I always felt like I was a good son, a good student, and a good citizen, but I also understood that the public and the press were more interested in the football and the fun.

I loved every minute of it. Because of the name I made for myself in football, I was able to hang out with movie stars and high rollers and show girls. I partied at the nation's best nightclubs and restaurants. And after I retired, I was one of the first athletes to move directly from the field to the broadcast booth, where I had a long and lucrative career.

So it's been a ball, and I really don't have any regrets. I was once asked, if I could come back from the dead as anybody, who would it be? My answer was . . . Paul Hornung. I'd be crazy to think otherwise. My life was all about games, girls, gambling, and gin joints, not necessarily in that order. I was the opposite of what's known today as "politically correct."

To be honest, I really wasn't much different from a lot of players in the 1950s and '60s. Guys like Bobby Layne, Billy Kilmer, Sonny Jurgensen, Casares, and, of course, McGee. They all played every bit as hard as I did, both on and off the field. I was just able to do a better job of capitalizing on it.

To this day, I sometimes think I'm remembered as much for my Miller Lite beer commercials as for the 176 points I scored in 1960, still the NFL record. For those of you who are too young to remember, a voice-over asked, "What's Paul Hornung's secret with women?" Wearing a tux, I opened the door to a limo—inside which you could see a pair of long female legs with a short skirt that was hiked up—and I said, "Practice, practice, practice."

That commercial was so popular that when I was walking down the street in New York or Chicago, cabdrivers would see me and yell, "Practice, practice, practice!" A lot of autograph seekers asked me to write the words under my name. With all due modesty, I'd say that commercial rivaled the pantyhose commercial that Joe Namath did when he was quarterbacking the New York Jets in 1974. Of course, the legs in mine were much better.

Since Namath's retirement, NFL playboys—at least in the traditional sense—have all but disappeared. Today's players tend to fall into one of two groups: squeaky-clean family men who never venture out, or clueless punks who end up arrested for getting into bar fights, beating up women, doing drugs, and fooling around with guns.

It's an amazing thing about pro athletes and girls. For the athletes, it's an easy road. The girls always are around. That obviously hasn't changed much, but the difference was that, in my day, it was fun for everybody, like a big game. Nobody was carrying guns, nobody was trying to set up athletes to extort money, nobody was beating up on girls, and nobody had AIDS. It was a more innocent time, I guess.

Once I went to Los Angeles right after the season to play in the Bing Crosby golf tournament. Bob Rosburg, then a pro golfer and later a prominent TV analyst, had two rooms for me. Rossy was playing with John Brodie of the 49ers, so he put me with Jimmy Colbert, a fine golfer who didn't really become a star until the Seniors Tour came along. The first day, I shot a 76. But the second round, after a hard night, I shot a 39–65 = 104. I must have had twenty penalty shots.

That night I was out with a star baseball player and we met these two girls. They asked us to drive out to their house and have a drink. Well, we ended up in the sauna with the girls. We were all naked and drinking and laughing when I noticed a male outside watching us through the glass door.

"Who are you and what are you doing?" I yelled.

"I'm watching you fuck my wife," the guy said.

Needless to say, we got out of there as quick as we could.

Dick Schaap once spent a week with me in Green Bay before we were to play the Cleveland Browns. He pretty well captured the way it was for me in those days.

"At three (after practice), he'd come home, mix a pitcher of martinis, and drink martinis until six o'clock with Ron Kramer and the others," Schaap wrote. "Then they'd go out and have dinner, a group of players. Scotch before dinner. Wine with dinner. Brandy after dinner. Then back on scotch. Every day. I lost count by the time it had reached more than 60. Also, he never went to bed before four in the morning, he never went to bed alone, and he never repeated himself."

The only thing I took exception to was that I would consume sixty drinks a day. That was a real stretch. But twenty? Well, that might have been in the ballpark.

My favorite of today's players is Brett Favre, the Packers' quarterback. On October 10, 1997, Favre took one of his off days to come to Louisville and appear on my cable TV show, *Paul Hornung's Sports Showcase*. He brought along his agent and their wives.

Brett had told me that he wanted to play golf at Valhalla, the world-class course outside Louisville that has twice been the site of the PGA Championship. So I called Rick Pitino, who was a member, and set it up.

So we're out there on the first tee at 8:30 A.M. and Brett says, "Can we have a few Bloody Marys?" So I got twelve of them and they were gone before we made the turn. Then Brett said, "How about some ice-cold beer for the back side?" So I got a case of beer and we killed that. Naturally, there were drinks after we finished and a couple of bottles of wine at dinner.

Brett shows up for the show in the same golf shirt and shorts that he had worn on the course. The restaurant, Damon's, was packed with Packer fans. There must have been 1,000 in a place that seats 250, and more were waiting outside. During the commercial breaks, the fans stormed the stage, looking for autographs, which really taxed the security guards the restaurant had hired.

The first question I asked him was about his addiction to painkillers, which had been a big story a few months earlier, and his love of booze. He looked me right in the eye and said, "I played the game, I got hurt, and I took something for it. But I don't blame the Packers or the NFL for my problems. We all choose to go down a certain road. But, Paul, I haven't had a drink for six months."

I swear, I about fell off the damned stool. It was exactly what the young Paul Hornung would have done forty years earlier. (All joking aside, Brett really did quit drinking and became a great family man.)

2.

THEY CALLED
ME "CUDDLES"

The great sports columnist Jim Murray once referred to my hometown, Louisville, Kentucky, as "America's bar rag." A lot of my fellow residents resented that, but I had to agree. The Louisville I knew as a kid in the 1940s and '50s was a city of whiskey distilleries, cigarette factories, and gambling at Churchill Downs, home of the Kentucky Derby.

As much as I love Los Angeles, New York, Miami, and Chicago, I've always kept my residence in Louisville, where I was born at 7:05 A.M. on December 23, 1935, in St. Anthony's Hospital. My mom, Loretta, grew up in Louisville—her dad operated a grocery at the corner of Seventeenth and Lytle in the western part of the city—and she was still such a home girl at heart that she left my dad, Paul Sr., at their apartment in Jackson Heights, Queens, so she could come home in her eighth month of pregnancy and have me in Louisville.

My godmother, Margaret Clifford, once told a reporter,

"Paul was a nice, large, lusty baby. He liked to play with balls in his crib."

My parents divorced when I was very young, only two or three years old, because of my dad's drinking. After he lost his job with the Metropolitan Life Insurance Co., first in New York and then in Louisville, he left mom and me. He took the car; she kept the furniture and me.

In 1939 she got a job with the Works Progress Administration as a clerk-typist, and later she worked in the personnel department at the Louisville Army Medical Depot. For years, mom and I lived in a two-room apartment above my grandfather's grocery at 523 North Seventeenth Street.

After my grandmother died (my grandfather was already deceased), mom sold the grocery and we moved in with a widow who didn't have enough bedrooms. So for a year, mom and I slept on two army cots in her living room.

We then moved to an apartment on Bank Street, but I didn't like it so we moved again, this time into an apartment owned by two widows at Twenty-second and Portland Avenue. That was mom's home until my senior year in college.

I can remember two things about growing up. One is carrying buckets of coal up the stairs to keep the living room stove going. The other is the way my mother tried to get me everything I wanted. When I was playing baseball, as most boys did in those days, she got me a Marty Marion fielder's glove and a Ted Williams Louisville Slugger bat, made right there in my hometown.

I kinda lost track of my dad until I was thirteen or fourteen years old, when he showed up one day after he had been drinking and acted like he was going to take a whack at my mother. I was big for my age, and I told him that if he laid a hand on mom, he'd have to deal with me. He didn't, thank God. That was the only confrontation I ever had with him.

He never came to any of my games in grade school, high school, college, or the pros, which was fine with mom. She always was afraid that he'd show up drunk and do something to embarrass us. In high school, I'd have dinner with him once a week. He was always clean and sober at those times, and he'd give me ten or fifteen dollars, which I took home and gave to mom.

The real father figure in my life was a kind, gentle man named Henry Hoffman. He and his wife, Edna, weren't related to us, but I called them "Uncle Henry" and "Aunt Edna." They had double-dated with my parents years earlier. As far as I was concerned, Uncle Henry was the perfect human being. He never lied to anybody.

Uncle Henry was the guiding male influence in my life until the day he died in 1984. He took me out to dinner at least once a week, every week, usually at the Blue Boar Cafeteria in downtown Louisville. He'd let me pile up my tray, and he'd always say, "Now Paul, you can have whatever you want, but what you take, you have to eat."

He liked to dress well, so he'd always buy me a nice sport coat at Christmas. He made sure I had nice clothes. He was a very conservative real estate man, and I always remember him telling me that I'd be a millionaire by the time I was thirty.

My mother was an educated person, having taken some college correspondence courses. Because of her job and my grandfather's grocery, we were considered better off than many of our neighbors in Portland, an Irish working-class neighborhood in western Louisville.

There was a lot of poverty around us. Once, when I heard somebody saying that there weren't any blacks in Portland, only Irish, I almost got into a fight by saying, "Yeah, there are no blacks because they want to move up, not back."

I took a lot of teasing when I was a kid because, like Cassius M. Clay Jr., another youngster growing up in Louisville around that time, I had a pretty face. One of my high school teammates, Mike McDonald, who went on to become a judge on the Kentucky Court of Appeals, once told a reporter that "Paul was not a tough guy. I never knew him to be in a fight, and that almost made you a pervert when you were from Portland." Actually, that's not true. I got into ten fights and got licked ten times.

My mom saved up enough money to send me to school at St. Patrick's Church at the corner of Thirteenth and Market. I was an altar boy for a couple of years, and I was always a pretty decent student. I was bigger than most kids my age, so, in the fifth grade, I was able to play for the eighth-grade team at St. Patrick's.

By the time I got into the eighth grade, I was the starting quarterback in football. Our coach at St. Patrick's, Father William O'Hare, let me call the plays because he knew absolutely nothing about football. Besides, he didn't have much choice. We only had sixteen boys (along with twelve girls) in our class.

Nobody else was much interested in kicking—American kids didn't play soccer in those days—so I decided to learn how to do that, too. I basically taught myself to kick at the playground across from the Marine Hospital in Portland. Once I started doing it, I found out that I liked it. Later, when I was at Flaget High School, I'd go by myself after practice to a playground on Bank Street and practice kicking the ball over the basketball goals.

Unlike the other aspects of football—running, passing, catching, blocking, and tackling—kicking is more of a solitary thing. So I could use my imagination. *There's only five seconds left and this is Flaget's last chance to win. Hornung sets up for a thirty-yard field-goal attempt . . . He kicks and . . . it's good! Flaget wins!*

During this time, I was encouraged by Bill Shade, one of the great athletes in the history of Louisville. The Louisville Colonels of the (Class AAA) American Association signed him to a baseball contract and he was hitting .350 for them when he got his wife pregnant.

He couldn't afford to play baseball and support a family, so he quit playing to get a "real job." He began playing fast-pitch softball. Bill took care of me. Besides teaching me a lot about how to play, he gave me jerseys, balls, and gloves.

I wanted to be a pitcher in baseball because I could throw hard. Unfortunately, I had absolutely no control. I once pitched a no-hitter where the final score was 13–12. To tell you the truth, I really liked basketball more than baseball or football in those days.

I always had fond memories of St. Patrick's, so when it went up for sale long after my pro career was over, I bought it in partnership with Frank Metts, my dear friend and fellow protégé of Uncle Henry. We wanted to turn it into a boxing arena with the help of city government. Hell, we were going to *give* it to the city. But somehow politics got involved, and we finally had to sell the old place, church and all.

From a young age, I liked the girls—some of them thought I was so cute they called me "Cuddles," if you can believe that. When I was thirteen, I lost my virginity to an older neighborhood girl who was something of an exhibitionist.

She always left her bathroom window open when she was taking a bath, and she knew that about six of us boys were hiding out watching her. One day she singled me out and took me down by the railroad tracks, where she gave me my first lesson in sex. Hell, I'm not going to lie about it. I enjoyed it.

Every kid needs a best pal, somebody to hang around with, and for me that was Sherrill Sipes. I met Sherrill when we were playing against his team from Christ the King in an eighth-grade football game. Compared to those of us in Portland, Sherrill came from an upscale neighborhood and background.

At first I didn't like him because he complained about how rough we played. Hell, what did he expect from a bunch of Irish-Catholic kids who came from a neighborhood where people shot craps on the street corners every night?

But we became friends at Flaget High and were inseparable, almost brothers, all the way through high school. Sherrill was a good-looking guy who was every bit as good an athlete as me, maybe better. He was the first white guy I'd ever seen who had "black speed," as he proved by winning the state track championships in the 100- and 220-yard dashes two years in a row.

The big difference between Sherrill and me was conscience.

I must have dated at least twenty girls in high school, but never went steady. On the other hand, Sherrill tended to fall in love and have deep relationships. He had one serious romance where I thought he was getting laid. But it bothered him so much that, I swear, he went to confession every other day. I consider myself a good Catholic, but I've never believed in confession and some of the other rituals.

During those days, you could find the best-looking girls on Sunday afternoons at either Tucker Lake or Lighthouse Lake. I always wanted to go where the girls were, but I had to coax Sherrill because he was afraid we'd get in trouble. It was pretty much the same when a bunch of us would throw in two or three dollars apiece and sneak into either Churchill Downs or Miles Park, a seedy little bush-league track in the west end.

At Derby time, Sherrill and I would get temporary jobs with the Andy Frain ushering service. Wearing our yellow coats, which were hot as hell even on a cool day, we'd take tickets for a few races, then begin letting people in for fifty cents apiece. We'd also steal mint-julep glasses while people were engrossed in the action and take them outside to sell them. At the end of Derby Day, after subtracting our gambling losses, we'd still come home with thirty or forty dollars each, which was good money in those days.

So I suppose you could say that I hadn't exactly lived a sheltered life when the fall of 1950 came and I began my sophomore year at Flaget. I became the team's starting quarterback midway through that year in a game against duPont Manual High, one of the big public schools in Louisville. The field was muddy and treacherous, and both the first- and second-string quarterbacks lost the ball on fumbles. Our coach, Paulie Miller, knew that I could run the split-T attack he had learned from Missouri's Don Faurot at the Great Lakes Naval Training Station during World War II.

The quarterback had the option to run, pass, or pitch out, much like the tailback in the single wing that was so popular in the 1930s and '40s. I handled the ball without losing it that night. We won the game, and I won the starting quarterback's job.

Miller was an outstanding high school coach who gave me my first taste of what I would experience years later under Lombardi at Green Bay. We knew he cared about us, but he hid it pretty well. He was a tough SOB who would raise hell with you when you screwed up.

"Even from the time he was a freshman," Paulie once said, "Paul had a tremendous amount of poise and coolness. He was easy to teach. He paid attention. He tried to do what you told him. Lots of times, when I laced him out, he looked like he wasn't listening. But you could tell he'd listened by the way he performed."

My best game came in a 61–7 win over Owensboro Catholic. I threw four touchdown passes, ran for two more, and kicked seven extra points.

When our junior team finished with a 7–2–1 record, Sherrill and I began getting a lot of attention from college recruiters. We made a pact that we would go to the same college.

After I turned sixteen on December 23, 1951, and got my driver's license, mom bought me a used black-and-yellow Chevy to replace my Schwinn bike. Showing off, I decided to take Sherrill and four girls out for a spin. Three of the girls were in the backseat and one was sitting on Sherrill's lap. I thought I was really cool until I backed the car around the corner and ran into another one.

Imagine how embarrassed I felt. My first day with a license, and I wrecked the car.

During the spring of our junior year, I broke my foot playing baseball. I still showed up for Paulie's Monday night practices during the summer of 1952, which wasn't too smart. The first time I ran the ball, I heard something pop and came up limping again. Miller immediately took me to the hospital, but first stopped by the school.

"I have to make a quick stop," Miller said. "Go into the chapel and start praying. I'll be back in a few minutes and I'll take you to the hospital."

Fortunately for both of us, the X-rays showed that I had a sprain instead of a break. My prayers had been answered.

3.

STIFF-ARMING THE BEAR

f I were given the chance to live three years over, the ones I'd pick wouldn't be when I played at Notre Dame or Green Bay or when I was on television. They would be my sophomore, junior, and senior years in high school. The early 1950s was a great time to be in high school. Our big thrill was to pack three couples into a convertible and go to a drive-in movie during the summer. It was difficult to make out while there were four other people in the car, but we managed. I went to a lot of movies, sometimes two or three a week, but never saw any of them if there were girls around.

At the beginning of my senior year at Flaget, my foot was still a bit sore, and so, in our first game, Miller put me into what's known today as a "shotgun" offense and all I did was hand off and pass. By our second game, however, my foot was fine and we went back to the split T.

Despite the graduation of end Howard Schnellenberger—

yes, the same guy who went on to a phenomenal coaching career in both college and pro football—our senior team at Flaget went 9–1–1, our only loss coming on the road in Oak Ridge, Tennessee, when the officials ruled that I missed a field goal that I still believe was good. To this day, our senior team is regarded as perhaps the best in the state's history.

We also were the biggest. We had some guys who weighed as much as 270 or 280, huge in those days. We'd put them all in when I was kicking an extra point or a field goal. One newspaper reporter wrote that our kicking team was bigger than the University of Kentucky's defensive team.

Paulie Miller talked me up for the sake of recruiters. "In his three years (as a starter) at Flaget," Miller said, "Paul could run the option play as well as Maryland or Oklahoma were running it at the time."

During the season, I got to know Paul "Bear" Bryant, the charismatic young coach who had taken Kentucky to the Orange, Sugar, and Cotton bowls in successive years. To this day, that remains the glory era of Kentucky football, the only time the Wildcats have been able to run with the big dogs for more than a year.

Looking back, I'd have to say Bryant is one of the five most impressive people I've ever met. He was as handsome as a movie star and had that deep, growly voice. He had been the "other end," opposite Don Hutson, on Alabama's great teams of the 1930s, so he also was bigger than most coaches.

Bryant visited Mom and me in our little apartment at least six times, and usually he was accompanied by Lawrence Wetherby, the Democratic governor of the state. Mom liked Wetherby. Of course, she was as devout a Democrat as she was a Catholic. If you were a Democrat, you got her vote.

Whenever Bryant and Wetherby would visit, they would always pull up in front of our apartment in the governor's official limousine. Then, once they were inside, the conversation would always be more or less the same.

> Bryant (in his famous growl of a drawl): "Fahn coffee, Mizzuz Hornung."
> Wetherby: "Fine to visit with you people around the state. You get so tied up with official duties that you don't get the chance to go around as much as you'd like."
> Bryant (looking at me): "Fahn boy."
> Wetherby: "Fine to visit with people around the state."
> Bryant: "Lawd, governor, but that's a real fahn stud. We got to keep that boy in the state."

Schnellenberger already was at Kentucky, and two of our best linemen, J. T. Frankenberger and John Noon, were ready to join him. But the players Bryant wanted most were Sherrill and me. He wanted me to be his split-T quarterback, replacing All-American Vito "Babe" Parilli, who was more of a pure passer than an option quarterback. He promised me I could try out for Adolph Rupp's basketball team, that I would start games as a freshman, and that he'd give scholarships to all nineteen of the seniors on our team.

While it would have been fun to have my high school buddies around me, I also knew that Bryant probably would run most of them off. He ran a preseason boot camp in Millersburg, Kentucky, which was the model for the one he later ran in Junction, Texas, for Texas A&M. Every year, he'd come back with about only half the players he took up there.

Heck, he also said he'd get a scholarship for Janie, my first heartthrob. She was a couple of years younger than me, but she could have come to all my games in Lexington. She and I dated off and on through my years at Notre Dame and even after I joined the Packers.

The Bear never offered me anything illegal, mainly because he had plenty of boosters to do that for him. Paul Karem, who owned the meat company where I worked a couple of summers, said that if Sherrill and I came to Kentucky, we would both be driving Cadillacs "because I'd buy them for you." There also wouldn't be any trouble landing cushy summer jobs. For a poor kid from Portland, it was all very tempting, especially since I knew how cold it got in South Bend, Indiana, during the winter.

Although I also was being recruited by coaching giants such as Notre Dame's Frank Leahy, Oklahoma's Bud Wilkinson, Maryland's Jim Tatum, and Michigan State's Clarence "Biggie" Munn, Bryant was the hottest thing in college football. I really gave him an eyeful on the night of November 14, 1952, when we won the mythical state championship with a 39–7 victory over Lexington Lafayette in the Recreation Bowl in Mount Sterling.

I had this old ball that I practiced kicking with. It was slick and I'd deflate it to the point that, if I hit it just right, I could placekick it seventy yards. I used it to try to intimidate opponents in warm-ups before the game. In those days, kickers had no hard-toed kicking shoes—I didn't get those until I was a senior at Notre Dame—so it was quite a feat to kick a ball that far.

By the last quarter against Lafayette, the game balls were gone because every time I'd kick an extra point, kids waiting behind the end-zone stands would grab the ball and take off with it.

All that was left was my old practice ball, so the officials had no choice but to use it.

On the kickoff, I had a little wind with me and I hit it perfectly. The ball was still rising when it went through the goalposts about ten or fifteen feet above the crossbar. It cleared the end-zone bleachers and sailed out of the stadium. It had to have gone ninety yards. Bryant was so shocked he almost fell out of the press box. I know because whenever I'd see him years later, he would always talk about that kick. I never had the heart to tell him the truth about my old ball.

After our season, Sherrill and I made our campus visits together. We went to Georgia Tech, because I thought I wanted to be an engineer, and to Florida, where they flew us into Daytona Beach, set us up in a condo on the beach, loaned us a car, gave us two hundred dollars to spend, and fixed us up with a couple of the prettiest coeds you ever saw. We even took the time to drive inland to visit the campus in Gainesville. Sherrill was sincerely interested in Florida, but I just went along because I had never seen the ocean.

In my senior basketball season, I averaged around 16 points as a 6-foot-3 forward and once scored a record 32 points in a Louisville Invitational Tournament game. We had a 28–4 record, but were upset in the first round of the state tournament in Lexington. Yet I remember that season more for the practices than the games, because we got to work out often with Ralph Beard, my hero when he was the All-American guard for "The Fabulous Five," the team that had won back-to-back NCAA basketball titles for Kentucky in 1948–49.

Ralph was a scrawny little guy, maybe 5-10 and 150 pounds, but he had made the all-NBA team his first two seasons in the league. But then he and thirty-two other players from around the country admitted to having taken money (in Beard's case while he was still at Kentucky playing for Rupp) from gamblers in college basketball's first major point-shaving scandal. The NBA banned him and the others for life. (The NCAA suspended the Wildcats for the 1952–53 season.)

So here he was, working out with us as he tried to figure out what to do with his life. Sherrill and I were thrilled. To be able to play ball with Ralph Beard was like a dream for us. We couldn't wait to get to practice. I still say Ralph is the fastest basketball player I've ever seen, faster even than Allen Iverson.

To this day, Ralph hasn't been inducted into the Basketball Hall of Fame and I think that's a damned shame. He admitted to taking the money, but swore he never did anything to influence the outcome of a game. I believe him. He's one of the most honest people I've ever known.

During the winter months, Sherrill and I finally narrowed our football choices down to Kentucky, because of Bryant; Notre Dame, because that's where my mom wanted me to go; and Indiana, because Coach Bernie Crimmins was a family friend from Louisville. We first eliminated Indiana because a rumor got started there that I had my hand out, and that sort of soured me on going there.

As what he hoped was a deal closer, Bryant sent Parilli, my football hero, to talk with me. That worried mom, because she knew how much I admired the Babe (who, by the way, was later a teammate at Green Bay in 1957 and '58). He was a great passer who was so valuable that Bryant told his offensive linemen they'd be punished if Parilli got any grass stains on his white pants during practice. In other words, don't let him get hit!

Many of his passing records stood at Kentucky until Tim Couch broke them in the 1990s.

Our weirdest visit was to Notre Dame. Leahy, who had won five national championships, talked in a very formal way. He wasn't nearly as young or as earthy as Bryant. We made our campus visit the weekend that Notre Dame played Southern Cal. After the game, we were taken to a room where Leahy was sitting on a big chair, like some kind of king.

The recruits were all lined up and filed past him one at a time. He had bushy eyebrows and a lyrical Irish voice. He would say a few quiet words to each of us, like the pope giving his blessing, and then it would be the next guy's turn. He called everyone "lad." I remember him looking at Sherrill and me and saying, "You lads would look splendid in green."

And that was it, the only contact we had with him. Here we had Bryant and all the other top coaches kissing our asses, and all we got from Leahy was a short audience. I remember saying to Sherrill, "Didn't that seem weird to you?"

Leahy offered us scholarships without ever having scouted us or seen us play. One reason could have been that he respected Paulie Miller's opinion and called him frequently.

"Hornung's going to be an All-American in college," Miller predicted.

"A lad like that comes along once every twenty-five years," Leahy said.

"If that's true," said Miller, "I guess I'd better retire from coaching."

In the early spring, a Notre Dame recruiter named Rog Huter drove Sherrill and me to South Bend for another audience with Leahy. It was still very cold there, and the students were away on spring break. It seemed like a pretty forlorn place.

"Let's don't go here," I said to Sherrill.

"Right," he said. "Let's get out of here."

But then we saw Leahy.

"Lads," he said, "Our Lady needs you here. Lads like you belong in a Catholic college. You belong to Notre Dame. You should matriculate at the finest university in the world. If you're going to play professional football, there's a back door and there's a front door. This is the front door. You'll be nationally recognized."

Then he looked at me.

"Paul," he said, "not only will you get a good college education here, but I think I can make you the greatest football player in the country."

That did it. Sherrill said, "Where do we sign?" And Leahy said, "We don't sign, we shake hands." And so we did.

It was hard to say no to Bryant. Still, when it was time to make the biggest decision of my life to that point, I told mom that she finally could stop praying on her rosary beads every night. Sherrill and I were going to South Bend to play for Leahy. On July 17, 1953, we confirmed our commitment in a wire to Leahy.

In the final analysis, I did it for mom. She had sacrificed so much for me that I felt I owed her at least this much. She was the kind of Catholic mom who could imagine no bigger honor than having a son who graduated from Notre Dame. To her, a football scholarship to South Bend was a blessing, almost a gift from God. If I hadn't picked Notre Dame, I think it would have broken her heart.

A year later, Bryant abruptly left Kentucky for Texas A&M, of all places. He left because he couldn't beat General Robert Neyland, the legendary coach at Tennessee, and because the Kentucky president had reneged on his promise to fire Rupp because of the point-shaving scandal. Angrily, Bryant took the only job still available, which was at Texas A&M. He had to be really mad at Kentucky because College Station was a dump compared with Lexington.

As I got to know Coach Bryant later, I learned that we had a lot in common. We appreciated a pretty woman and a stiff drink. He also liked to gamble, which got him into a world of trouble in the early 1960s. The old *Collier's* magazine ran a story in which the writer claimed to have eavesdropped on a telephone conversation between Bryant, then at Alabama, and Georgia coach Wally Butts, arranging to fix the outcome of a game.

Bryant denied the charges, saying that he and Butts were engaged only in football small talk, and he sued *Collier's* for libel. After a highly publicized trial, a jury eventually acquitted him and awarded him so much money that *Collier's* soon went out of business.

Whenever Bryant returned to Kentucky for a speaking engagement, he would tell his audience that he left Kentucky because he couldn't sign me. Once, when I heard him say that, I collared him and said, "Yeah, you didn't get me, but those two oil wells they gave you at Texas A&M didn't hurt, either, did they?" We both had a good laugh over that.

4.

THE GOLDEN BOY IS BORN

I wish I could tell you that I fell in love with Notre Dame the first time I laid eyes on its stadium, the most famous in college football, but that wasn't the case. In fact, it took me a while to warm up to Notre Dame and to understand the place's history, tradition, and spirit.

I don't know why. Maybe I was still wishing that I'd gone to Kentucky. I'd have been playing on Bryant's varsity, probably starting, and I'd have had a car and plenty of dates. In South Bend, I spent much of the first semester dreading the cold, depressing winter to come. Hell, I didn't even own a topcoat.

Notre Dame wasn't coed in those days, and the girls at St. Mary's were a couple of miles away from campus, meaning that even a date for the movies required a lot of bus rides. So the goal was to date a "townie," a girl who lived in South Bend and had access to a car. That's what I did as a senior, but by then I also was dating some Chicago showgirls.

Before my freshman season in 1953, we all had to fill out
questionnaires for Charlie Callahan's sports information department. When I came to the part that asked you to name your he-
roes, I put Babe Parilli in football and Ralph Beard in basketball.
That didn't go over too well with Charlie, but I really didn't have
any Notre Dame players that I admired that much.

I also switched uniform numbers. I'd worn No. 20 in high
school, but under Notre Dame's policy at the time, quarterbacks
wore lower numbers. So I picked No. 5 in honor of Joe DiMaggio, my favorite baseball player, and I wore it for my entire career
in college and the pros.

After about two months in South Bend, Sherrill and I wrote
a letter to the University of Miami, in Florida, saying that we
wanted to transfer. But we never sent it, thank heaven, even
though we both were miserable.

The only thing that saved me that fall was football practice.
Although freshmen were ineligible to play varsity football,
Leahy brought me up to scrimmage against the varsity, mostly
because of my kicking. I don't know what it was, but suddenly I
could kick a lot farther than I did in high school. Leahy did more
than anybody else to give me my first taste of national recogni-
tion. He bragged to the newspaper guys about my kicking and
running. I was told he had never talked like that about anyone.

That year Notre Dame had a helluva team, led by Ralph
Guglielmi at quarterback and Johnny Lattner at halfback.
Lattner, a senior out of Chicago, won the Heisman Trophy that
season. Every freshman was assigned an upperclassman to be a
sort of "big brother" and Johnny was mine. He used to say, "Want
to go downtown to a movie or get a cheeseburger and a Coke?"

But Sherrill and I would say, "Let's go downtown, but how about a beer?"

That wasn't Johnny's thing, of course. He was the opposite kind of guy from me. He used to say, "Hornung knew more about life as a freshman than I did as a senior . . . He took me to bars in Mishewaka that I didn't know existed." Mishewaka was a suburb of South Bend—you didn't know South Bend had suburbs, did you?—where a lot of students and athletes went to blow off steam.

Our season was going along perfectly until November 21, when Don Penza, our captain and senior end, dropped a pass wide open in the end zone, which enabled Iowa to escape with a 14–14 tie in Notre Dame Stadium. (In those days, there was no such thing as overtime.) That was the only blemish on our record. Heading into the final game against Southern Methodist in South Bend, we were 8–0–1 and in the running for the national title.

The week before the SMU game, Leahy had me portray the Mustangs' Freddie Benners and run the spread offense against the varsity. They couldn't touch me in the first half. At halftime, Leahy came up to me and said, "Good job, lad, keep it up." Then he went to the varsity and said, "If Hornung's on his feet at the end of the third quarter, I'm going to run you out of the stadium." So I got beat up pretty good, but I guess it was worth it.

The Friday night before the game, Sherrill and I went to the pep rally in our old field house. It was a musty old place with wooden bleachers and a running track encircling the dirt floor. Since Sherrill and I were freshmen and not members of the varsity, we had to stand with the regular students.

When it was time for captain Penza to speak, he was very emotional as he faced the student body for the first time since blowing the catch that would have beaten Iowa. The first words out of his mouth were, "I just want to say to my teammates and fellow students, I'm sorry . . ."

And that's all he was able to get out. The place went crazy and stayed that way for about twenty minutes. Penza was crying and so was everybody else. The students were telling Penza that he didn't have to apologize. He was one of them and they knew he was trying his best for Notre Dame. The noise was unbelievable, and it just went on and on.

I'm not an emotional guy, but I got choked up. I looked at Sherrill and said, "This is the most amazing thing I've ever seen or heard." Suddenly I understood why grown men grew weepy over Notre Dame Stadium, the fight song, and "Touchdown Jesus." Never again did I think wistfully about playing for Kentucky. From that moment on, I was a Notre Dame man to the core.

Well, we drilled SMU, 40–14, and were voted No. 2, behind only Maryland, in the final polls. In those days, Notre Dame had a policy against playing in bowl games because it represented "overemphasis," or some bullshit like that. So we had to sit home and watch in agony while 10–0 Maryland got upset by Oklahoma, 7–0, in the Orange Bowl. In those days, the national championship was decided by regular-season play only.

As freshmen, Sherrill and I roomed together in Cavanaugh Hall. Once I learned how to study and allocate my time, I did pretty well academically at Notre Dame, except for accounting, which I almost flunked. The coaches discouraged me from studying engineering because it had afternoon labs that conflicted with football practice. So I majored in business, which turned out to be very useful, especially after I retired from pro football.

"Paul has never felt he couldn't do what he set out to do," my mom once told a reporter. "He was no trouble to raise. He always made good grades in school."

Mom and some of her friends made the trip to South Bend to watch me play in the 1954 Old-Timers Game, which always was a big deal at Notre Dame. Besides being the culmination of spring practice, it was the first time the freshmen played on the varsity against the graduating seniors and stars from the past.

Mom was very nervous. As she told her friends, "I'm afraid I'll drop dead when he runs out on that field. Maybe I belong home saying the rosary. Paul never writes me about how he's doing. He just tells me to pray for him and not worry."

I sat on the bench the entire first quarter. Waiting to get in the game seemed like an eternity. In fact, the first quarter seemed so long that when it was over, I thought it was halftime and almost headed for the locker room.

Once I got the chance, though, I lived up to Leahy's expectations. In fifteen minutes at quarterback, I threw three touchdown passes as the varsity beat the alumni, 40–26. Tommy Fitzgerald of the *Courier-Journal*, my hometown paper, was there to cover the game, and he dubbed me "The Golden Boy."

I was really looking forward to playing for Leahy as a sophomore in 1954, but Father Theodore Hesburgh, the young, new Notre Dame president, and Father Edmund P. Joyce, his right-hand man, forced Leahy to resign for "health reasons." That was a crock.

Sure, Leahy was having health problems, but the reality was

that he was run off because Hesburgh and Joyce felt he had gotten bigger than the university. (They may have been right.) The
final straw for Leahy was when they cut his scholarships to
twenty-four a year, which wasn't nearly enough to compete
against the national schedule of teams that Notre Dame always
played.

So Leahy retired with an 87–11–9 record, five national
championships, six undefeated seasons, and a 39-game winning
streak in the late 1940s. His successor was young Terry Brennan,
who had been our freshman coach.

I liked Terry. He was very bright and a damned good coach.
His only problem was that he wasn't Leahy, a cardinal sin in the
minds of some of Notre Dame's "subway alums." Still, we had
enough talent returning from the varsity and coming up from
our freshman team that we were picked high in the preseason
polls.

In those days, you had to play both ways in college football, so
I had learned to play defensive back. I was 6-foot-3 and about 195
pounds, big for a back, but I could run. In practice, I could stay
up with Aubrey Lewis for forty yards or so, and he almost made
the 1956 Olympic team as a hurdler. On the depth charts, I was
listed as the fourth-string quarterback and second-team fullback.

We opened the 1954 season against Texas in Notre Dame
Stadium. Brennan had told me before the game that if the Long-
horns won the toss and elected to receive, I'd kick off to them. I
told Guglielmi what the coach had said. "That's wonderful,"
said Ralph. "Your first game, 59,000 people looking on—suppose you go charging up to kick and miss the ball altogether?"

Well, Texas did win the toss and elect to receive. So on my
first varsity play for Notre Dame, I kicked off before 57,594 rabid

fans in the most hallowed football stadium in the nation. Before I kicked, Ralph whacked me on the butt and said, "Don't miss it." I didn't, and, after that, the butterflies disappeared. We beat Texas, 21–0.

At home again against Purdue, I returned a kick 58 yards, one of the few bright spots in a 27–14 loss. We then went to Pittsburgh and drubbed the No. 8 Panthers, 33–0. Sherrill, who had won the starting job at right halfback, scored on a 24–yard pass from backup quarterback Tom Carey, and I scored on an 11–yard run. Amazing! Sherrill and I both scored our first college touchdowns in the same game.

But a few games later, Sherrill suffered a hip injury, the same kind that Bo Jackson had years later. Sherrill thought he could come back from it, but he never really did. He no longer could take a hit on his hip, so he was relegated to spot duty and holding for kicks. He lettered three years and always pulled for me. Yet, as I became more successful, I knew he had to be thinking, "That could be me." And it easily could have been.

As the season progressed, I played some fullback on offense and safety on defense, but mostly Brennan began grooming me to replace Guglielmi, a first-team consensus All-American, at quarterback. My best game as a sophomore came in a 42–13 win over North Carolina. Playing the entire second half at quarterback, I completed five passes and ran seven times for 72 yards. I also intercepted a pass on defense and returned it 70 yards before being overtaken from behind at the one-yard line.

George Dixon, our quarterbacks coach, was so upset at me being caught from behind that he instituted what came to be known as "the whistle drill" the next week in practice. "Never again will that happen, Hornung." So he made me get down in a three-point stance on the goal line. When he blew his whistle, I'd sprint until he blew it again. Then I'd get back down in the stance immediately and sprint again when he blew the whistle. Sprint and stop, sprint and stop. After about eight times up and down the field that way, I collapsed. He made me get up and start again. It was brutal, but I was never caught from behind again.

We finished the season at 9–1, our only loss to Purdue.

After we hung up the pads for the winter, Johnny Jordan, the Notre Dame basketball coach, invited me to come out for the varsity. He knew I could play a little because he had seen Sherrill and me play intramural ball for the Air Force ROTC team.

Jordan had lost so many players from the previous season that I quickly became the sixth or seventh man, averaging 6.1 points for a 14–10 team. Whenever I got the ball, I wanted to shoot it. Hell, I was from Kentucky, and that's the way I learned to play. In my best game, I scored 13 points against DePaul.

Jordan liked to tip a few, and sometimes, on the road, he'd take me out drinking with him. He could do that because I wasn't on a basketball scholarship. I earned my monogram, but never again played basketball for Notre Dame because Brennan was afraid I'd neglect my studies and become academically ineligible for football.

I had another sensational spring in 1955, and, even though the varsity lost to the alumni in the Old-Timers Game, Leahy heaped some pressure on me, proclaiming, "Paul Hornung will be the greatest quarterback Notre Dame ever had. He runs like a mower going through grass. Tacklers just bounce off of him. His passing is tops and his kicking is, too."

An overwrought writer reported that "Hornung runs like a berserk elephant trampling through a banana patch."

That summer I stayed in South Bend, where I attended summer school and worked at Drury's Brewery for the handsome sum of three dollars an hour. I also expanded my social horizons. Guglielmi had introduced me to Julius Tucker, a trucking company executive who took such a liking to me that he let me use his car, a little green Studebaker.

Julius, in turn, introduced me to a couple of Chicago guys named Abe Samuels, a millionaire bachelor who was a huge Bears fan, and Manny Scar, who owned a nightclub and was rumored to be somewhat connected to the mob. It was through them that I was introduced to the Pump Room, Chez Paree, and the other top nightclubs in Chicago. I briefly fell in love with Pat Lee, a Chicago showgirl who had been Miss Photo Flash.

My name began appearing in the gossip columns as well as the sports columns. Through Samuels, I got to meet show-biz celebrities such as Tony Bennett, Phil Silvers, Sammy Davis Jr., and Dean Martin. That was pretty high living for a poor kid from Louisville.

I had a helluva season in 1955. The team went 8–2 and was ranked No. 9 in the final Associated Press poll. I ranked fourth nationally in total offense (1,215 yards passing and rushing), and on defense I made a team-high four interceptions.

We had to fight against injuries the whole season. Ray Lemek, our captain and guard, played on one good leg. Our other guard, Pat Bisceglia, also had a bad leg. We had one center, Jim Mense. Gene Kapish, an end, had a bad knee. And we didn't have too many subs. We just played the same group, game

in and game out, and if they got hurt, they played the next week
anyway.

We won our first three games before being upset by Michigan State, 21–7. We bounced back the next week to beat Purdue, 22–7, but I broke my nose in a pileup. On the sidelines,
they jerked the nose back straight, stuffed cotton up it to stop the
bleeding, and when I went back into the huddle, one of the guys
looked at me and said, "Oh, hell, there goes Hornung's Hollywood contract."

Before the next game, against Navy, I was interviewed by
Jimmy Cannon of the *New York Post*, who was then one of the
most influential sports columnists in the nation. He noted my
self-confidence. "They must be conceited, but the good athletes
conceal it and use it as a skill," Cannon wrote. "It is a quality big
gamblers develop when they work at their vice a long while. It is
unique in a kid such as Paul Hornung . . ."

The crowd included Admiral Arleigh Burke, the chief of
naval operations. Although Navy quarterback George Welsh had
a good day, completing 13 of 25 passes, we won, 21–7. I scored
one TD and set up two others with a 24-yard run and an interception. Wrote Cannon, "I think Hornung is one of the best
players of our time."

Against Iowa, with us trailing 14–7 in the fourth quarter, I di-
rected a touchdown drive that ended when under heavy pressure
I dropped back to the Hawkeyes' forty-yard line and then hit Jim
Morse with a TD pass. I also kicked the extra point to tie it.

After we regained possession with less than five minutes to
play, I hit Morse with a 35-yard pass that set up my game-
winning, 28-yard field goal. The fans were so excited that they
carried me off the field.

The next day, Brennan called me into his office to tell me I had made history. He said he had never known a player to be carried off the field in Notre Dame Stadium. But he also told me not to expect it to happen again. "We don't do that at Notre Dame," he said.

A week later, we played Southern Cal in the Los Angeles Coliseum and lost, 42–20. But I passed and ran for 354 yards, the single-game high for the season, and probably got at least another 100 yards returning punts and kickoffs. I also played fifty-nine minutes. I don't think I've ever felt as tired after a game, at least until I got to Green Bay.

In the Heisman voting, I finished fifth behind Ohio State senior Howard "Hopalong" Cassady. The other three players ahead of me in the voting—Jim Swink of Texas Christian, George Welsh of Navy, and Earl Morrall of Michigan State— also were seniors, so that made me the front-runner for the '56 Heisman.

That '55 season we became the first Notre Dame team to play three televised games (one national, two regional), so that gave me some unprecedented exposure. Plus, I had the Notre Dame mystique behind me. Notre Dame is the greatest place in the world for a football player. As I used to tell ex-Michigan All-American Ron Kramer after we became teammates in Green Bay, "Michigan football may be popular in Michigan, but Notre Dame has a following in every state."

After the season, I was named to the *Look* magazine All-American team, which meant I got to fly to New York to appear on the popular *Ed Sullivan* TV show. I got to meet a great bunch of guys in New York: Cassady, Kramer, Jim Parker of Ohio State, Calvin Jones of Iowa, and many more.

Before I met Parker and Jones, I hadn't been around too many black players. We had only a handful at Notre Dame when I was there, even though Notre Dame was considered progressive for that time. Hell, Notre Dame didn't have a black All-American until Alan Page in 1966.

I fell in love with New York. I got to know Toots Shor, who owned a restaurant where a lot of athletes and entertainers hung out. Toots was the king of New York's nightlife, at least partly because he was an easy touch for everyone he cared about. If he had twenty-five thousand dollars in his pocket, it would be gone in two days. And what he didn't give away, some of his bartenders and captains stole from him.

He was just a beautiful guy with a big heart. After he went bust, Frank Sinatra took care of everything for him. When John Daly was the moderator of the popular *What's My Line?* television show, he hung out at Shor's, and Toots convinced him to give Colonel Harland Sanders his first national exposure for Kentucky Fried Chicken.

I loved the stories I heard in Shor's. Such as the time that Jackie Gleason bet Toots a thousand dollars that he could beat him in a race around the block. Poor Toots huffed and puffed his way around, but when he staggered into his bar, there was Gleason, sipping a drink.

"I took a cab," Jackie said.

Toots affectionately called all his friends "bums." But when I walked in there one day, he boomed, "Here comes my loud-mouth buddy!" When I asked him what he meant, he said, "A loudmouth is a martini. It's a man's drink, and the more you drink, the louder you get."

On that trip to New York after my junior year, our hostess was actress Kim Novak, who had just made the movie *Picnic*. She was so gorgeous that a lot of the guys wanted to ask her out to dinner. But the only one who had the nerve was, well, guess who?

So I introduced myself and told her that my man at Notre Dame had given me carte blanche at the Stork Club, then one of the hottest nightclubs in New York. "Sure, Paul," she said, "but let me talk to my agent." She came back and said that if she went, her agent, his wife, and a couple of others had to go. I knew my carte blanche at the Stork Club didn't stretch that far and I had only forty-four dollars in my pocket. So she smiled and said she was sorry, and that was that.

Later, I went to the Stork Club with Don Schaeffer, one of my Notre Dame teammates from Pittsburgh. "Damn, Schaeffer," I finally said, "I could be here with Kim Novak, and, instead, I'm with an ugly son of a bitch like you."

Somehow, it just wasn't quite the same.

5

"MOM, I WON THE HEISMAN!"

The funniest story I've ever heard about the Heisman Trophy involved Glenn Davis, the great Army running back for Colonel Red Blaik in the 1940s. He was "Mr. Outside" to full-back Doc Blanchard's "Mr. Inside." I used to go to the Norman Theater in Louisville to see those two guys on the *RKO News of the Week*. Both won the Heisman, Blanchard in 1945 and Davis in '46.

Davis played his pro ball with the Los Angeles Rams. He was a good-looking guy who got some bit parts in a few movies. After he got divorced, he began dating actress Terry Moore. She was a knockout, but she knew absolutely nothing about football.

One night at Davis's house, she noticed this huge trophy of a football player throwing a straight arm.

"What's that?" she said.

"The Heisman Trophy," said Davis. "It goes every year to the best player in college football."

"And you won it?" said the actress.

"Yes," said Davis. "I was very fortunate. It's a really special trophy. There aren't too many of them out there."

The next week, she and Glenn went to the Blanchards' to have dinner. As she was looking around their house, Terry noticed a trophy identical to the one that Davis had.

"Did you send your trophy over here?" she asked.

"No," said Davis. "Doc was fortunate enough to win one, too."

The next week, she and Davis went to have dinner at the home of Dr. Les Horvath, who was Glenn's dentist, and damned if Terry didn't see another Heisman. Horvath was the 1944 winner while playing at Ohio State.

"Glenn, you've been lying to me," she said. "This trophy isn't special. Everybody you know has one!"

Heading into the 1956 season, I was considered the front-runner for the Heisman, although there wasn't nearly as much publicity about the award then as there is now. Nobody even mentioned it until November at the earliest.

After another summer of going to school and working at the brewery, I was ready to have a great senior season. We were ranked in the preseason top ten by many of the magazines. I saw no reason why we shouldn't challenge for the national title again.

My senior year got off to a traumatic beginning. As I was leaving Cartier Field, where we practiced, I saw a girl whom I had been dating. I had met her over the summer. When I saw her standing there, I was flabbergasted.

"What are you doing here?" I said.

"I need to talk with you," she replied.

After I had showered, we went to get a cup of coffee and she told me she was pregnant. She said it had been confirmed by a doctor at home, but I asked her to go to a doctor friend of mine in South Bend, just to be sure. He also confirmed it. She wanted to have an abortion, and I told her to do whatever she wanted but to keep it quiet because neither of us needed the publicity.

As she told me later, she went back home and "took care of it." I never asked her what that meant. I saw her a few times after that, but it was never the same.

It became quickly apparent that our preseason ranking was due to Notre Dame's tradition, not our talent. My only reliable receiver was Jim Morse, a great football player and a helluva guy. When we were juniors, I used to babysit for him and his wife.

Jimmy probably did better than anybody in Notre Dame's class of '57. He owned shopping centers all over the country, and made so much money that he gave Notre Dame more than $5 million.

(Jimmy wanted his son, Bobby, to play football at Notre Dame, but the admissions office turned Bobby down. So he went to Michigan State, where he played from 1983 to 1986 and became the main blocker for Lorenzo White, the Spartans' all-time leading rusher. During Bobby's four-year varsity career, Michigan State beat Notre Dame twice. As a proud dad, you couldn't blame Jimmy for having a secret little chuckle over that.)

We lost our 1956 opener on the road to third-ranked SMU, 19–13, but came back home to beat Indiana, 20–6. But then we dropped three straight at home to Purdue, No. 2 Michigan State, and top-ranked Oklahoma.

Before the season, I asked for tickets to the Michigan State and Oklahoma games, our biggest home games of the season. I got about thirty, and I sold the Michigan State tickets for about seventy-five dollars each. But I'm lucky nobody asked for their money back because the game was a disaster. We were tied 7–7 at halftime, but then the Spartans blew us out in the second half, rolling to a 47–14 win behind the running of Clarence Peaks and Dennis Mendyk.

I dislocated my left thumb against Michigan State while making a tackle that saved a touchdown. Despite the Michigan State blowout, I made my first appearance that week on the cover of a relatively new magazine named *Sports Illustrated.* I might have been the first victim of what came to be known as the *SI* "cover jinx." But I must say that Oklahoma was the best college team I had ever seen. They had All-Americans in Tommy McDonald and Jerry Tubbs. The Sooners kicked our ass, 40–0, our worst loss ever.

I also lost in the wallet because, after the Michigan State loss, I could get no more than fifty dollars each for the Oklahoma tickets.

We went on the road and lost to Navy (33–7) in Baltimore and to Pittsburgh (26–13). But I set what surely must be an NCAA record by dislocating my right thumb against the Panthers. Has anybody else ever played with two dislocated thumbs?

We finally ended our losing streak with a 21–14 win over North Carolina at home, a game in which I scored all our points. But then we dropped our last two, both on the road, to No. 3 Iowa (48–14) and No. 17 Southern Cal (28–20).

Before the Southern Cal game, our former coach Frank Leahy asked me to leave our training site in Santa Barbara and come to Los Angeles to appear on a TV show where he was to an-

nounce the All-American team he picked for Chrysler. I wanted
to do it because Chrysler would have paid my mother's way out
to California and back.

I told Leahy I'd have to get permission from Coach Brennan.
However, Terry said no because I'd have to miss a practice and I
wouldn't get back to Santa Barbara until late. Well, Leahy was so
pissed that he came out that week and told the media that our
team "lacked the spirit of past Notre Dame teams."

The so-called "feud" between Brennan and Leahy was still a
big story when we took the field against Southern Cal. My
thumbs were so sore that Brennan moved me to halfback and
put in Bob Williams at quarterback.

Under the circumstances, I had another great game against
the Trojans, including the only three pass receptions of my college career and a 95-yard kickoff return for a touchdown, which
tied for the sixth longest in Notre Dame history up to that time.
Said Brennan, "If there's a better back in the nation than Hornung, I'd like to see him."

Bob Waterfield, the veteran Los Angeles Rams quarterback,
scouted the game and sent a two-word message to his employer:
"Get him." I wish he had given the same message to his wife, the
sultry actress Jane Russell.

Although we finished a stunningly poor 2–8, Notre Dame's
first losing season since 1933 and its worst record ever to that
point, I finished second nationally in total offense (1,337 yards).
I also led the team in rushing, passing, scoring, punting, total offense, field-goal kicking, kickoff return average, and minutes
played. Oh, yeah, I also was second in tackles.

I was an All-American again, although a couple of the wire
services demoted me to second string because of our record. I

didn't think much about the Heisman because nobody from a losing team had ever won. But on December 4, 1956, I got a call from Charlie Callahan, who told me to come to his office. When I walked in the door, he handed me a telephone and said, "Here, tell your mother that you've won the Heisman Trophy."

That made me Notre Dame's fifth Heisman winner, following Angelo Bertelli, Johnny Lujack, Leon Hart, and Johnny Lattner. (John Huarte and Tim Brown won it after me.)

I was amazed, really, especially considering the competition. The runner-up, by only twelve votes out of more than three hundred cast, was Johnny Majors, the star tailback on a 10–0 Tennessee team that had finished second to 10–0 Oklahoma in the polls. (The polls proved accurate when the Volunteers were upset by Baylor in the Sugar Bowl.)

Third and fourth in the voting were halfback Tommy McDonald and center-linebacker Jerry Tubbs of unbeaten national champion Oklahoma. The rest of the top ten were Jim Brown of Syracuse, Ron Kramer of Michigan, John Brodie of Stanford, Jim Parker of Ohio State, Ken Ploen of Iowa, and Jon Arnett of Southern Cal.

Brown was, and still is, the best football player ever, period, but he didn't win the Heisman, because blacks were only starting to enter the mainstream of college football. My friend Dick Schaap was so upset that he swore he would never again participate in the Heisman voting.

Many years later, when Lindsey Nelson and I were doing some college games for WTBS, Ted Turner's cable station in Atlanta, I was assigned to do a Tennessee game when Majors was coaching in Knoxville.

During the interview, I said, "Coach, we have about 19 million people watching, and many of them would like to know why you didn't win the Heisman Trophy in 1956." I caught him completely off guard. While he was fumbling around for something to say, I said, "Personally, I thought Tommy McDonald should have won it."

I was trying to put him on the spot and I did. I acted like I was just kidding, but I really did think McDonald was the guy to beat, considering the season Oklahoma had, and I was a little surprised that I beat him.

In December I took my mother to New York for the Heisman ceremony, her first trip to that area since she had come back to Louisville to have me. I made a second trip to New York that month for the *Look* magazine All-American team.

This time our hostess was Kathryn Grant, a former Miss Texas who had started dating Bing Crosby. I didn't even take a shot at her. Bing was worth $40 million or so and all I had was a forty-pound trophy. However, I wasn't completely shut out. She let me take her to church at St. Patrick's Cathedral.

I got a big thrill by being invited to the Sullivan TV show again, where Oklahoma coach Bud Wilkinson and I were introduced from the audience. But what I remember most about that trip was the night that Arnett, Calvin Jones, and I went to hear some jazz in Greenwich Village.

After the festivities in New York, Jimmy Morse and I went to San Francisco for the East-West All-Star Game. When we began practicing, Brennan, who was East head coach, picked me to be the punter and Oklahoma's Tubbs, not my friend Dave Kuhn from Kentucky, to be the long snapper, even though Kuhn and I had practiced together before we left for San Francisco.

I knew I was in trouble when, at our first practice, Tubbs

looked back at me and said, "Paul, do you have to stand so far back?" I told him I normally stood fifteen yards behind the line of scrimmage when I punted. Tubbs's first snap hit five yards in front of me and dribbled back. I chalked it up to nerves. But when the second did the same thing, I asked him if he was all right.

"You have to understand, Paul," Tubbs said, "we never punted at Oklahoma."

From there, Morse and I went to Hawaii for the Hula Bowl, another all-star game. Along with Jon Arnett and John Brodie, we took over the penthouse of the Reef Hotel in Honolulu. The game sponsors said they would pay for everything except clothes, so we decided to throw a luau at the hotel. We did it right— Hawaiian punch, Polynesian food, a calypso band, the whole deal. We invited about fifteen or twenty girls that we had met. I particularly had my eye on an airline stewardess from Minnesota.

It turned out to be the first time I ever went out the night before a game and the first night I slept on a beach. I didn't wake up until the sun hit me in the face at about 8 or 9 in the morning. I still was hungover at game time, but I was in better shape than Brodie, who was so sick that he didn't play a down. We didn't have any other quarterbacks, so I had to play the whole game.

We College All-Stars lost, 55–21, to the Hawaiian All-Stars, who consisted mainly of moonlighting Los Angeles Rams and San Francisco 49ers, but, amazingly, I played well enough to be named the game's MVP.

Jim Morse and I had to get back to school early, so we were at the airport when I heard this announcement on the public-address system: "Paul Hornung, please report to Pan-American

Airlines." When I did, I found a sheriff and three policemen waiting for me.

"We have a bill here from the Reef Hotel for $800 in clothes and you didn't pay it," the sheriff said.

"I didn't buy any clothes," I said.

"Well," he said, "you signed for them."

I looked at the signature and it wasn't mine.

I finally talked them into letting me board the plane with the promise that I'd send them a check for the clothes when I got back home. I kept my word. To this day, I know that either Brodie or Arnett set me up. I'm sure they thought it was a great gag.

6

THE SIBERIA OF SPORTS

Early in my career at Notre Dame, Ralph Guglielmi had advised me to make sure I got on the dean's list by my last semester, because then I'd have unlimited classroom cuts, giving me time to pick up a lot of easy money through speaking engagements. He knew what he was talking about.

I did a bunch of them, getting about $200 to $250 for each. One I remember in particular was in Harrisburg, Pennsylvania. A guy named Joe Bekelja, who ran a steel company in Harrisburg, kept me in spending money at Notre Dame. I'd get him a sideline pass and he'd give me $100. So when he asked me to give a speech in Harrisburg, I was happy to say yes.

For Joe, I would have done it for nothing. But he gave me $500 to speak to about twenty of his buddies in a private room at his country club. It was a piece of cake. And to top it off, he fixed me up with the prettiest girl in town. She showed me the sights, one of which was the view from the top of the mountain.

The view was a beauty and so was she. I thoroughly enjoyed my-self.

I used part of the money from the speaking engagements to move mom into a nicer apartment in Louisville, near the Audubon Country Club. I also paid a prelaw major, a guy named Eddie, to handle my fan mail for me, which turned out to be a mistake.

After graduation, Sipes and I found that we were six weeks away from two years of active duty in the Air Force. So my mother used some of her Army connections to get us into the Army Reserve, which would require six months of basic training followed by five years of monthly meetings and two weeks of camp every summer.

The NFL draft was held in late spring, and I knew I was going to be the No. 1 pick, then known as the "bonus" pick. That pick would go to either the Packers or the Chicago Cardinals, who both had told the media they would pick me if they won the coin flip.

I really had wanted to play for the Bears, but I thought the Cardinals would be OK because at least I'd be in Chicago. I fig-ured there would be better opportunities in a big city, both for business and for dates. I knew from my days in South Bend that a small town could be tough on a single guy.

But the pick went to Green Bay, which selected me to be the savior for a team that existed in the NFL's smallest city and had endured ten straight losing seasons. I had one other football op-tion, Vancouver of the Canadian League, which offered me $35,000. Once again, I eventually deferred to mom.

"I'd rather have Paul play in the U.S. than Canada," she told a reporter. "If I cared about money, I wouldn't have sent my boy to Notre Dame in the first place."

I also had a movie offer on the table from Twentieth Century Fox. It offered me a seven-year contract for $25,000 a year. The only catch was that I couldn't play football. I decided to stick with football, but I had second thoughts years later when Jim Brown, who retired from the Cleveland Browns a year before I retired from pro football, became the first actor to earn $1 million for a single movie when he signed to do *The Dirty Dozen*.

On January 9, 1957, I met with Packer management to sign my first contract. I was represented by Julius Tucker, my friend from South Bend who had let me use his green Studebaker. It took us only eight minutes or so to sign a three-year contract for $15,000 the first year, $17,500 the second, and $19,500 the third, plus a $2,500 signing bonus.

I used some of the bonus money to buy mom a mink stole, and another $800 to buy a '49 Ford convertible that could do eighty miles an hour in second gear.

I drove it to my first preseason training camp at Stevens Point, Wisconsin. On the way, I stopped off in Chicago for a week to play for the College All-Stars in the annual charity game against the defending NFL champs, which this year happened to be the New York Giants.

The All-Stars' coach was Curly Lambeau, who had been the Packers' coach from 1921 through '49, when he resigned to become vice president and head coach of the Chicago Cardinals. He lasted only two seasons there before retiring.

Lambeau's main offensive assistant was Otto Graham, who had been a great quarterback for the Cleveland Browns in the late 1940s and early '50s. Let's just say that he and I didn't exactly see eye to eye about the importance of this game.

Chicago was my town. I knew the clubs, I knew the show-girls, I knew everybody. After a week of practice, I was ready to go out. So was the rest of the team. Unfortunately for us, Graham decided to have a bed check, and the only rooms he checked were mine and Jim Brown's. So the next day, he ratted us out to Lambeau and said we should be benched for the game.

That put Lambeau on the spot, not only because we were two of his best players, but also because he had been at the Chez Paree the previous night. I saw him come in while I was waiting for my date. He was with Jane Russell, the beautiful actress married to Bob Waterfield.

Somewhat sheepishly, Curly let Graham have his way, and Brown and I started the game on the bench. The team didn't miss me a lot because we had other great quarterbacks in Lenny Dawson from Purdue and John Brodie from Stanford. But not to play Brown was ridiculous.

With two minutes left in the second quarter, and the Giants holding a 7–0 lead, Lambeau put Brown and me into the game. All I did was hand it off to Brown and throw him swing passes. Nobody could stop him one-on-one in the open field. We scored to tie it up at halftime.

Lambeau wanted to start us in the second half, but I told him I was hurt and couldn't play. So during the second half, as Brown and I were sitting on the bench by ourselves, Brown said to me, "Let's you and me get dressed right now and leave. The hell with this."

I was tempted to go along, but I knew that such an act of protest would hurt us with the NFL. Jim was especially vulnerable because he was black, and there weren't too many blacks in the league then. So I said, "Let's not start our pro careers this way."

Jim finally agreed and we sat on the bench the second half, watching the Giants roll to a 22–12 victory. From then on, Jim Brown and I were good friends. But I didn't have much use for Otto Graham.

I got even with him, though. Years later, he came to Louisville for a clinic or something, and he wanted to be fixed up with a date. So I obliged by setting him up with this hooker I knew. I told her only one thing: "Spend the night with him, if he wants, but whatever you do, don't screw him."

The next morning I saw Graham and he looked a little puzzled.

"What's wrong?" I said.

"Good question," he replied. "Beats the hell out of me."

The morning after the all-star game, I drove to training camp with Michigan's Ron Kramer, who was to become my teammate and one of my best friends. When I got there, this girl—she seemed as big as one of our fullbacks—was waiting for me on the steps to the dorm. I was stunned until I finally figured out that Eddie, the prelaw major at Notre Dame, had screwed me over.

I got a lot of fan mail that year, mostly from girls. To give you an idea, I even had a fan club of about forty-five girls in France. Sometimes, unfortunately for me, Eddie got a little too amorous with his replies. That was the case with this poor girl. He had told her that I wanted to meet her when I got to camp.

It embarrassed the hell out of me and I ran her off, but the damage had been done. In looking for me, she had gone into the office and asked Coach Lisle Blackbourn how to find me. Naturally, knowing about my reputation, he was furious. After that, we never hit it off. I didn't like him and he didn't like me, as he demonstrated during a press conference by failing to mention me as he talked about his players.

"What about Hornung?" a writer asked.

"Smart aleck," said Blackbourn.

That's what a lot of my new teammates thought before they met me. They were prepared not to like me because of Notre Dame, my confidence, my reputation as a ladies' man, and my bonus. At first they teased me in a sarcastic way, and tried to kill me in practice. They called me derisive nicknames such as "Heisman" or "Plum" (because of the bonus) or "Golden Dome." One name that stuck was "Goat," because of my thin, narrow, billy-goat shoulders.

But I won them over by always bouncing back up and smiling.

I roomed with Kramer that first training camp, and we agreed that Stevens Point was a real pain in the butt, to be blunt about it. There just wasn't a thing to do except practice football. There was one little bar where you could get a beer and that was about it. If you had $500 in Stevens Point, you could go two weeks and not spend $200. Yet it was a fitting place for the Packers to get ready for another dismal season. The Packers hadn't had a winning record since 1947, when the team went 6–5–1 under Lambeau.

Before camp, the Packers had traded quarterback Tobin Rote to Detroit and obtained Parilli, my old hero, from Cleveland. He was backed up by Bart Starr, a second-year player out of Alabama who had been the very last draft pick in 1956. Blackbourn worked me at three positions—quarterback, halfback, and fullback—which pissed me off because I never knew where I was going to be playing.

The truth was, Blackbourn believed I didn't pass well enough to play quarterback, run fast enough to play halfback, or hold up well enough to play fullback. So, in his mind, that left only one place for me: the bench.

The mood at Green Bay was radically different from what I had known at Notre Dame. Even when we went 2–8, Notre Dame played with pride because we had all that tradition to uphold. But the Packers were so used to losing that all the veterans cared about was their statistics and their next contracts.

The team was so bad that after home games, the players brought their wives into the locker room and unwound there because they didn't want to be seen in public at bars and restaurants. I said the hell with that; I wasn't going to change my lifestyle just because we lost.

Before our last exhibition game in 1957, Max McGee, a three-year veteran end out of Tulane, got out of the Air Force. When he checked into training camp, he found out that he had been assigned to room with me. I was playing cards the first time I saw him, and I was winning a lot of money. Max took one look at all the chips in front of me and said, "That's my roomie."

Max came from a family of good athletes in Longview, Texas. One of his brothers, Coy, played football at Notre Dame in the late 1940s and graduated No. 1 in his class in engineering. Max was smart, too, but he just didn't care much about going to class. At Tulane, I think he majored in Bourbon Street.

We went out after every home game, sometimes to a rock 'n' roll strip joint named Picadilly's. One fan wrote the paper, "Why should I pay to see Hornung in the afternoon when I can see him at night partying at Picadilly's?"

We had some great times at Picadilly's. One night Max and I were in there with the owner, Bobby Harrell, playing cards and minding our own business. But here came these bad-ass motorcycle guys, about thirty of them, wearing their black leather stuff and looking for trouble.

They came strolling up to the bar to get drinks, and one of them looks me squarely in the eye and says, "McGee, you eat shit." While I was figuring out what to do, Max leans over and says to me, "McGee, you going to let him say that?"

Well, the two of us and Harrell started laughing so hard that the motorcycle guys thought we were crazy. They were getting pissed when Harrell brought out a gun from under the bar, where he also kept a baseball bat and a billy club, and said, "Boys, you either get over there and enjoy your drinks, or get the hell out of here."

I hated Green Bay back then. When I got there, Green Bay was the Siberia of sports. Sportswriter Jim Murray once described Green Bay as "the city where the mackinaw is formal wear." Besides being located in the smallest city in the NFL, the Packers also were the only franchise that was publicly owned. The stockholders were the fans, and the team was run by a board of directors. All this meant that Green Bay was the place where nobody wanted to play.

We opened the season with a 21–17 win over the Bears in the new City Stadium, which would be renamed Lambeau Field in 1965. (The featured speaker at the dedication the day of that Bears game was Vice President Richard M. Nixon.)

I played spasmodically in what turned out to be a no-fun 3–9 season. Blackbourn was conservative and bland, the exact opposite of me. I did as well as I could for a coach I couldn't stomach, and in a rare win, 27–10 over the Steelers on November 24, I tore up every muscle and ligament in my left ankle.

I couldn't walk without crutches, so the team gave me four or five days off. I came home to Louisville for a couple of days, went to South Bend to see Notre Dame beat Southern Cal, 40–12, then returned to Green Bay to fly with the team to California for a two-game swing against the Rams and 49ers.

I was hoping the warm weather would help my ankle get better, but it didn't, so I was on the bench for the Rams game in the Los Angeles Coliseum on December 8. Late in the game, with the Rams leading 35–0, Blackbourn put in Starr, who took us on a long drive.

I was sitting there next to Howie Ferguson when I felt a tap on the shoulder. I turned around to see this gorgeous girl in a tight sweater and a short skirt. "I'm not going to leave until I get a photo with you," she said.

I got up and turned around for the photo. Blackbourn didn't see me because he was watching the field. We scored just as the photo was being taken, and Blackbourn turned around just in time to see the girl walking away with her friend, and me easing back down on the bench. He put two and two together and got furious.

"Hornung," he screamed, "get in there and kick off!"

I could barely walk, much less kick, but I went out there because I didn't want to give him the chance to talk about what a bad attitude I had and how selfish I was. I always kicked with my right foot, but my ankle was hurting so much that I couldn't plant my left foot and so I kicked it only a few yards, after which

I got leveled by the Rams' guard who was assigned to get the kicker.

I was in terrible pain when I limped off, but, more than that, I was really pissed. There was no reason for Blackbourn to humiliate me like that, especially in a meaningless game that we lost 42–17.

As soon as the season was over, Sherrill and I went into the Army to do our six months of basic training. We were sent to Fort Knox, only twenty-five miles or so south of Louisville. I actually enjoyed the Army because we spent most of our time playing basketball, softball, and volleyball for our battalion's team.

In December 1957, a story broke that an aspiring actress, Pat Mowry, a former Miss New Hampshire whom I'd dated, claimed that she was engaged to me. She had also dated Elvis, and she reportedly said she liked me better than him.

Naturally, it was only a publicity stunt. A friend of Pat's had concocted the story and "leaked" it to a disc jockey, who put it out on the air. Quickly, it became a national story. Pat later wrote to apologize to me, but we never dated again.

That sort of thing was fairly common back then. The stars and star-wannabes hired press agents to get their names in the gossip columns and the movie magazines. But the press did very little snooping of its own, at least compared with what goes on today. I don't know how some of today's stars put up with the paparazzi.

Being in the Army was a helluva way to spend the off-season, but I was in the best shape of my life when I reported to the Packers' training camp for the 1958 season.

7.

THE GOLDEN BOY
GOES HOLLYWOOD

While I was doing my duty to my country, Blackbourn refused an offer from the Packers board of directors to resign, so he was fired and replaced by Ray "Scooter" McLean, who was a much better guy but just as bad a coach. At preseason camp, McLean announced that we all would be on the "honor system" as far as bed check was concerned. To Max and me, that was a license to party. We established curfew at total exhaustion or 4 A.M., whichever came first.

We went 1–10–1 my second year, the worst record in Packers history. As the columnist Red Smith put it, we "overwhelmed one opponent, underwhelmed 10, and whelmed one." About the best that could be said for me was that I was the best of a bad lot. And even at that, I lost my starting job at fullback for our last two games to rookie Jimmy Taylor of LSU.

McLean's system was just as screwed up as Blackbourn's had been. It was so confusing that nobody could understand it, especially Taylor. When McLean finally started him in my place on the two-game West Coast swing that ended the season, Taylor gained 146 yards without really knowing what the hell he was doing.

The football situation in Green Bay was so bad that our daily poker and gin rummy games were a lot more competitive and exciting. On trips, we played on the planes and in our hotel rooms. At home, we'd get together at somebody's house or a bar.

The games got pretty expensive, too. One time, when we were playing "Boo-ray," a card game from Louisiana where you had to match the pot if you lost, the pot had grown to eight thousand dollars and it was up to Nate Borden, one of our defensive ends, to match it. But he didn't have any money. We forgave him, because he was a good guy, but he also didn't play with us anymore.

Max and I always did pretty well at cards, and maybe that had something to do with us being tempted to bet on football. The Colts were favored to beat us by nineteen in Baltimore only a few weeks after Bart had played a great game against them in a 24–17 loss in Green Bay. Max, Bill Howton, and I were going to bet five hundred dollars each on us plus the nineteen points. (In other words, the Colts would have to beat us by twenty or more in order for us to lose.)

Howton was a former All-Pro end, a real loose cannon, who shared a house with us the previous year. He was the only guy we had who hated physical contact worse than Max. They both hated to block and had a contest to see who could finish the season with the most blocks. In the final game, Max got two blocks to edge Howton, 3–2, for the season.

We all agreed there was no way Baltimore could beat us by

nineteen. I tried to call my man Abe Samuels in Chicago, but I couldn't reach him so we didn't get the bet down.

Well, we fumbled away the opening kickoff and the Colts scored. We fumbled the next kickoff and they scored again. Then, after we ran a couple of plays, we fumbled again and they scored again. The game was four minutes old and we were already down 21–0.

The Colts went on to clobber us 56–0, by far the worst loss I suffered in my Packer career. Those were the days when a white horse circled the field after every Colts touchdown, and we almost killed him that day. I'm surprised we weren't arrested for cruelty to animals.

That should have been a great gambling lesson for me, but it wasn't. Mostly, my betting was limited to the racetrack and card games. I've never made, or lost, much betting on football games.

I was so discouraged that I was really thinking about retiring at the ripe old age of twenty-two. Believe me, football sucks when you're losing. Uncle Henry told me I should think about coming home to Louisville and going into the real estate business with him and Frank Metts. I was thinking seriously about it, but I was also getting in pretty tight with the movie crowd in Hollywood.

By then I had turned into a sort of vagabond. A fairly well-off vagabond, mind you, but one who just didn't stay in one place too long. As soon as the season ended, I'd spend a month or so in L.A. or Hawaii, doing photo shoots for Jantzen sportswear.

The shoots took only a week or so, but I'd stretch them out so I could hang around L.A., going to the Hollywood Park or Santa Anita tracks in the daytime, then running on Sunset Strip into the wee hours. After a few weeks of pure pleasure, I'd go home to

Louisville for a couple of weeks to check on mom and my business interests with Uncle Henry and Frank, most of which were in real estate. Then I'd move on to Miami, where I usually stayed at the Racquet Club and spent a lot of time playing the horses at Gulfstream Park.

I played a lot of golf with Eddie Arcaro, perhaps the greatest Thoroughbred jockey of all time. He won the Triple Crown twice with Calumet Farm horses, Whirlaway in 1941 and Citation in '48. After he retired, Eddie didn't hang around the racetrack much. All he cared about was his golf game.

In Florida, Eddie belonged to La Gorce, and we'd play there a lot. He was a competitor who didn't like to lose at anything, and I can't ever remember losing a golf match with Eddie as my partner. He was a classy guy, and I always enjoyed his company.

One night in Las Vegas, we got drunk and I gave Eddie my diamond cufflinks to remember me by. I also fixed him up with a date. At first she said, "What am I going to do with this little guy?" The next day she came up to me and said she'd never been with anyone like him before. "He's hung like a stallion," she said.

When the weather warmed up in Chicago, I might hang out there awhile and I'd even drop in on Green Bay to play a little gin with Pat Martin, a Notre Dame graduate who had befriended me. His wife, Mary Ellen, came from a great family. Her grandfather had helped start Kimberly-Clark and the Fort Howard paper company. We got so close that they asked me to be the godfather for one of their five children.

To be honest about it, I had more friends than money. I'd gotten into the habit of sending my paychecks home to Uncle Henry, who would take out taxes and invest the rest of it except for four or five hundred dollars that he would send back to me for spending money.

That's all I needed, really, because everywhere I went I had friends who would put me up for a few weeks, loan me a car, pick up the dinner checks, introduce me to girls. It was about as good as it gets. In Honolulu, for example, I stayed with Nick Nicholas, who owned a club called the Red Vest. Like me, Nick was single, and we had a blast. He later franchised a chain of seafood restaurants called Nick's Fish Markets.

I liked wherever I was, but Hollywood was really exciting in those days. I loved it all—the weather, the lifestyle, the people, the excitement of meeting a lot of the movers and shakers in the movie industry.

I got to know Frank Sennes, who owned the Moulin Rouge nightclub; Tony Owens, an executive at Columbia Pictures, who was married to actress Donna Reed; Frank O'Connor, who was a big shot at Universal Studios; and Elmer Valentine, a former cop from Chicago who came up with the idea for Whisky a Go-Go, the biggest nightclub in L.A. in the 1960s.

Goddamn, we did have some parties at the Whisky. It was the hottest spot on Sunset Strip for about ten years. When I first met Elmer, he owned a place called The Party Room that was about to go bust. I loaned him some money, which earned me a friend for life.

When a guy from Atlanta offered to loan him the money to start Whisky a Go-Go, Elmer told me, "I don't know what I'm going to do, so I got to take a shot." Well, Johnny Rivers came in and opened the place. A few weeks later, Janis Joplin played there. The place was on its way. One of the regulars was Steve McQueen, a good friend of Elmer's.

Sometime during this period I fell in love with a cocktail waitress named Donna. I'd take her to dinner, then she'd go to work and I'd go to the Whisky. One night, I came to her club to pick her up, and Hoagy Carmichael was playing the piano and singing for her. He was crazy about her. He'd come in three or four nights a week, just to play and sing for her.

She liked to drink and she'd never let me drive home. So she'd get in my Corvette and get it up to a hundred miles an hour. She would laugh like crazy, but I was scared shitless. But, hell, we were young, and L.A. was the place to be in those days.

I ran around with the Crosby boys—Bing's sons—and with Jon Arnett, whom I'd played against when he was at Southern Cal. Every night, we'd go see Sammy Davis Jr. or Dean Martin, somebody like that. Or maybe we'd catch Don Rickles at a little club on La Cienega called Slate Brothers.

It became a kind of status symbol to get attacked by Rickles, and he used to rip me every time I was in the audience. "There's Paul Hornung," he would say. "Big football player, big ladies' man. Let me tell you, he's the biggest fag in the country." That was funny back then; today you couldn't get away with that kind of humor.

I knew I had to get out of L.A. and clear my mind if I was to make an intelligent decision about my future, so I flew back to Louisville to spend a few days at my mother's place.

But trouble waited there, too. As I said earlier, I still dated Janie, my girlfriend from high school, when I was in Louisville. Well, she missed a period and thought she was pregnant. Unfortunately for me, she told her parents, so one day I walked in to find the parents, Janie, and my mom sitting in my mom's kitchen. Everybody was upset.

Amazingly, however, Janie hadn't been tested by a doctor. When she got tested, it turned out she wasn't pregnant. But the circumstances between us had been so strained that we stopped dating and drifted apart.

On the football front, McLean resigned before the Packers board of directors could fire him, which was good, but by the time the NFL winter meetings rolled around in January, the Packers still hadn't named a head coach.

When contacted by Green Bay management, both Commissioner Bert Bell and Paul Brown of the Cleveland Browns recommended the same man: Vincent Thomas Lombardi, a relatively unknown New York Giants assistant. So the Packers took a shot, which turned out to be the greatest decision in the franchise's history.

"Do you know anything about him?" mom asked.

"Not much," I said, "but I know he's got a good reputation."

The papers said that Lombardi was the son of an immigrant Italian butcher. He had played as a 172-pound guard in the famed "Seven Blocks of Granite" line at Fordham in the 1930s. His coach, Jim "Sleepy" Crowley, was one of Coach Knute Rockne's famed "Four Horsemen" at Notre Dame in the early 1920s. The writer who gave the "Four Horsemen" their nickname, Grantland Rice, was a New York columnist who often wrote about Fordham during Lombardi's playing days.

Lombardi's background also included a stretch on Colonel Earl "Red" Blaik's staff at West Point in the late 1940s and early '50s. He had hoped to get the Giants job when Steve Owens was fired in 1953. Instead, the Giants hired Jim Lee Howell, who picked Lombardi to coach the offense and player-coach Tom Landry to be in charge of the defense.

Later I learned that Lombardi had turned down the Philadelphia Eagles job in 1957, which meant that his last game with the Giants was the 23–17 sudden-death overtime loss to the Colts in the 1958 NFL title game. Many historians now claim that game made the NFL because a record audience saw it on TV.

Knowing that the Packers board of directors was notorious for second-guessing the coach, Lombardi demanded—and received—full control to run the team as he saw fit. He made the trades, negotiated all contracts, and determined who deserved a bonus and how much. The whole time he was in Green Bay, to my knowledge, the board of directors never overturned one of his decisions.

At the same time I was thinking about Lombardi, he was thinking about me. Almost as soon as he arrived in Green Bay in early 1959, he began watching films. He quickly noticed that I had the same kind of versatility as Frank Gifford, the former Southern Cal star who had been his left halfback with the Giants.

"The more I saw of Hornung in those movies," Lombardi said later, "the more I figured he was the man. He didn't have Gifford's moves, but he was bigger and could run harder. Actually, he had better running ability than I thought. And I knew he could throw."

I could tell pretty quickly that under Lombardi it was going to be very different in Green Bay. The first time we talked on the phone, he told me, "You're going to be my left halfback or you're not going to be a player in the NFL." I liked that. I figured that if Gifford could play left halfback, so could I.

I suppose the thing that impressed me the most was how assertive and confident he was. He told me the same thing he had told a group of Wisconsin sportswriters: "I've never been part of a losing team and I'm not going to start now." This was the kind of coach I wanted.

Lombardi never said anything about my reputation as a playboy, even though I'm sure he knew about the photo incident in L.A. All he said was, "I'm going to be all over your ass because you need it and you can handle it." He knew that others couldn't, so he treated them according to their personality and needs. That was the core of what he did. He knew that everyone wasn't the same, so they couldn't be motivated the same. So defensive tackle Henry Jordan wasn't being quite accurate when he said, "He treats us all alike—like dogs!"

Lombardi made me look at football in a whole new light. I realized I wasn't done with it yet. It was still in my blood, and I wanted to know what it felt like to play for a winner again. Plus, having tasted the nightlife in L.A. and New York and Miami, I wasn't ready to settle down to being a Louisville real estate man. And I figured the movies could wait.

Looking back, it was a good thing I didn't go to Hollywood. I don't know if I'd have been strong enough to take it out there. Sunset Strip was hot in those days, and I was *always* on the Strip. There were so many great-looking women in L.A. that I used to say that if you played for the Rams, you should get a medal just for showing up on Sunday.

Given my interests in gambling, football, and my home state, I was interested in the news about George Ratterman, a former backup quarterback to Otto Graham with the Cleveland Browns who had retired after the 1956 season. He plunged into politics and ran for sheriff in Newport, Kentucky, just across the Ohio River from Cincinnati.

Ratterman was an anti-gambling crusader, which naturally made him the enemy of the guys who ran the corner handbooks, distributed gambling cards, and operated high-stakes games at Vegas-style casinos such as the Beverly Hills, the club in Southgate, Kentucky, that burned to the ground in a horrible 1977 tragedy.

The gamblers tried to ruin Ratterman one night by slipping a mickey into his drinks, hauling him to a hotel, and photographing him in bed with a stripper named April Flowers. Naturally, all hell broke loose when the photo was printed in the papers. I remember that Ratterman began his press conference by saying, "You know, a funny thing happened to me on the way to work last night . . ."

As we'll see later, it was my misfortune to join Ratterman as a victim of a drugged cocktail.

8

MEET THE GUYS

Of the eleven members of the Pro Football Hall of Fame who played for the Packers from 1959 to 1967, when we won five championships in nine years, including the first two Super Bowls, I was the only No. 1 draft pick, the only Heisman Trophy winner, and the only first-team consensus All-American. The rest either escaped the notice of the pro scouts or were underrated by them. But we were all Lombardi's kind of guys— unselfish, hard-working, determined, and proud.

For example, consider Willie Wood.

Coming out of Southern Cal as a quarterback in 1960, Wood wasn't drafted, so he sent postcards to several NFL teams, asking for a tryout. Lombardi liked this sort of initiative, so he decided to take a look. And that's how he got a guy who turned out to be the best free safety in the league and an eight-time Pro Bowl player.

Willie had a good, strong arm, but there was no way he was

going to beat out Bart Starr in Lombardi's system. So he didn't complain when Lombardi asked him to become a different kind of player.

In 1961, Willie led the league with a 16.1-yard average on punt returns, and in '62 he led it with nine interceptions. Along with Max McGee and Bart, he played a starring role in Super Bowl I in 1967, intercepting a Len Dawson pass and returning it fifty yards to the Chiefs' five, from where Elijah Pitts scored on the next play.

Somehow, Lombardi snookered Paul Brown of Cleveland into a couple of trades that brought future Hall of Famers Henry Jordan and Willie Davis to us. In 1959, Lombardi got Jordan, Lew Carpenter, Bobby Freeman, and Bill Quinlan in exchange for end Bill Howton, who retired after only a year with the Bears. The next year he got Davis from the Browns for end A. D. Williams.

Willie Davis was a great guy to be around. He was always jivin' around in the locker room, so I called him "Doctor Feelgood." He was serious in games, though. He was so quick off the football that offensive tackles had a hard time blocking him. When we won our first championship in 1961, Willie was our defensive captain and center Jim Ringo our offensive captain.

Ringo was the Packers' center from 1953 to 1963. He was a tough SOB, but after he had made a few Pro Bowls, he got a little too big for his britches. He was at the point where he would dog it in practice or beg off with an injury. With Lombardi, that was a no-no. He liked his players to practice.

Before the 1964 season, Ringo happened to run into Lombardi at the Packers' office. After they had exchanged greetings,

Vince said, "Jim, we haven't signed your contract yet, so why don't you step into my office and we'll get it done?"

Unknown to Lombardi, Ringo had been the first of us to hire an agent to negotiate for him. So you can imagine Lombardi's surprise when Ringo said, "Coach, you'll have to talk with my agent. I'm sure he'll be glad to work with you to get it done."

Then Ringo walked off to shoot the bull with some people working in the office. As he was leaving, he ran into Lombardi again.

"Don't forget to call my agent, Coach," Ringo said.

"Jim," said Lombardi, "you better tell your agent to call Philadelphia because I've just traded you to the Eagles."

That was Lombardi for you. No way he was going to put up with any damned agent. You dealt directly with him and you took what you were offered. In the winter of 1961–62, I used a weekend pass from Fort Riley, Kansas, where I was on active Army duty as a member of the Reserves, to meet Lombardi in Hot Springs, Arkansas. I signed my contract the next day on a golf course.

He also told me that he would never pay me as much as Bart Starr or Jimmy Taylor were getting because I made so much more than they did from commercials and endorsements. To him, that seemed perfectly fair. Can you imagine a player's agent accepting that sort of reasoning today?

Of course, Starr and Taylor deserved every cent they got and a lot more. When the AFL challenged our league by starting a bidding war for the best college seniors, we gave six-figure bonuses to players such as Donny Anderson and Jim Grabowski. Understandably, that bothered a lot of the veterans.

Take Forrest Gregg, for example.

He was our best offensive lineman and perhaps the best all-around athlete on the team. Lombardi loved him because he always executed his assignments perfectly. The coaches had certain criteria they used to grade the offensive linemen, and Forrest always graded high. He was almost as good as Jim Parker of the Colts, who I thought was the best offensive lineman in the league. Off the field, Forrest was a quiet guy whose only real fault, in my eyes, was that he was as close with the dollars as any SOB you've ever seen.

One year the team was in the locker room cutting up the purse we had earned for winning the NFL championship. In those days, the players held a closed meeting to vote on who would get full or partial shares. Sometimes we'd give a share to the cleanup guys or the trainers or the water boys.

When Ringo asked me if I thought anybody outside the team deserved a share, I said, "Yeah, how about those four hookers in San Francisco that everybody laid? I think they should get a share." Well, everybody laughed except Forrest Gregg.

"I don't think that's funny at all," he shouted. "I don't want to give an extra share to anybody, especially some of Hornung's hookers."

He was adamant about it and from then on he always told me, "Hornung, I don't want to hear any talk this year about giving our money away." I guarantee you that Forrest has the first dollar he ever earned.

But he was that way only about money. As a player, Forrest was as good a teammate as you could ever hope to find. All he cared about was executing properly, grading high, and winning. He was completely unselfish, as most of us were.

The only exception was Jimmy Taylor, the hard-running fullback from Louisiana. At LSU, he had played for a national championship team in 1957, but he was overshadowed by Billy Cannon, who won the '59 Heisman Trophy. Then, at Green Bay, he didn't get as much publicity as me, and I think he resented that.

In the locker room after a game, the first thing Taylor wanted to know was how many yards he had gained. Then he wanted to know how many yards Cleveland's Jim Brown had gained.

In the nine seasons between 1957 and '65, Brown won the NFL rushing title eight times. The only year Taylor beat him was 1962, the season Taylor also ended my streak of league scoring titles at three in a row. For their careers, Brown gained 12,312 yards to Jimmy's 8,597, even though Taylor played one more season.

Pound for pound, there wasn't a tougher bastard who ever played than Jimmy. He was big and he was tough, the sort of back who loved to run off tackle and dare anybody to stop him. Compared to Jimmy, I was more of a finesse runner—except when I got inside the ten-yard line.

Jerry Kramer tells a good story about that.

"I remember one game early in my career where we needed to win the ballgame to win the division," Kramer says. "I look over and I see Hornung walking through the hotel lobby with a sweet pea on each arm and a martini glass in each hand. This was on Saturday night.

"So I go over there and get in his face. It was very unusual for me to get on Paul's ass, but I felt pretty strong about it. So I said, 'Hey, bud, this ballgame is terribly critical for us and it doesn't look to me that you're going to be ready for it.' I really challenged his ass.

"And he looked me in the eye and he said, 'You watch me tomorrow. You watch me inside the five-yard line. You watch me in short-yardage situations to see if I'm ready or not.' So I said, 'Good enough.' The next day, I watched him very closely in those situations. He was great. So that's when I learned that Paul came to one o'clock differently from the rest of us, but he always showed up ready to play."

The only time I really worried about losing my starting job was when we drafted Herb Adderley out of Michigan State in 1961. He had played running back for the Spartans, and that's the position where Lombardi put him for the first few days of practice. He was big and he was fast.

And he was also smart, as he proved after about a month of practice when he went to Lombardi and told him he wanted to play defensive back. I guess he figured that he might get more playing time there than he would playing behind me at left halfback. It turned out to be the decision that paved the way for Herb to make the Hall of Fame.

(Under Lombardi, we sometimes used a three-back set with Don McIlhenny as the right halfback. But we soon switched to a mostly two-back set, with me at left half and Taylor at fullback, because Lombardi thought we were at our best with another receiver in the lineup instead of a right halfback. That other receiver was flanker Boyd Dowler.)

Adderley was the first to define the corner position as we still know it today. Adderley had great athleticism, and he was in such good shape that I don't ever remember seeing him breathing hard. He could run faster backward than a lot of guys could run forward, and he aggressively went after the football.

Adderley made thirty-nine interceptions with the Packers from 1961 to 1969. In our 33–14 win over Oakland in Super Bowl II, he returned an interception sixty yards for a touchdown. After being traded from Green Bay following the '69 season, he played three years for the Dallas Cowboys. But perhaps Herb's main claim to fame is that he played in four of the first six Super Bowls, winning three championship rings.

Once, after I had retired and Herb was playing for the Cowboys, a big TV executive loaned me his ranch outside Dallas for a few days. I called up Herb to see if he wanted to have dinner there and he said, "Sure, but I have to ask you a question: do you mind if I bring a white girl?"

Well, that was certainly no problem for me, so I got a date and the four of us had dinner right there at the ranch. It was a helluva place, with servants and all the amenities. There was even a theater where we watched a movie after dinner. Herb and I felt like Howard Hughes.

When I asked Herb how he liked playing for the Cowboys, he told me something that I thought was the key to our success at Green Bay.

"Paul, they have more talent on this team than we ever had on any of ours at Green Bay," he said. "But these guys are different. Once practice is over with, they're gone. There's no such thing as going out to have a beer or hanging around together. I've been here awhile, and there are still a couple of my teammates who haven't spoken to me. I can see now why Dallas could never beat us."

While Adderley and Wood intimidated rival pass receivers with their quickness and aggressiveness, Henry Jordan teamed with Willie Davis to give us two of the best pass rushers in the league. Offensive linemen hated to block Henry, a country boy from West Virginia, because he was even quicker than Willie.

Of course, the anchor of our defense was Ray Nitschke, our Hall of Fame middle linebacker. For the first few years that we were teammates, he was a real pain in the ass. But, then, after he stopped drinking, he turned into the greatest Packer of all. To his dying day (March 8, 1998), Packer fans loved him. So did his teammates.

Ray came up the hard way. He was raised in Cicero, Illinois, by his older brother, and the two of them were tough guys who didn't mind getting into bar fights. They didn't always win. After we won the '61 NFL championship, for example, the Nitschke brothers got the shit beat out of them by two of Ray's teammates, Dan Currie and Bill Quinlan. It wasn't over anything in particular. Just a bunch of drunk jocks blowing off steam after a big win.

Last, but hardly least, was Bart Starr. When I talk about Bart, I tend to gush. He was one of the most perfect men I've ever met in my life. We lockered next to each other for ten years and I never heard him curse. I took care of that for our corner of the dressing room.

I first saw Bart play when I was still in high school. Another school in Louisville, duPont Manual High, had a quarterback named Bunky Gruner, who was the main reason his team was ranked No. 1 in the state. That season Manual played at home against the top-ranked team in Alabama, Sidney Lanier High of Montgomery. I went to watch Gruner, but I ended up marveling at Starr. Bart's team won, 39–0.

After a decent career on some bad, pre-Bryant Alabama teams, Bart was the 356th and last pick in the 1956 NFL draft. At

Green Bay, coaches Blackbourn and McLean used him as a backup. He didn't move into the starting lineup permanently until 1960, Lombardi's second year, but he remained the Packers' starter until he retired after the 1971 season.

One of the great myths about being an NFL quarterback is that it's imperative to have a strong arm. As Bart proved, that's simply not true. How far you throw the ball isn't nearly as important as how accurate and smart you are.

Bart would listen to his offensive linemen. If one of them told Bart that he could dominate his defensive opponent and block him either left or right, Bart would take him at his word. But the lineman had better be able to do what he said he could, or he'd have to answer to Bart.

His wife, Cherry, was a beautiful lady and a damned good cook. Like most girls from the South, she knew that fried chicken wasn't any good unless it was cooked in lard. A couple of times every season, she'd invite Max and me over for fried chicken. It was as good as any I ever tasted.

On Saturday mornings, when we'd do a no-contact run-through, Bart would bring his sons, Bart and Bret, into the locker room with him. A lot of the players did that, but there was something different about Bart's kids. While the others were running around and screaming, Bart and Bret were perfect gentlemen. Everything was "yes, sir" and "no, sir." If Bart told them to sit on stools and talk to Mr. Hornung while he was taking a shower, they'd do it.

Bret, in particular, really liked me. Cherry liked to talk about the time that she took him to a grocery store and another kid came up to him.

"I bet your dad plays for the Green Bay Packers," the kid said.

"Yes, he does," said Bret.

"I bet I know who he is," the kid said.

"I'll bet you don't," responded Bret.

"Who is it?" said the kid.

"Paul Hornung," said Bret.

Tragically, Bart and Cherry lost Bret to a drug overdose when he was in his twenties. Of all the terrible things imaginable, it was Bart who found him. I felt so badly about it that I felt almost as though I had lost a son of my own.

We had a few other guys who I think deserve to be in the Hall of Fame. Our guards, Jerry Kramer and Fuzzy Thurston, were the lead blockers on our bread-and-butter play, the "Green Bay sweep." Both played their positions about as well as anybody in the league at that time.

So did Ron Kramer, our tight end. He was such a great athlete that he was drafted by both the Packers and the Detroit Pistons of the NBA. He won something like twelve letters and he never had a coach raise his voice at him until he played for Lombardi. If he'd run a bad route or miss a block, Vince would let him have it. It took a while for Ron to get used to Vince.

He certainly wasn't alone.

9

THE LEADER OF THE PACK

Lombardi moved our training camp from Stevens Point to St. Norbert College in West De Pere, just outside Green Bay. When I met him face to face before that season in 1959, I wasn't particularly impressed with his appearance. He was maybe 5-foot-10 with graying hair and a bit of a paunch. When he smiled, which wasn't often in those early days, he had a gap-toothed grin. But there was something about him, a no-nonsense approach to football, that hadn't been seen in Green Bay for many years.

It didn't take long for Lombardi to show us there was a new sheriff in town. We were supposed to be in bed at 11 P.M., and one night Lombardi showed up at 11 on the dot in the room that Jerry Kramer and Jimmy Taylor were sharing. Taylor was sitting on his bed with his socks and shorts on. Lombardi fined him twenty-five dollars for not being in bed. The next day, he fined Nitschke fifty dollars for being in the phone booth a couple of minutes after 11.

After a few weeks, I'd had enough. I asked Kramer if he wanted to sneak out with me, and he signed up. Naturally, Max was game. At 11:30, the three of us started sneaking down the hall.

We stopped to get Jim Ringo. "Hog" Hanner, Ringo's roommate, said he couldn't sleep alone, so he joined us. When we passed Bill Quinlan's room, he woke up and joined us, as did his roommate, Dan Currie, who claimed he was afraid of the dark.

So the seven of us sneaked out. The only place still open was a pizza joint, so we went there and spent a few hours laughing and talking, pleased that we had put something over on Lombardi. But we hadn't. It turned out that Lombardi knew everything. His spy system was amazing. But rather than fine us, he gave us a warning: "People have been phoning me saying that they've seen some of you guys out after curfew, but I don't pay any attention to those crank calls."

But Max was stubborn. A few weeks later, Lombardi found out that he had sneaked out and fined him $125. He promised that the next violation would cost $250, a hefty sum considering what we were making.

Before camp, Lombardi did two things that convinced me he knew what he was doing. First, he sent an assistant coach, Red Cochran, to spend a month with Taylor in his hometown of Baton Rouge, Louisiana, so Taylor would know the offense by the time he got to training camp. The previous year, under McLean, the rookie Taylor never did catch on to our confusing offense.

Second, he began trading for veteran players who had an understanding of what it took to win. A good example was his acquisition of veteran free safety Emlen Tunnell from the Giants.

Tunnell was the king of Harlem because he spent every quarter he ever earned there. He invested in businesses and was a soft touch for somebody who was down on his luck. If anybody from the streets needed fifty dollars, they knew where to go. I promise you that at that time, if Tunnell had been walking down one side of 125th Street and Sugar Ray Robinson down the other, Tunnell would easily have drawn the bigger crowd.

One night he took some of us to a club in Harlem. Nitschke, the perfect bully, was sitting at the bar and smarting off. Finally this really tall black guy got up and said, "Hey, white boy, sit down and shut up or your ass will be out the door." It was Wilt Chamberlain. Nitschke didn't make another peep.

The rest of us were having a great time when up gets Dinah Washington, the talented black singer who was married to defensive back Dick "Night Train" Lane of the Detroit Lions. She put on a helluva show. Afterward, Tunnell told us that if any of us wanted to buy a mink stole, just let him know. We all bought one. I gave mine to mom. They were hot, no question about it.

Emlen was kind of a father figure to the young black players. Emlen didn't see black players or white players, he just saw ballplayers. He did a lot of good for Willie Wood, who had a chip on his shoulder when he joined the team. Tunnell proved to be a stabilizer, and that's the same reason that Lombardi had brought in Bill Quinlan from Cleveland.

Soon after he joined the team, Quinlan showed us why Lombardi had acquired him. After practice one day, he told us, "No wonder you guys aren't champions. You don't talk like champions. You talk like you enjoy getting beat." Then he turned on defensive tackle Dave "Hog" Hanner.

"You're not smart enough to be an end," Quinlan barked.

"You don't have the speed. You can't diagnose the plays. You're not tough enough. You don't have the ability or the brains."

"OK, Quinlan," said the fuming Hanner, "let's go outside and settle this."

"That's the way, Dave," said Quinlan, grinning. "Now you're talking like a champion."

That first camp, Lombardi made the personnel changes that put me and Taylor in the backfield with Boyd Dowler. Just as important, Lombardi also gave us a simplified system that suited our talents. His philosophy was keep it simple and avoid mistakes. That was far different from Blackbourn and McLean. Lombardi didn't care whether somebody knew a certain play was coming or not. He knew that if we executed properly, we couldn't be stopped.

We had about eighteen offensive plays—ten runs and eight passes—and Starr called them all. He really was an extension of Lombardi. The best one, as far as I was concerned, came to be known as the "Green Bay sweep." I'd get a handoff from the quarterback and take off around end at about three-quarters speed so I could give guards Jerry Kramer and Fuzzy Thurston time to pull and get ahead of me.

We had the most success running it to the strong side, where tight end Ron Kramer was. Kramer could manhandle most of the strong-side linebackers in the league, and Taylor would block the defensive end. I'd find the hole and run to daylight. We ran it over and over again. Our offensive team was really smart, and our guys seldom missed an assignment.

Jerry Kramer once said that I had a "wonderful ability to set up a blocker." By that he meant that I'd stay behind the blockers and see how a play was developing before making my cut. When

Elijah Pitts joined the Packers as my backup in 1961, it took him a while to learn that. When Elijah was running the pitch, he wouldn't wait for his blocks. He'd overrun them and not get nearly as many yards as he should have.

Finally Kramer said, "Elijah, I can't outrun you, but I can block for you. So goddammit, wait for me." To make the sweep work, everybody had to do his job. When it worked perfectly, it looked so easy. In Wisconsin, artists have made a lot of money by making paintings of our sweep. I've seen only one I thought was inaccurate. It had McGee making a block, and, hell, that was ridiculous.

Lombardi also saw to it that we all were in good shape. Our biggest linemen weighed no more than about 250 or so. That's one difference I notice between our NFL and today's NFL. You see these big ol' fat linemen weighing 350 or more. That can't be good for their health. A lot of them will be lucky to make it to fifty.

I don't know how rampant steroid use is in today's NFL, but you have to look at some of these guys and wonder. In our day, there also was drug use, but it was mainly uppers and downers. Jim Ringo used them a lot. He was our offensive captain, and when he went out to the middle of the field for the pregame coin flip, I don't know how he was able to get "heads" or "tails" out of his mouth.

The "pep pills," as they were called, really got the adrenaline flowing and put a lot of guys on edge. The linemen got me to try them once. I didn't sleep for three days, and that was the end of the "pep pills." Besides, Lombardi would have been furious if he had known about it.

What Lombardi changed the most in Green Bay was the atmosphere. Laziness and carelessness weren't tolerated. He de-manded that we begin thinking and acting like winners. Lom-bardi believed fear was the best motivator and he used it constantly. One of his favorite sayings was "Fear will make cow-ards of us all."

Most of the Packers were scared to death of him, no matter how big and mean they were. Of all the Packers, nobody was more scared of Lombardi than Max McGee. He never ques-tioned any of Lombardi's decisions, not even when Lombardi, as general manager, offered him the usual parsimonious salary. Max would simply accept it, thank him, and get out of his office as fast as he could.

But, to be fair to Lombardi, Max never had reason to com-plain. Every year Lombardi would give Max a fair raise because he knew he deserved it. Despite all of our pranks, Max was one hell of an end, even though he hated contact so badly that I re-member a game where he caught four important passes without ever hitting the ground. He'd either score or run out of bounds.

Away from Lombardi, however, the meek little lamb turned into a tiger. Max probably was the most oversexed individual I've ever known. His appetite for women was nearly insatiable. Natu-rally, with a roommate like him, I had no incentive to behave myself. So the tales of our nightly exploits became legendary among our teammates.

We were always being caught at the wrong place at the wrong time. One time, we were out in the early hours of the morning with two spectacular airline stewardesses when we ran into a cou-ple of assistant coaches who were looking for us. We didn't have to pay, but we did have to turn the girls over to the coaches.

Unlike Max and the rest of the Packers, I was never scared of

Lombardi, even though I argued with him constantly. I never won a single argument, although I know—and he knew—that I was right many times.

Once, when we were in training camp, he was watching film when he got a call from his wife. "Happy anniversary, shithead," she said. Lombardi had forgotten his wedding anniversary, and it put him in such a foul mood that he decided to take bed check. Lombardi rarely took bed check, usually leaving it to his assistant coaches.

We heard him coming so Max and I quickly put our beds together and took off all our clothes. When Lombardi opened the door, Max and I were locked in an embrace. "Please, Coach," I said. "Would you close the door and leave us alone?" Lombardi was dumbfounded. He backed out of the room and closed the door. Then he stood out in the hallway until he finally bellowed, "What's going on in there? I'm coming in."

This time Max and I were laughing so hard we were almost crying. Lombardi finally understood that he'd been had. He said, "What am I going to do with you two?" But at least he had forgotten his foul mood.

We started the 1959 season with Lamar McHan at quarterback, and we won our first three games under Lombardi. The way our offense was set up, the quarterback would throw it twenty-five to thirty times a game, Taylor would run it about that many, and I'd run it maybe twelve times a game, in addition to receiving, passing, kicking, and blocking.

But I was moved to fullback for an October 11 home game against the San Francisco 49ers because Taylor had suffered a burned arm. He said his wife had gotten so mad at him that she threw a pan of grease at him.

At LSU, Jimmy had gotten in the habit of lifting weights, and he started us lifting at Green Bay. At 5-11 and 215 pounds, he was one of the strongest backs in the league. I didn't really appreciate how strong he was until that game against San Francisco.

I carried the ball around twenty-eight times for more than 140 yards. But my body really wasn't strong enough to take that much abuse. Leo Nomellini, the 49ers' 295-pound All-Pro defensive tackle, pounded me play after play. We won, 21–20, but after the game I was so beat that I checked myself into St. Joseph's Hospital and spent the night there. My mother and her friends Jinx and Lil, who were up for the game, were worried about me.

But I was back at practice the next day because I was so excited about what was happening. The players' attitude, the organization, and the coaching were all different. I was especially pleased with my improved blocking. I took Lombardi at his word when he said, "Unless you can block and tackle, you don't belong on the team."

I told Taylor to get well in a hurry because I couldn't take getting beat up every week. But he missed the next two games, both losses. And even when he returned, we lost three more. Had our fast start been only an illusion? Was the old Pack back? These were the questions being asked in the newspapers.

After the fourth straight loss, in an effort to turn things around, Lombardi replaced McHan with Starr for a game against the Colts in Milwaukee, where we sometimes played. He also gave Dowler his first start at flanker. The crowd was announced as only 25,521, the smallest ever to see us play in County Stadium, and we hardly rewarded the faithful, trailing

21–3 at halftime. But we rallied behind Starr in the second half and the league's defending champions beat us only 28–24.

So Bart started the last four games and we won them all to finish 7–5, which tied San Francisco for third in our conference. In the final game of the season, a 36–14 win over the 49ers in Kezar Stadium, I entered the game trailing defending champion Pat Summerall of New York in the scoring race. I scored three touchdowns and added four extra points to finish with ninety-four points for the season, highest in the league.

Under Lombardi, no player thrived more than me. The left halfback spot turned out to be perfect for me. Running, throwing, and catching, as well as handling the placekicking, I made the Pro Bowl for the first time and scored a record thirteen points then with a touchdown, a field goal, and four extra points.

What had gotten into me?

"I didn't make Paul," Lombardi told the media. "He was a good football player when I got to Green Bay. Success brought confidence to Paul, and since he possesses great pride, he played with even greater effort as the season progressed."

Jerry Kramer once said of me, "He was, I think, the best short-yardage runner I've ever seen. He was smart. He used his blockers so well. It was almost like you could go blindfolded around the corner and just run like hell and Paul would draw the tacklers to you."

Under Lombardi, I had been reborn as a football player.

"After playing under Lombardi for a while," I said after my first season with him, "I felt like a new player. He had me concentrating on my position so heavily that I forgot everything else. I even forgot my movie hopes. After a while, with everything going great, I wouldn't have wanted to be a movie star if they'd handed the job to me. There's only one thing I want to be. I want to be the best player in this league."

Ironically, I lost my Kentucky driver's license in the spring of 1960. The NFL scoring champion had accumulated too many points for speeding in his home state.

10

FOOTBALL AS IT WAS
MEANT TO BE

As far as I'm concerned, and I'm admittedly prejudiced, the 1960s was the golden era of the National Football League. At the beginning of the decade, there were thirteen teams in the NFL and eight more in the brand-new American Football League. By the end of it, the NFL and AFL had merged into a 26-team league and the Super Bowl, first held in 1967, was fast becoming bigger than baseball's World Series.

We didn't pay much attention to the AFL until the bidding wars for college players got crazy in the mid-1960s. Heading into the 1966 season, for example, the AFL had beat out the NFL for such exciting young stars as Joe Namath, Daryl Lamonica, Mike Garrett, and Lance Alworth.

The upstart league also had a bunch of veterans who had made their names in the NFL, most notably George Blanda, the ageless quarterback and placekicker for the Oakland Raiders.

The AFL just seemed more exciting than the NFL, which came off as rather stodgy in comparison.

Although we were the NFL's "Team of the '60s," we didn't exactly win our championships by default. Nobody gave us more trouble defensively than the Detroit Lions, especially such formidable players as Alex Karras, Roger Brown, and Joe Schmidt.

The Lions also had one of the game's all-time great defensive backs in Dick "Night Train" Lane. In 1963, Lane's wife, singer Dinah Washington, died suddenly the week before the Lions were to play the Bears in Chicago.

The Packers were pulling for the Lions because, if they won, Green Bay and not the Bears would go to the NFL championship game against the Giants. But without Lane, who was so saddened by his wife's death that he couldn't play, the Bears' receivers had a field day in the secondary and earned the right to play the Giants, whom they later beat, 14–10.

"The Bears seemed to me to be really lucky that year," Jerry Kramer once said. "They were playing good and they were a good football team. But it's also true that the ball always seemed to bounce into their hands when they needed it.

"I remember saying to Doug Atkins, 'You lucky sonofabitches. Every time you turn around, the ball bounces right.' And he said, 'Jerry, you're absolutely right. I remember one game where we fumbled, but the ball bounced into one of our guys' hands. That's when I said, "Boys, it's our year, it's our turn." Everything we did turned out right.' "

Atkins, who played college ball at Tennessee, was the best defensive end I ever played against. He was 6-9 and maybe 275 pounds, and he could run. You couldn't block him, and he was such a wild man that Bears coach George Halas couldn't coach him. Atkins and I developed a relationship based on mutual respect because of what I did once when we were playing the Bears.

Atkins had a knee injury, and, on this one play, I had a great shot to put a crackback block on him. He didn't know I was coming. If I had hit him, it would have been all over for him. I could have really wiped out his knee. Instead I yelled, "Doug, I'm coming!" That gave him time to protect his knee.

He really appreciated that. To pay me back, he never "clotheslined" me. That was the technique by which a defensive player would come up on an unsuspecting runner and hook him with his arm around the neck. It was devastating when you weren't expecting it, and Doug was a master at it. The NFL subsequently outlawed it.

Once, after Doug had clotheslined Elijah Pitts, Pitts came to the bench and said, "Damn, Hornung. He must not like blacks. That's the only reason I can figure that he clotheslines me every chance he gets and never clotheslines you."

I told Elijah what I had done for Doug, and he understood.

The Bears hit almost as hard as the Lions did. They had guys like Atkins, Dick Butkus, and Bill George. Because of our long history together and the proximity of Chicago and Green Bay, they always were our most hated rivals. We would always go to Chicago or Milwaukee by train, and that gave us a great chance to gamble on card games. We loved the train. We'd play blackjack and poker up and back.

I always felt the Packers had a good draft when they got me as the "bonus" pick and Ron Kramer as the No. 1 pick in 1957. But the Bears had the greatest draft in NFL history in 1965 when they got Gale Sayers and Dick Butkus.

Before we played them at home on October 3, 1965, somebody knocked on our dressing room door. When Bud Jorgensen,
our trainer for more than forty years, opened it, there stood
Halas. "Tell Coach Lombardi I want to talk to him," he said.

After checking with Lombardi, Jorgensen ushered Halas
into a small room in the locker room, where Lombardi was waiting. "Vince," said Halas, "I just want to tell you this: you'd better
have your boys ready today because we're going to kick your ass."
And then he left.

Lombardi was so flabbergasted that he was distracted all during the game, wondering why Halas had done that. This, of
course, was exactly what Halas had intended. He wanted to get
into Vince's head. But besides that, he knew he had a couple of
rookie superstars in Sayers and Butkus.

Sayers was in the league for five years, but he was healthy for
only the first three and a half. He wasn't the same when he came
back from the leg injury that eventually forced him to retire.

When Sayers was healthy it was unbelievable to see him run.
Every time he got the football, you edged up to the front of your
seat because he was a threat to score. I thought Hugh McEl-
henny of the 49ers was the best open-field runner I ever saw until
Sayers. And once he would shake loose, he had Mike Ditka
ahead of him to block the safety or a defensive back.

I could see greatness in Sayers when we played them in '65.
We won, 23–14, but after the game I put an arm around Sayers as
we were walking off the field and told him, "Gale, if you do
things right, you can be the greatest running back ever to play in
this league."

A few months later, when I picked up the papers the morning after I'd scored five touchdowns against the Colts, I saw that

I'd gotten second billing to Sayers, who had scored six against the 49ers, tying the NFL record. From then on, I called him "the upstaging SOB" whenever I saw him.

As good as Nitschke was for us, Butkus was the best middle linebacker I ever saw. He still may be the best ever to play that position. The first time we played against him in 1965, Lombardi's face lit up with eagerness.

"I want you to take a look at this Butkus," he told us in a film session. "He's a big, sloppy-looking kid. Forrest, you'll be able to kick his ass. He plays way too deep. Jerry and Fuzzy, when we go up the middle, you should have a field day blocking him."

Well, although we had the angles on him, he just threw the blockers away. He was everywhere. The Bears held Taylor and me to a little more than fifty yards on about forty carries, and Butkus made thirty-two unassisted tackles. As we were reviewing the films after the game, Lombardi finally shut off the projector and said, "I'm sorry, boys, but this Butkus may be something special." It was the only time I ever heard him apologize.

From 1960 through '67, we went 12–4 against the Bears and 10–4–2 against the Lions. The only other team that gave us much trouble was the Colts, and we had an 11–5 margin over them.

Many experts regard Johnny Unitas as the greatest quarterback of all time, and he may well have been, but I also think that, like me, he was lucky enough to be surrounded by great players. He had great receivers and runners in Lenny Moore and Jimmy Orr, and Raymond Berry was so smart and disciplined in his routes that he always beat cornerbacks who were faster. Jim Parker was a Hall of Fame offensive guard, and anybody would have wanted John Mackey at tight end.

In 1967, the Colts signed Bubba Smith, the huge defensive end from Michigan State, and he played against the Packers in the College All-Star Game. The newspapers made a big deal of his matchup with Jerry Kramer, and the *Chicago Tribune* even ran an ad that said, "Come see Bubba Smith beat up on Bart Starr." Well, early in the game, Smith lived up to the hype by getting through Kramer and sacking Starr. As he was going back to his side of the line, Bubba said to Jerry, "All night long, old man, all night long."

Jerry is a proud man and that really pissed him off. So he began calling the plays in the huddle. He'd tell Bart, "Give me a '41 trap." After that, he'd say, "Now give me a '51." Every play we trapped Bubba and drove him back. When we got down to their twenty, after seven or eight straight plays right over Bubba, Smith took himself out. He didn't know what to do because Jerry had just whipped his ass.

I was glad that I had retired and didn't have to play against the 1968 Baltimore team that went 13–1 and ripped Cleveland, 34–0, in the NFL title game. The Colts were coached by Don Shula and had a roster of All-Stars, including several friends of mine. So how in the world did the '68 Colts lose to the Jets in the Super Bowl? Especially since they were 19-point favorites? Namath just had a career day, that's all. Plus, Jets coach Weeb Ewbank, who had been the Colts' coach when they beat the Giants in that historic 1958 overtime game for the title, did a masterful job of preparing the Jets for his former team.

If the Colts had kicked the crap out of the Jets, as everybody expected, I don't know where the NFL would be today.

We never lost to the Giants or Browns during those years, which must have made Vince happy. He liked to beat the Giants because they were his hometown team and he had worked for them, and he liked to beat the Browns because their coach, Paul Brown, was recognized as the league's most brilliant innovator.

When I was growing up in Louisville, we used to get the Browns' games on TV because WAVE, the only station that carried the NFL, did their games instead of the Bears or Cardinals. So I remember watching players such as Otto Graham, Lou "The Toe" Groza, Dub Jones, Bob Gain, Mac Speedie, and Ray Renfro. Just as the Brooklyn Dodgers had led Major League Baseball in integration, so did the Browns in football. They had great black players such as fullback Marion Motley, end Lenny Ford, and pass receiver Horace Gillom, who had been a track star at Ohio State.

But Paul Brown and Jimmy Brown were the greatest Browns of all. The first time I saw Jimmy at the College All-Star Game in Chicago, he was playing basketball. He could jump well enough to touch the rim and he had this incredible chiseled body. He also was an All-American lacrosse player in college. I really think that if he had ever fought Ali, he could have beaten him. He was that kind of talent.

Black players made a great game better, and they did it at a tough time in our nation's history. I'm sure the white guys, for the most part, didn't have a clue about what those guys were going through in those days.

Today, when a guy makes a routine tackle or a catch, he "celebrates" as if he had done something really significant. That just wasn't done in football, although the taunting antics of my fellow Louisvillian, Cassius Clay, who had joined the Black Muslims and changed his name to Muhammad Ali, were beginning to be mimicked all through the sports world.

From a sheer talent standpoint, I think the guys that I played with or against could more than hold their own against today's stars, especially considering that we didn't have the year-round weight-training programs and exercise facilities that every NFL team has today. Many of us had to work off-season jobs to make ends meet, and that meant that staying in football shape was hard.

Still, the players of our era set standards for future generations. No running back has ever had better balance than Jon Arnett of the Bears. Deacon Jones of the Rams was one of the first defensive ends to be as fast as a back. Nobody won more championships than Otto Graham of the Browns. Chuck Bednarik of the Eagles was the last to play both offense and defense, and Norm Van Brocklin had one of the strongest arms ever.

If I had to pick an all-opponent defensive team, I'd probably go with Doug Atkins and Deacon Jones at the ends; Bob Lilly of the Cowboys and Alex Karras at tackle; Chuck Bednarik at middle guard; Butkus, Bill George, and Joe Schmidt at linebacker; and "Night Train" Lane, Jim Patton of the Giants, and Yale Lary of the Lions at defensive back. Lary is also the best punter I've ever seen. He didn't get as much publicity as Ray Guy got years later, but Lary was better—he kicked for a better average.

I guess the all-opponent offense would be Unitas at quarterback; Sayers and Jim Brown at running back; Ditka at tight end; Del Shofner of the Giants and Raymond Berry at wide receivers; Bednarik at center; and Jim Parker, Rosey Brown of the Giants, Dick Schafrath of the Browns, and Abe Gibron of the Bears in the offensive line.

When I look at the NFL today, I don't see any coaches who can come close to Lombardi or Halas or Paul Brown. I can't put

Weeb Ewbank in their class, even though he won championships both with Baltimore and the New York Jets.

When he was with Baltimore, Ewbank would substitute his guards on every play, a ploy he learned from Paul Brown. But the guards weren't bringing in the plays to Unitas because John called his own plays.

Once, after a timeout in the final minutes of a close game, the guards were huddled with Weeb and then ran out to the huddle on the field. It looked to the fans as if they were bringing in the game-winning play. Unitas, who had never even gone to the sideline during the timeout, asked the guards, "Got anything from the bench?" They said, "Weeb said to tell you to score."

So Unitas called his own play, as usual, and it won the game. Naturally, the writers all called Weeb a genius.

11.

THE BREAKTHROUGH YEAR

Before the 1960 season, we got a scare in practice when a photographers' stand collapsed on Nitschke and a bolt penetrated his helmet, coming within an inch of his skull. Only a few moments earlier, he had been standing bareheaded in the same place. But that was about the only scare we had in the preseason, when we won all six of our exhibition games.

We were confident that we could build on our success of '59 and seriously contend for the championship in what turned out to be one of the most historic seasons in pro football history.

This was the year that Pete Rozelle, an innovative former publicist with the Los Angeles Rams, replaced Bert Bell as commissioner. Rozelle was the genius who knew how to marry the NFL to Madison Avenue and the television networks. Under him, the players in my era did more to promote the league than ever before.

This also was the year the American Football League started

play with eight franchises. The NFL owners turned up their noses at the AFL, which proved to be a big mistake. That first year, the Houston Oilers beat the Los Angeles Chargers, 24–16, in an AFL title game that drew a crowd of 32,183. That was less than half of the 67,325 that would watch us play the Eagles for the NFL title.

Starr opened the season as the starting quarterback, but Lamar McHan replaced him after we lost to the Bears at home, 17–14. That loss really had a deflating effect on me. I was in the first year of a new three-year contract that paid me twenty-one thousand dollars a year, plus bonuses for scoring, but I swore it would be my last Packer contract because of the limited business opportunities in Green Bay.

But I regained my spirits the next week when we defeated Detroit, 28–9, behind McHan. With an 11-yard touchdown run, a 16-yard TD on a reception from McHan, and four extra points, I personally outscored the Lions, 16–9. The next Sunday, after I had been limited to only five conversions in a 35–21 win over the mighty Colts in Baltimore, a writer asked Lombardi if I might be better if I concentrated on only one talent instead of so many.

"He could kick better if he didn't have to run so much," Lombardi said. "But he wouldn't be a better runner if he didn't kick. Besides, who else would I use to do the things he does?"

The next week I proved Lombardi's point in a 41–14 win over the 49ers. I gained 72 yards rushing in 13 attempts and scored two touchdowns on the ground; completed one pass for 20 yards and caught another for 10; kicked two field goals, including a personal longest 47-yarder; and tacked on five extra points.

On October 23, McHan was still the starter when we went to Pittsburgh to play the Steelers. Although McHan was a better athlete than Bart, it was inevitable that Starr would get the job full-time. Bart was an extension of Lombardi on the field. He could pick you to death with his pinpoint accuracy and throw the ball on the money to any spot.

Late in the first half of a 0–0 game against the Steelers, I told Lamar I could get open on a down-and-out-and-up. Sure enough, I did, and McHan put it right in my hands. A certain six. Except that I dropped the ball. My usually sure hands failed me. All through the first half, for some strange reason, guys were dropping Lamar's passes.

So Lombardi decided at halftime to put in Bart, and he led us to a 19–13 victory. That was the beginning of Bart Starr's legend. Except for a handful of games he had to miss because of injuries, he was the Packers' starting quarterback through the 1970 season.

Whenever I see Bart now, I like to kid him that I dropped that pass on purpose just so he could play.

We had a four-game winning streak going when we played the Colts in a rematch on November 15 in Milwaukee. I always enjoyed playing Baltimore because they had about as much talent as we did. Their Hall of Famers from that era were Raymond Berry, Art Donovan, Coach Weeb Ewbank, John Mackey, Gino Marchetti, Lenny Moore, Jim Parker, and, of course, the incomparable Johnny Unitas.

They also had some players who aren't in the Hall of Fame, but who should at least be included in any discussion about really good players who haven't been inducted: Jimmy Orr, Lenny

Lyles, Art Spinney, Bert Rechichar, and Gene "Big Daddy" Lipscomb.

The love affair between those players and the Baltimore fans was so great that it took a real jerk, Robert Irsay, to ruin the whole thing. He bought the Rams in 1972, and then swapped teams with Colts owner Carroll Rosenbloom. He pissed me off in 1974, when he fired Howard Schnellenberger, my old high school teammate, after three games because Howard refused to replace Marty Domres with Bert Jones at quarterback.

But that was a minor blip compared with what Irsay did in the spring of 1984, when he sent a bunch of trucks to the Colts' offices in the dark of night, packed up everything, and moved the franchise to Indianapolis. Had somebody tried to pull that in Green Bay, he would have been lynched.

In our rematch with the Colts in 1960, Unitas and Starr had a sensational passing duel that Baltimore eventually won, 38–24. I also had another outstanding game, gaining 99 yards rushing, four more than the entire Colts team, and scoring 18 points on two touchdowns, a field goal, and three extra points.

After a win at home over the Cowboys, we lost to the Rams and the Lions, giving us a 5–4 record to take to Chicago for a must-win December 4 game against the Bears. I had one of the better games of my career in our 41–13 victory, scoring 23 points on two touchdowns, two field goals, and five extra points to give me 143 points for the season, surpassing Don Hutson's single-season league record of 139.

After scoring a TD in the final quarter, I hotdogged it for one of the few times in my career, flipping the ball toward the fifth row. Some said I was flipping it to my date for the evening, but that was a lot of nonsense. If I'd had a date, she wouldn't have been sitting behind the goalposts. It was a spontaneous gesture. Everybody was chanting "Throw the ball, throw the ball," so I did.

George Halas, the "Papa Bear," wasn't amused. He said I owed Chicago twenty-five dollars to cover the cost of the ball. I refused to pay, but Lombardi offered to pay for me. Halas quickly forgot about it, though.

I loved to play the Bears in Wrigley Field. Chicago was so close to South Bend that I was pretty popular there. Plus, I relished playing against Halas, the greatest name in the history of the game. I think Vince would have agreed with that.

I respected Halas, and I loved it when he cussed me out from the sidelines. He was violent in his language. His favorite word was *cocksucker*. I used to love getting into a stance on his side of the field. I'd lean to the left and he'd yell at his players, "Watch Hornung! He's going left!" But then I'd cut to the right, and Halas would go nuts.

When he'd get upset with the referees, Halas would sometimes come all the way down to the end zone to protest. I'd yell at the refs, "Get him out of here! He can't be down here!" Naturally, that would piss off Halas even more. But I'm sure he understood that it was all in the spirit of competition. He was very special, and I just relished the opportunity to play against the man who made the NFL what it was.

The night before we played the 49ers in San Francisco in our next-to-last game of the 1960 regular season, I had dinner with Barney Shapiro, a millionaire bachelor whom I'd met when I played in the East-West All-Star Game in college. He fixed me up with a showgirl and showed me around town.

He also introduced me to a guy named T. W. Richardson,

who had owned the Royal Nevada hotel and casino. He later sold it and it became part of the Stardust. Anyhow, Richardson asked about the 49ers game.

After I told him what I thought, he said, "Hell, you got a $5,000 free ride," meaning he was going to bet $5,000 for me. We were 6½-point favorites to beat the 49ers, but what the bookies didn't count on was that rain had turned Kezar Stadium into a quagmire on game day. But we won, 13–0, covering the spread, and I scored all our points.

The next week we beat the Rams in L.A. 35–21, to win the Western Division with an 8–4 record. It was the best year of my career. I scored 176 points, still the NFL record, on 15 touchdowns, 41 point-after conversions (out of 41 attempts), and 15 field goals (out of 28 attempts). Believe it or not, I've held that record longer than Babe Ruth held his record of sixty home runs in one season.

To this day, some sportswriters think it'll never be broken, but I disagree. We played twelve regular-season games. Now they play sixteen and you can bet it's going to eighteen. Plus, every team in my day had two running backs who could score. In today's game, everybody uses one back, so today's runners should have more chances to score.

At the same time, I must say that I disagreed with an ESPN online poll about the NFL's ten greatest records taken in 2002. My record came in only eighth, which bothered me. But here's what ESPN said:

"There are *teams* that have had trouble scoring as many points as the great Packer halfback and kicker did in 1960, when he ran for 15 touchdowns, kicked 15 figgies [field goals], and punched home 41 PAT [point-after attempts]. That's in 12 games, folks, and just one of the reasons Vince Lombardi called him 'the most versatile man who ever played the game.' Hornung's record, if it's broken, will almost certainly be done sans touchdowns, by an ace kicker behind a great offense and a wimpy coach."

After celebrating in L.A., we flew back to Green Bay to begin preparing for the NFL title game against the Philadelphia Eagles. We figured we could run on them. We were a pretty cocky outfit; we moved the ball against anybody. The main thing we were concerned with was stopping the passing of their quarterback, Norm Van Brocklin.

We didn't get in a lot of field practice in Green Bay because it was below zero and the field was frozen solid. We flew to Philadelphia on Christmas Eve and found it was cold there, too. We spent the night in our hotel and had a brief workout on Christmas Day.

We played the Eagles for the NFL championship on December 26, 1960, at Franklin Field in Philadelphia. They had a veteran team led by Chuck Bednarik, the iron man who played center on offense and linebacker on defense.

It was a helluva game. I kicked field goals from Philadelphia's 20- and 23-yard lines to give us a 6–0 lead early in the second quarter. But the Eagles fought back to take a 7–6 lead on a 35-yard touchdown pass from "The Dutchman," Van Brocklin, to Tommy McDonald, my former Heisman competitor.

Bob Walston kicked a 15-yard field goal to extend Philadelphia's lead to 10–6, and I missed a 13-yarder just before halftime.

The third quarter was scoreless and uneventful for everybody but me. Tom Brookshier, the Eagles' safety and later an announcer for CBS, put a pop on me that pinched the nerve in my neck leading to my right shoulder, the beginning of the physical problems that would plague me throughout the rest of my career.

When I got hit, I fell to the ground, my right arm quivering as I felt a twinge in my neck. I figured, hell, it's just a pinched nerve and the numbness will go away. I picked up the ball, but couldn't grip it. About ten minutes later, I tried to throw the ball again, and my arm was just numb. I had no control over it.

Still, we took a 13–10 lead early in the fourth when Max McGee noticed that the Eagles weren't rushing him and so took off on a 35-yard run that set up Starr's seven-yard pass to him and my conversion. But Ted Dean, a rookie fullback for the Eagles, took my kickoff and returned it to our thirty-nine before being knocked out of bounds. With Dean and Billy Barnes pounding away at us, the Eagles took a 17–13 lead when Dean scored from the five and Walston added the extra point.

As the final minutes ticked away, Bart led us on a long drive that made the Eagles' fans nervous. On the last play that tough old SOB Bednarik stopped Jimmy Taylor on the Eagles' ten. They won the title, but we had impressed everyone with a young team that promised to get only better.

After the game, Vince gave one of his better speeches. He said he was proud of us, that we had played well enough to win, but were beaten by a veteran quarterback who had a great day. But he also said, "This is the last time we'll lose in a championship game." And he proved to be right.

The night of the game, I flew from Philadelphia to L.A. to play in the Pro Bowl. I roomed with Bill George, the Bears' linebacker, in a big hotel downtown on Wilshire Boulevard. He later reported that I was the perfect roommate because I was never there. I was running the nightclubs with Rick Casares of the Bears.

At the beginning of the week, Rick and I agreed that I'd pick up the checks and that he'd settle up with me after the game. As it turned out, we blew about $1,500 each, or twice as much as each member of the winning team got.

"Shit," said Rick, "aren't you going to Vegas after the game?"

We weren't about to lose money on the deal, so we agreed to bet on the game in Vegas. I called Barney and asked him to get the bet down for us. We won our bet, more than covering our expenses for the week, so I went to Vegas to collect.

I also looked for T. W. Richardson to collect on that $5,000 free bet he said he was going to make for me on the 49ers game. But he had lied, and I never got paid.

12.

HOW JFK SAVED
THE DAY

After the 1960 season, I made my usual off-season visit to Hollywood, where my friend, the executive Tony Owens at Columbia Pictures, got me a bit part as a cop on a TV sitcom, *My Sister Eileen*. Then Tony said to me, "I've got you an agent, but he's only handled one person in his life." The agent turned out to be Aaron Rosenberg, who had made a fortune for Bing Crosby. He also had produced *Mutiny on the Bounty*, starring Marlon Brando.

I sure had the right team in place if I wanted to pursue a show-business career, but the only team I really cared about was the Green Bay Packers. I wanted a championship ring more than an Oscar. So I put Hollywood on hold again and returned that fall of 1961 to St. Norbert College, where I got a lot of razzing from Max about my venture into TV.

One day, after beating me in a hand of gin rummy, Max sang, "He used to be my roomie, but now he's my sister Eileen."

"Deal," I growled.

The preseason games were an important part of Lombardi's philosophy. He thought we needed to get away from training camp, so we sometimes played in out-of-the-way places such as Winston-Salem, North Carolina; Columbus, Georgia; and Cedar Rapids, Iowa, in addition to big cities. And he wanted us to win the exhibitions because he felt it had a carryover effect.

He usually played the starters at least three quarters, leaving precious little playing time for rookies. Nevertheless, his system worked. During Lombardi's era, the Packers had a 39–8 record in preseason games. We went a combined 17–0 before the 1960, '61, and '62 seasons.

Our expectations high, we opened the 1961 season being upset by the Lions, 17–13, before 44,307 fans in County Stadium in Milwaukee, the largest crowd ever to see a football game in Wisconsin. Afterward, we had a wedding party for Max, whose stunning decision to get married forced me to line up two new roommates: Jesse Whittenton, who was single, and Ron Kramer, whose wife was home in Michigan awaiting the birth of their second child.

Stung by the loss, we roared back with lopsided wins over the 49ers and Bears. After I had scored eighteen points in a 24–0 win over Chicago, Lombardi told the media, "Hornung has three things that make him special. First, he's got heart. He's got all the heart in the world. Second, he's handsome. And third, he's a great big ham."

In a 45–7 drubbing of the Colts on October 8, I scored three touchdowns, six points-after, and three field goals for thirty-three points, a Packers record and the third highest single-game total in NFL history. A week later, we went to Cleveland and shocked the proud Browns, 47–14.

As we piled up the score, Lombardi came up with another innovation. A photographer on the roof of Cleveland Stadium took Polaroids of the teams' formations and threw them down to the Green Bay bench in a weighted sock for the chain-smoking Lombardi to study.

We were so far ahead in the third quarter that when Bart called "63," a play for me, I said, "No, this is Jim's game, so let him do the scoring." Which he did, without ever thanking me for being an unselfish teammate. After outgaining Jim Brown 158 to 72 and outscoring him 24–0, Taylor plopped down on our bench and said, "Who's Jimmy Brown?" Afterward, Lombardi said, "This was the best game we've ever played."

The day after the Browns victory, a Milwaukee sportscaster reported that Ray Nitschke, Boyd Dowler, and I had been ordered to report for active Army duty, effective October 30, because of the Berlin crisis.

Hostilities between the U.S. and the Soviet Union had escalated to the point that the East Germans, who were controlled by the Russians, built a steel and concrete wall in Berlin to stop the flow of immigrants into the western part of the city, which was controlled by the U.S. and its allies.

Lots of Packer fans immediately got lathered up about the Army taking us. As our reporting date drew near, a couple of Wisconsin politicians, U.S. Senator Alexander Wiley and Representative Alvin E. O'Konski, asked the Defense Department to reconsider our call-up, to no avail.

Because of my neck injuries, I probably could have gotten a

4-F classification that would have disqualified me for service. But the Army didn't want a repeat of what had happened during the Korean War, when Mickey Mantle was classified 4-F because of osteomyelitis in a knee, leaving him free to play baseball for the New York Yankees while many less athletic men his age were fighting a godforsaken war halfway around the globe.

Still, instead of reporting directly to Fort Riley in Kansas, I was ordered to take a physical in Milwaukee. I flunked and returned to Green Bay, where I played sparingly in a 33–7 win over the Vikings, due to a recurrence of my neck injury. The next week I got another call from the Army, telling me to report to the Great Lakes Naval Training Station for another round of examinations.

The night of my first day of tests, I was supposed to stay on the base. But I had Rick Casares, my buddy with the Bears, pick me up, and we went to Chicago to have dinner.

I took the physical the next day and the doctor laid it out for me. "You can either go in now," he said, "or they'll keep sending you around the country until you pass." So I said, "No, I don't want that, so let's get this over with."

I played in two more games before reporting to Fort Riley on November 14, 1961. I was slotted to be a truck driver and radio operator for the 896th Engineering Battalion based in Louisville. Pat Martin, my Notre Dame buddy from Green Bay, flew me to Kansas in his twin-engine Cessna 310, and I had a buddy from Louisville drive my Cadillac out there.

My commanding general initially said that I would get no weekend passes. That hardly seemed fair, considering that Nitschke and other players, such as Bobby Mitchell of the

Browns, had commanders who were willing to let them play on the weekend.

So at a time when I was a point ahead of my record 1960 scoring pace, I had to miss a November 19 home game against the Rams because I was stuck in Fort Riley. But my commanding general relented and offered me a helluva deal: If I'd stay out of trouble and make eight speeches a year for him, he'd give me weekend passes so I could play football. The rest of the season, Pat Martin would pick me up at Fort Riley and fly me to wherever we were playing.

In our next-to-last game, we played the 49ers in San Francisco. Before the game, Lombardi left the locker room so anybody who wanted to could say something. When Jim Ringo, our center and captain, asked me if I had anything, I stood up and said, "Guys, I came here from Fort Riley, and believe me, you don't want any part of that. Practices are a snap compared to the Army. I came out here to get two things. I got the first one last night; now let's go out and kick the 49ers' ASS!!"

Well, the team cracked up. The laughter was so loud I knew that, outside the locker room, Lombardi had to be wondering what the hell was going on. He didn't like his players laughing before such a big game.

So when he came back in, he said, "What's so funny?" I said, "Coach, we're just laughing about how we're going to celebrate after we win this damned game." But the last laugh was on us. The 49ers upset us, 22–21.

I had to miss our final game against the Rams in L.A., but we still won the Western Division title with an 11–3 record, best in the league. I had scored 146 points to lead the NFL for the third consecutive year. Back at Fort Riley, I was informed after the regular season that I had been voted the league's most valuable player.

The honor came as a great surprise to me because my Army duty had caused me to miss the two games against the Rams. I also realized that three or four other players on our team deserved the honor as much as I did.

So here I was, biding my time in the Army as I awaited another championship game, this time against the New York Giants. It figured to be an emotional game for Lombardi, a native New Yorker and longtime former Giants assistant.

But a problem developed at Fort Riley.

I was supposed to begin a six-day leave the Tuesday after the championship game. I asked my captain if I could switch the leave to December 27–January 3 so I'd be able to play in the NFL title game. Much to my surprise, the SOB said no.

I immediately called Lombardi and told him we had a problem. He listened, then said, "Let me make a phone call and I'll call you back in twenty minutes." When he called back, he said, "I think your captain is about ready to get a phone call that will get you off to play."

Damned if he hadn't called President Kennedy. Sure enough, the captain got an immediate call from the White House. At first, he didn't believe it was really JFK on the line. Heck, everybody was impersonating Kennedy's Massachusetts accent back then. But when it dawned on the captain that it was, indeed, Kennedy, it wasn't long before Private Hornung was on his way to Green Bay to play in the championship on December 31.

This time the flight in Pat Martin's plane was really rough.

The weather was so bad that we got lost and ended up landing in Rochester, Minnesota, instead of Detroit, our destination. The plane was jerking from side to side and our radio went out. It was scary as hell. I promised God that if He got me out of this mess, I'd never sin again. So when we finally landed in twenty inches of snow that caused the plane to skid off the runway, I called up this girl who was waiting for me in Milwaukee and told her, sorry, but I couldn't make it.

Pat and I rented a car and got into Green Bay about 9 P.M. Our first stop was Speed's bar. All the guys were there and they weren't expecting me. The first to see me was Bill Quinlan, who grabbed a microphone, jumped up on the bar, and said, "AWOL Paul is back."

The 1961 championship game against the Giants was the first NFL playoff game ever held in Green Bay, and CBS sent Lindsey Nelson and Chris Schenkel, its No. 1 team, to do the national television broadcast. As the announcers chattered on with their pregame analysis, they didn't know what was happening, from a psychological standpoint, down on the field.

The Giants had great defensive ends in Jim Katcavage and Andy Robustelli, but their quarterback, Charley Conerly, later said they became kind of mesmerized when we came out on the field. Jimmy Taylor and I went out to warm up in the freezing cold, and we just had on T-shirts. They were freezing, and we were running around as if we were in L.A. We did it on purpose. They had to say, "Look at those crazy mothers out there. They have to be freezing their butts off." What we were saying to them was, "This is our kind of weather. It isn't bad. It's perfect. Let's play ball."

Ron Kramer had been out drinking the night before the

game with a friend of mine from Kentucky, and he smelled like a brewery. He usually put on a rubber suit under his uniform so he could sweat off some extra pounds in the warm-ups before the game. But I told him not to do it. He must have drunk a half quart of whiskey the night before, and I think the smell would have killed us all.

By this time Kramer must have weighed about 280. He was the biggest and most feared tight end in the league. And on this day, he also had a beard, just to make himself look meaner and tougher. He looked dirty, and he liked that.

"Follow me," growled Kramer, "and you'll win the Corvette."

He was referring to the new $5,000 Corvette that *Sport* magazine awarded to the game's most valuable player.

Well, on a bitterly cold and windy day, we kicked the Giants' butts. After a scoreless first quarter, we got on the board on the first play of the second period when I scored from the six and added the extra point. Within five minutes, it was 14–0. Nitschke intercepted a Y. A. Tittle pass at the Giants' thirteen, which set up a 13-yard scoring pass from Starr to Boyd Dowler, our standout wide receiver out of Colorado, and my second conversion.

The rout was on. An interception by our Hank Gremminger led to a 13-yard TD pass from Bart to Ron Kramer, who played one of his greatest games that day. He ran all over Sam Huff, the Giants' great linebacker. Chris Schenkel and the media made it seem like Sam was the greatest linebacker who ever played, but, hell, he couldn't carry Ray Nitschke's jockstrap.

In that game, Huff was a nonentity. We kicked his ass, and he knows it, too. I never said a word to Huff. I like Sam. We're friends. He is a big man in horse racing in West Virginia and I used to see him all the time at Saratoga. But we felt we could run against him, and we went right up the guy, with Ron Kramer cracking down on him.

The Giants played the same flex defense that they had learned under Tom Landry when Vince was with them. We just matched up better against them. In pro football, you have to match up. We matched up because we did things properly and didn't make mistakes. They might have known the sweep was coming, but they couldn't stop it.

On the last play of the first half, I kicked a 17-yard field goal to send us to the locker room with a 24–0 lead. In the second half, I added two more field goals and another extra point (for a total of 4) to give me 19 points for the day, a league championship-game record. The final score—we won, 37–0—was the most one-sided in a title game since Otto Graham quarterbacked Cleveland to a 56–10 win over Detroit in 1954, and it was the first championship-game shutout since the Eagles had defeated the Rams, 14–0, in 1949.

Conerly was at the end of his career. In fact, he had been replaced by Tittle, who had thrown thirty-six touchdown passes that year. But when Tittle played against us, he was horrible. Couldn't do anything. So in the third quarter, Conerly was standing on the sidelines, freezing. We didn't have any heat blowers in those days. We were winning 37–0 when Tittle came over to Conerly and said, "Charley, you want to take a couple of series?" He wanted out. But Charley said, "Yat, you took us this far. Why don't you take us the rest of the way?"

It would have been a lot worse if Lombardi hadn't called off the dogs. Hell, I wanted to match the 73–0 whipping that the Bears had put on the Redskins in the 1940 title game. But Lombardi didn't want to completely humiliate his former team, which really pissed me off.

"Today," a choked-up Lombardi told us in the locker room, "you were the greatest team in the history of the National Football League."

I was named the game's most valuable player, which meant I received the Corvette. The way I saw it, the car could just as easily have gone to Ron Kramer. He would have won the trophy if the writers had known anything about football.

In the locker stall next to mine, Kramer was sipping on a pint of whiskey brought in by his dad.

"And I had to tell you to follow me," he said.

A few days after the game, Pat Martin flew me from Fort Riley to New York City, where I received my Corvette in a ceremony at the Waldorf-Astoria Hotel. I was seated at the head table with an Army lieutenant colonel, who did everything but salute me.

Naturally, after I accepted the keys to the car, a member of the media asked me what I was going to do with it.

"I'll have someone drive it down to Louisville," I said. "My mother will use it until I get out of the service."

"How old is your mother?"

"She's fifty-five, I think."

"Isn't a sports car a little jazzy for a woman her age?"

"It probably is," I said. "But I can't take a Corvette to Fort Riley. It would be too conspicuous."

"More conspicuous than a Cadillac?"

"Of course," I answered. "My Cadillac is an old one. It's a '59."

When it came time to file my taxes, instead of just ignoring the Corvette as other previous winners had, my accountant tried to claim it as a gift so I could get a tax break on it. But the IRS wouldn't allow it, which started a legal fight that went all the way to the U.S. Supreme Court, where I lost. I could have killed my accountant.

During the rest of my stay at Fort Riley, I flew to Miami to do some commercials, home to Louisville for the '62 Derby, and to New York for Ralph Guglielmi's wedding. On the way home from the wedding, I suffered a sudden attack of appendicitis in Kansas City and underwent emergency surgery.

The doctor said it would be at least two weeks before I could return to Army duty, so I got mom and went to Miami to recuperate. Just like any other All-Pro Army private would have done, right?

13.

GOLDEN BOY INC.

When I first came into the league in 1957, there were few nationally televised NFL games and television was still available mainly in black and white. By the end of the 1962 season, however, the NFL was threatening to replace Major League Baseball as the national pastime and color TVs were no longer considered a luxury. It was part of the genius of Pete Rozelle that he not only envisioned the potential of TV long before anybody else in sports, he positioned the NFL to take full advantage of it.

In a sense, then, I suppose I came along at the right time. The camera always had been kind to me, and my playboy image didn't hurt, so suddenly I was one of the most marketable athletes in the country. At one time or another, I had contracts to promote such products as Jantzen leisure wear, Chevrolet, shaving cream and after-shave lotion, and many more.

And then there was Marlboro cigarettes.

I used to smoke five packs a day in my playing days. Almost

everybody except Bart smoked. At halftime, the locker room would be filled with smoke. Lombardi was good for at least four cigarettes at halftime.

I got cartons of free cigarettes from Marlboro, so, on the road, guys would come to my room to get some. It was unbelievable how much we smoked. I didn't stop smoking until almost twenty years after I retired, when a doctor discovered some lesions in my mouth.

At least I could endorse Marlboros in good conscience.

I had so many accounts going that I even hired a New York agent to represent me, Frank Scott, who handled Mickey Mantle and Roger Maris. In the winter of 1961–62, although I had been the NFL's most valuable player and leading scorer, I finished second in all the major sports awards to Maris, who had broken Babe Ruth's record with sixty-one homers for the Yankees.

So every time we appeared together on the rubber-chicken circuit, I always played second fiddle to Maris. I figured Scott must be doing something right, but I was wrong. Scott did very little for me.

But because of my contract with him, I wasn't able to sign with Mark McCormack, a young Cleveland attorney who wanted to represent me. McCormack's International Management Group went on to make fortunes for many athletes, most notably golfers Arnold Palmer, Jack Nicklaus, and Gary Player.

I especially enjoyed the work for Jantzen, which also employed such athletes as Frank Gifford, Bob Cousy, Jerry West, Bobby Hull, Don Meredith, Ken Venturi, and Dave Marr in what it called the "Jantzen International Sports Club." We'd spend a few days, usually at the Royal Hawaiian Hotel in

Waikiki, posing for photos that would be used in Jantzen cata-
logs or magazine ads. The photographer was Tom Kelly, who always had a lot of beautiful girls around him because he had done
the Marilyn Monroe calendar.

We had to pose in literally hundreds of outfits, which required a lot of back-and-forth trips between a men's room in the
hotel and the beach. Gifford and Cousy finally got so tired of the
routine that they began changing behind a huge potted plant in
the hotel's lobby, only a few feet away from where society ma-
trons were strolling.

In our off time, we played a lot of beach volleyball and basketball. When we played hoops, I was still a gunner. Here I was,
playing with future Hall of Famers, and they all complained that
they couldn't get a shot because Hornung wouldn't give up the
ball.

Once I talked West, the best player ever to come out of West
Virginia and a star with the Lakers, into playing me one-on-one,
head-up. I insisted that I get the ball first, and somehow I slopped
in my first shot. I walked off the court and refused to play anymore so I could always say I had beaten Jerry West.

I really appreciated the ad that Jantzen ran after I was reinstated. It said: "The NFL welcomed back Paul Hornung . . . We
at Jantzen never left him."

Years later, the Jantzen International Sports Club was given
credit for proving that the public liked to see athletes in sporting
attire and that a group of stars, working as a team, could sell a
product. So the Namath pantyhose commercial, the Jim Palmer
Jockey underwear campaign, and the wildly successful Miller
Lite Beer campaign owed a lot to us.

I got into the Miller Lite commercials a little late. Before I signed on in the fall of '76, the McCann-Erickson public-relations agency already had done 17 commercials, most of which featured retired athletes such as Mantle, Dick Butkus, Matt Snell, Tom Heinsohn, and Wilt Chamberlain. Hell, even Ray Nitschke was in one, with Rosey Grier and Ben Davidson. The theme was always a play on the motto "Tastes great, less filling."

My first Miller Lite commercial was a total dud. They taped it in the New Orleans Superdome, and the idea was to play on my playboy image. So they had me saying things like "See this face? It's gorgeous!" until I was mobbed by a group of cheerleaders, who wrestled me to the ground. It was killed after only a couple of national showings.

But I made one of the great comebacks in commercial history with "Practice, practice, practice." It was possibly one of the most popular commercials Miller ever did, and it gave me a national identity with a new generation of fans. In fact, it was such a hit that they made a sequel starring me and Steve Mizerak, the great pool player. After I'm the last of several guys to lose, I say, "Steve, how did you do that?" Then, as he walks off with a model, he looks back at me and says, "Practice, practice, practice."

That was the last Miller Lite commercial I did. I got pissed at McCann-Erickson because I didn't like the fact that to do a Miller Lite commercial, you had to negotiate through one of their guys instead of being able to negotiate for yourself. That sounded unfair to me, so I became the first one of the bunch to quit.

Like my mom, I was a staunch Democrat until the era of double-digit inflation and skyrocketing interest rates during the

Jimmy Carter administration. I was in an 82 percent tax bracket. That's right, if I earned $200,000, I had to pay $160,000 in taxes. But Ronald Reagan changed all that with his supply-side economics.

Under Reagan, I had more money to put back into the economy and invest in new businesses. So I bought into things that began providing a nice annuity for me. That's how I became a Republican. Even my mom couldn't say much about that.

Of course I never earned nearly as much money as later NFL players, but I don't begrudge them the incredible money they're making today. I can't help but wonder sometimes, though, what a player like me or Starr or Nitschke—any of us, for that matter—could command in today's marketplace.

In my day, we had to rely on outside income because we were never paid enough to retire on. I made a joke about it a few years ago, when I was on a Super Bowl panel with Joe Montana, Jerry Rice, and Michael Strahan, a defensive end for the Giants.

"Hell, I *had* to gamble," I told them. "That was the only way I could make any money."

But unlike some of today's athletes, who have lost their money because of prior investments, I was independent financially, all because of Uncle Henry and Frank Metts. Whatever money I made during my playing career, whether from salary or endorsements, they invested wisely for me in the stock market, real estate, and various business ventures.

Frank was the smartest real estate guy I ever met. I doubt that he graduated from high school, yet he usually managed to outsmart guys with Ivy League educations. He just had a knack for saying or doing the right thing to close a deal. Plus, he worked his ass off.

Before he died of a heart attack on August 20, 1990, Frank had gotten me into a great deal that gives me a nice annuity to this day. We bought the old Seagram's Distillery in Louisville, which had close to two million square feet. We sold half of it and kept the other half to establish Golden Foods/Golden Brands, a state-of-the-art vegetable and soybean company.

By 2003, it was doing $200 million a year in business, thanks to clients like McDonald's and Pillsbury.

I also own a building with six hundred apartments, ground leases on several businesses, and a shopping center in partnership with Lenny Lyles. My stocks have done well, and I still make speeches and commercial appearances for longtime clients such as the Ford Motor Company.

In fact, most of the old Packers have done a good job of using the publicity they got from football as a springboard to successful business careers. Willie Davis got a helluva job with Schlitz and owns three or four radio stations. Bart and Adderley and Max . . . hell, they've all done well.

I used to tell Pete Rozelle that the NFL should study how players do in business after they leave football. I guarantee you there are far more successes among guys who played on winning teams than those who played on losing teams. I think there's a carryover effect from both winning and losing.

As a hobby and an investment, I collect celebrity art. I have pieces signed by Tony Bennett, Red Skelton, and Peter Falk. Their value should only increase over the years. Hell, maybe Max and I should do a few paintings and try to sell them. We should be great with nudes, considering all the experience we've had.

Although I played too early to make the really big money in

the NFL, I came along at just the right time to cash in on the sports memorabilia craze. Like many of the stars from my era, I've made more money in retirement than I did as a player. The demand for autographs, photos, equipment, and other artifacts is insatiable. I even had two thousand bobblehead dolls of myself made and sold them out.

I have a cheap little trophy that I got in high school. I don't know why I kept it all these years, but I did. I'll bet I could put that thing on eBay, and some crazy Notre Dame or Packers fan would pay five hundred dollars for it.

I still go back to Wisconsin five or six times a year just to sign stuff. I could probably go back twenty-five times, if I wanted, and get paid every time. I try to do what I can for charity, too. If somebody sends me something to be signed, I'll send it back with a note asking the person to make a donation to the Sister Visitor Program in Louisville, which provides food and clothing for the poor.

About twenty years ago, at the beginning of the memorabilia craze, I came up with an idea for Joe DiMaggio that I was certain would be a huge moneymaker. I offered him $1 million to autograph ten thousand baseballs, provided those would be the last balls he ever signed.

A lot of people apparently found DiMaggio to be aloof and difficult to deal with, but he was always nice to me, maybe because I wore No. 5 in tribute to him. He rarely gave interviews, but he once gave me a half hour when I was doing a *Greatest Sports Legends* show for CBS. We shot it in Philadelphia and he had only one condition: that we not talk about Marilyn Monroe.

We had a preview of the show at Gallagher's Steak House in Manhattan, and it seemed like five hundred sportswriters showed up. They had never gotten so close to DiMaggio. Afterward, Joe asked for a copy of the show. Then he took it and showed it all over Japan, charging for showing it.

DiMaggio was certainly not averse to capitalizing on his name and fame. He had made a bundle as the national spokesman for Mr. Coffee, and he was definitely interested in my idea. At the time, however, he was suffering badly from arthritis and finally said, "Paul, I'm sorry, but I just can't do it." I tried to sweeten the deal by offering to take him on a ten-day cruise on which he would sign only one hundred balls a day. But he still said no.

I also noticed that whenever I went back to Canton, Ohio, for a Hall of Fame induction ceremony, the biggest ovation always would go to Joe Namath. Always. So I began thinking about ways that Joe and I could do business together.

When he came to Louisville to do my weekly television show *Paul Hornung's Sports Showcase*, which we taped live the day before it aired, he always hung around to sign every autograph. He was great with the public. I guess he had really grown up a lot since his early days in New York. My wife, Angela, thought he was great. Even now, he has a way with the women.

I didn't want to be in front of a camera anymore, but I was interested in producing a show. Namath still owns New York. So I got the idea of doing a show called *Namath on Broadway* that would be done from Gallagher's Steak House. He would interview sports celebrities, of course, but he also would do shows with politicians, actors, Broadway producers, and TV stars.

I had Joe really interested, not to mention several sponsors. He said that if he would agree to do it, I'd have to come and pick the games on one segment of the show. I told him I'd do that much. Still, I could never quite pull it all together. He had just gone through a divorce that was very painful for him and he was drinking a lot. Before he and I did a TV interview show together in Atlanta, he was drinking boilermakers. He noticeably slurred his words on the air, so I took him aside and said, "Joe, you just can't do this."

He decided not to do the show until he had straightened out his life. Apparently, he was still struggling when he appeared drunk on ESPN at the thirty-fifth reunion of the 1969 Jets team that had shocked the Colts in Super Bowl III. On camera, he told a female reporter twice that he wanted to kiss her. I told Angela, "He's half smashed." It didn't take Joe long to apologize and enter a treatment program.

But I still haven't given up on doing a show with him. All he would have to do is fly to New York on Friday night, tape the show on Saturday, and fly back home on Sunday morning. If he did that for thirteen weeks, I promised him, he and I would split $1 million. I still think it's a great idea.

14.

MONEY WON IS TWICE AS SWEET AS MONEY EARNED

I wasn't deactivated from the reserves in 1962 until late summer, which meant I went directly from Fort Riley to the Packers' training camp. The only sad thing about ending my ten months on active duty was that I had to say good-bye to a gorgeous black girl I had met through the man at the base who helped me stay in shape with heat treatments and rubdowns.

She was a knockout. Sometimes I'd take her to Kansas City, Missouri for weekends. Back then, this kind of relationship was strictly a no-no. Every time I'd call the manager of the Muelenbach Hotel, he'd say, "Again?" I'd tell him that if he didn't get me a room, I'd get the NAACP on his butt and I'd be one of the picketers.

But it was great to be a civilian—and a Packer—again. Naturally, there was a lot of speculation in the papers about whether I had gotten out of shape or lost my timing in the Army. I told the press I had stayed in good shape, but it was a lie. It wasn't that I was too heavy at about 222 pounds; it was that my legs felt like lead pipes.

And that wasn't all. On August 25, 1962, Commissioner Pete Rozelle visited us before an exhibition game against the Bears to warn us against gambling. This was no big deal; every year the commissioner visited all the teams. But this time, when he was done, he asked me to meet him for a cup of coffee.

"You're going to have to watch yourself," Rozelle warned me. "You're going to have to watch your associations. You have to be extra careful, Paul, because you're a bachelor and some people are always anxious to shoot down someone of prominence."

Our first outing since our championship romp over the Giants was against the College All-Stars on August 4 in Chicago. Since the game I had played in five years earlier, Otto Graham had been elevated to the Stars' head coach.

They played us tough for three quarters, but then we exploded for three touchdowns and a 42–20 victory. I gained thirty-three yards on only six carries. The star was Bart, whose passes to Dowler and McGee confounded the Stars' defense. Typically, Lombardi noted that Starr and Dowler were in better shape than the rest of us. I got the hint and really worked to get back into football shape.

One night during camp, Max sneaked out and got stopped for speeding by the Wisconsin State Police. He promised them anything if they would keep the ticket out of the papers, but they didn't. When Lombardi saw it, he erupted and called a team meeting.

"Max," screamed Lombardi, "that'll cost you five hundred dollars! And if you go again, it'll cost you one thousand dollars!"

The room was completely silent, but suddenly Lombardi smiled a little smile.

"Max, if you can find anything that's worth a thousand dollars to sneak out for, hell, call me and I'll go with you," he said.

After the exhibition season, I got off to a hot start in 1962 by scoring twenty-eight points in a 34–7 win over the Minnesota Vikings. After a victory over the St. Louis Cardinals, we ripped the Bears 49–0 in Green Bay. A week later, I kicked a 21-yard field goal with 0:33 remaining to beat the Lions, 9–7.

With 1:46 remaining, the Lions were beating us, 7–6, and had the ball at their own 49-yard line with a third-and-eight situation. Linebacker Joe Schmidt, the Lions' captain, had told quarterback Milt Plum to eat up some clock by running the ball, and then let Yale Lary punt it to us deep in our territory.

Instead, Plum tried one more pass on third down, a mistake that proved to be fatal. Herb Adderley intercepted the pass and streaked down the sideline right in front of our bench. The Lions finally tackled him at their twenty-two. After we ran a few runs to kill some time, I kicked the field goal that won it for us and ended up costing the Lions a crack at the NFL title.

I couldn't help but feel sorry for Schmidt, a friend and one of the toughest competitors I ever played against. Years later Schmidt told me he never got over Plum's "dumbass call." In his book, it was a blunder that could never be erased. He might have hurt Plum's feelings, but at least everybody on the team knew that Schmidt was dead honest. He never said anything he didn't believe.

After we retired, Schmidt was a regular at the annual golf tournament I used to have in Las Vegas. Joe liked to sing and he was pretty damned good at it. No matter what bar or club he was in, he'd get up and sing with the band. So I decided to pull a prank on Joe. One night I grabbed one of the hotel employees and introduced him to Joe as the head of entertainment at the Golden Nugget. I also told Joe this guy was looking for a singer to front for Alan King that fall, and maybe he could be the one.

When I got back home, Joe started calling me on a regular basis to ask if I had heard anything from the Golden Nugget. I told him that I was still talking with them, and that they were still interested in him. Once I sent him a letter on hotel stationery saying that they were thinking about asking him to open for King the next year, and that they'd pay him thirty thousand dollars a week in addition to picking up everything for him and his family.

This went on for six months. Everybody in Detroit knew about it because Joe told them. "And to think," he would say, "that I was told I couldn't sing." When he finally found out the truth, he was hot. He called me, raising hell. I told him I was getting him back for all the times he clotheslined me. He'd really done it to me.

But don't get the idea that Joe was a dummy. Just the opposite. Hell, he should have been named president of the Lions years ago. They love him in Detroit, which, by the way, is the greatest city in the country to play pro sports in because of the automobile industry. If you play in Detroit and don't get involved with the car companies, you must not like money. I've had a great relationship for years with the Ford Motor Company. If I'd played in Detroit instead of Green Bay, I'll bet I'd be worth $100 million today.

I'm not sure how many game-winning touchdowns or kicks I made during my Green Bay career, but Lombardi always said,

"The bigger the game, the better Hornung plays." He had a soft spot for Max and me because he knew we were "gamers," guys he could depend on to come through in the clutch.

I've always thought that Lombardi was secretly interested in news about my womanizing. I once dated a girl from Louisville named Doness. She was gorgeous, and had more personality than any woman I'd ever met. I took her to Green Bay and Lombardi really flipped over her. After that, he'd always ask me how she was doing and when I was going to bring her back for another game. I mean, he melted right in front of her.

She could really dance, and we danced the night away on many occasions. I thought I might marry her, but she caught me at the wrong time. She had a daughter to raise, and I was just starting to run around the country. But I stayed in touch with her for a long time. She was quite a girl.

In the season's fifth week, we were well on our way to a 48–21 victory over the Vikings in Minneapolis when, late in the second quarter, I got hit by Vikings linebacker Bill Livingston, twisting my right knee. I left the game and never returned.

Livingston made a clean tackle; I just happened to be planting my right foot for a pivot when he hit me. It was the worst injury I had suffered in my five-plus years of pro football. But I still hoped that I'd be ready in time to play against the 49ers in San Francisco the following week.

But the knee was still so sore that I sat on the bench, wearing a coat and tie, while we clobbered the 49ers, 31–13. Tom Moore started in my halfback spot and Jerry Kramer took over as our placekicker, a job he held for the rest of the season because of my knee. Sometimes I could kick as well as ever, but other times my knee would lock and I couldn't kick ten yards.

The injury caused me to miss the following two games as well: a 17–6 win over Baltimore that gave us our first road win over Johnny Unitas and the Colts since 1957, and a 38–7 victory over the Bears in Chicago. We were 8–0, and I had played only four and a half games.

One Sunday night, my date and I had dinner reservations at the King's X, a restaurant owned by Jesse Whittenton, one of our defensive backs. As we were arriving, two guys were walking around outside, smoking cigarettes. I'd already had a few martinis, and I was in a foul mood because I hadn't been playing.

One guy said, loud enough for me to hear, "Well, Golden Boy might not be playing anymore, but he can still get the women." I said, "Pardon me?" As he walked up to me, I put my 1961 championship ring on my right hand. When he got close enough and started to say something, I swung and hit him.

We wrestled each other to the ground, and the guy's buddy joined in. I had a heavy overcoat on and I couldn't do a thing. They were half stoned, or they could have really done a job on me. Fortunately my date ran into the bar, where Max was waiting for us.

"Max," she screamed, "some guys are beating up Paul in the parking lot."

To which Max replied, as only he could, "Hon, don't worry about it. The Horn can take care of himself." Anybody else, I'd have been mad at. But not Max. He always swore he didn't get into fights because he had a "paper-thin body."

Luckily for me, Ron Kramer also was there. He rushed outside and broke it up. He held one of the guys for me to hit with the big ring on my right hand, but I swung and missed, hitting Ron instead.

It was really stupid on my part. I could either have had a law-suit on my hands, or gotten beaten up badly. That was the only fight I ever had while I was in Green Bay, and, thank heaven, it didn't make the papers.

I saw limited duty in a 49–24 romp over the Eagles, and played only sparingly again in a 26–14 Thanksgiving Day loss to the Lions in Detroit that ended our eighteen-game winning streak. That was the game where Fuzzy Thurston invented what we came to call the "look-out block."

The Lions had a helluva defensive team. It was always knock-down-and-drag-out when we played. In those years, the Packers and the Lions were 1–2 in the league, and the Lions hated us be-cause they were always No. 2.

The Lions' defensive tackles, Alex Karras and Roger Brown, always gave fits to our offensive guards, Jerry Kramer and Thurston, because our guys just weren't strong or quick enough to handle them.

So this one game, Roger Brown sacked Bart about six times. It got to be a joke. Finally, Fuzzy got set to pass-block and just as Bart was getting ready to take the snap, Fuzzy looked over his shoulder and yelled, "Look out, Bart." That cracked up every-body.

Fuzzy could outdrink anybody I ever saw. He was the cham-pion, the best, and I never even saw him throw up. In fact, we used to arrange contests matching Fuzzy with the champion drinker from another team. The Redskins, for example, had a tackle named Fran O'Brien. He owned his own bar, and he could drink. So we made a huge bet with some of the Redskin players that he couldn't outdrink Fuzzy.

We got to the bar before the Redskins. Fuzzy was thirsty so he said, "Let me warm up with three beers." I tried to talk him out of it because I was afraid he'd give O'Brien an advantage. "Fuzzy, don't screw this up," I warned him. He knocked back the three beers.

When Franny got there, they started the contest with martinis. After an hour and a half or two, as the Redskins were literally carrying Franny out to keep him from falling down and passing out, Fuzzy was up on the bar, doing push-ups. And he kept on drinking.

Another time, just to get out of Green Bay for a while, a bunch of us were planning to go to Appleton, Wisconsin, to have dinner at a place owned by Jack Skau. Fuzzy and I met in Green Bay before lunch and had two or three drinks. But when I went home, Fuzzy didn't. He drank all afternoon at Spot's, one of our favorite hangouts.

Jerry Kramer, Max, and I met Fuzzy at 4:30 to have a few drinks before we left for Appleton, which was about forty-five minutes away. I took a "roadie" with me, and Fuzzy had the bartender mix up some martinis and put them in a milkshake glass for him to drink on the trip down.

At the restaurant, we decided to drink champagne and Fuzzy had at least a whole bottle before going to stingers, a lethal combination of brandy and crème de menthe. Then he had the bartender fill up the milkshake glass full of martinis for the trip home.

Back in Green Bay, he stole a jug of wine from under the bar at Speed's, another of our hangouts, and chugged half of it. Then we went to the Picadilly to play cards and check out the band. There Fuzzy switched to scotch. On the way to our house, he bought a case of beer and downed about six of them before he went home.

We all had to go to a funeral at 8:30 the next morning, and damned if Fuzzy wasn't back at our house, knocking on the door and waking us all up. I said, "You must feel like shit." He laughed and said he felt great. Sure enough, he was the least hungover of all of us. He was just amazing.

The Thanksgiving Day loss to Detroit gave us a 10–1 record heading into a game against the Rams in Milwaukee on December 2. I returned to the starting lineup and helped us to a 41–10 win with a 30-yard touchdown catch, a 35-yard reception to set up a TD, and nine carries for 30 yards.

During my absence, Taylor took up the slack in a big way. Ever since he came into the league, Jimmy seemed more concerned with gaining more yards than Cleveland's Jim Brown than with anything else. In that respect, he wasn't much of a team player. But with me on the sidelines for so many games, he became both the league's leading rusher (1,474 yards) and scorer (114 points).

We closed out the 1962 regular season with a 13–1 record that earned us a rematch against the 12–2 Giants for the title on December 30 in Yankee Stadium. It was so cold and windy that day that the turf was frozen, making it difficult for runners to cut and passers to throw accurately. Taylor and I later agreed that we had never been hit as hard as we were that day.

The conditions forced both teams to be more conservative than usual on offense. We took a 10–0 lead into the locker room at halftime on the strength of Jerry Kramer's 26-yard field goal in the first quarter and a 7-yard touchdown smash by Taylor in the second, followed by Kramer's conversion. I set up that TD with a 26-yard pass to Dowler.

In the third quarter, McGee was called upon to punt from our fifteen, but the Giants' Erich Barnes blocked it and Jim Collier recovered in the end zone for a TD. Don Chandler's conversion cut our lead to 10–7. But that was as close as they came. Our fired-up defense—cornerback Willie Wood was so angry about a call that he got ejected—shut them down the rest of the way and Kramer added two more field goals to give us a 16–7 win and our second consecutive title.

I'll always think that '62 team was our best one. We scored at will, averaging more than thirty points a game, while our defense only gave up seven or eight. We were so good that we placed eleven players on the twenty-two-man All-Pro team.

On offense, they were Ron and Jerry Kramer, Gregg, Thurston, Ringo, and Taylor; on defense, it was Willie Davis, Henry Jordan, Dan Currie, Bill Forester, and Herb Adderley. And get this: Starr didn't make the All-Pro team even though he led the league in passing, and Wood didn't make it despite leading the league in interceptions.

Although my winner's check for $5,888.57 seems paltry by today's standards, it was a nice supplement to my income, which had grown to $45,000. Although the Packers were owned by the city of Green Bay, the franchise was run by a board of directors who had loved to meddle and second-guess before Lombardi arrived. As president and general manager, Lombardi ran the whole show. The board never questioned one of his decisions.

So Lombardi and I came to have an understanding: he always would give me an extra $5,000 for a good season. But the most important thing was that I was able to take advantage of the lucrative marriage between television and the NFL.

On Tuesday, January 8, 1963, I was in L.A., having dinner with Bart Starr and his wife, Jimmy Taylor and his wife, and Jerry Kramer and his wife. They were all out there for the Pro Bowl. I wasn't in it, so I was doing some Jantzen clothing ads. During dinner, I got a message to call Commissioner Rozelle at his home in New York.

"When can you come to New York?" he said. "I'd like to talk to you. It's important."

I had an idea what it was about. So I took the red-eye and was in New York the next morning.

15

IF YOU WANT TO DANCE, YOU'VE GOT TO PAY THE FIDDLER

Pete Rozelle had a huge smile, a great tan, and a persuasive personality. His background as a PR man taught him how to handle the media, which was one of his greatest assets as commissioner. I wasn't sure what he wanted with me, but I suspected it would have something to do with my gambling. If so, I was ready to argue that it wasn't a big deal because I had never bet against the Packers.

The meeting was so hush-hush that Rozelle wanted to hide me away in some fleabag hotel in Manhattan. But I said the hell with that, so I checked into the St. Moritz on January 9. Mickey Mantle was living there then and I met him in the bar. We had a drink but he never asked me what I was doing in New York.

The next day I met Rozelle in the Plaza hotel. I didn't bring a lawyer with me, so it was just the two of us. That was a mistake. At first, I denied gambling on anything. But I knew he had me when he told me the league had been conducting a secret investigation for ten months and had tapped my phone in Green Bay.

I was so naïve that I didn't even think about whether the wiretaps were legal or not. So I told Rozelle that, yes, I had bet on two or three games in the late 1950s. Since 1960, when Rick Casares and I went to Las Vegas after the Pro Bowl, I'd been betting through one man, Barney Shapiro, who had become a very close friend.

Well, actually a teammate and I also were betting on the NFL with a guy he knew down in his home state. We won about ten thousand dollars, which was serious money back then. The guy was slow to pay, and I wanted my money so I said, "Tell that SOB to pay us." Well, my teammate came back and said the guy wouldn't pay. What recourse did I have? I couldn't call the police on the guy.

Other than that, however, I only bet with Barney. I never went to either San Francisco or Vegas without seeing him. He had a wonderful sense of humor, and he was always trying to date my girlfriends. It got to be kind of a joke. I remember a tall, gorgeous showgirl in Vegas named Sanita. I really liked her. But as soon as I left town, Barney was after Sanita. He was *always* with a pretty lady.

Barney owned all the pinball machines in the San Francisco area, which made him enough money to move his office to Vegas. He built up his business to where he owned almost all the slot machines in Nevada; invented the electronic blackjack game and put those machines into bars, restaurants, grocery stores, and drugstores all over the state; and owned a lot of property in the Reno-Tahoe area.

Because of his business, Barney did have a gambling stamp, as required by Nevada state law, but that hardly made him the big-time bettor that the press made him out to be. He loved to bet on football, and he might ask me how I felt about a game. Sometimes he'd listen to me, sometimes he wouldn't. I didn't think it was any big deal. Just a couple of friends talking about football.

I'd tell Barney what I wanted to bet, and he'd get it down for me in Vegas. I'd bet seven or eight games a year through Barney. The biggest bet I ever made in those days was $800, and I *always* bet on us to win. But it was just for fun, more than anything. I don't think I ever won or lost more than $2,000 on a season, which was peanuts for a guy making $100,000 a year to film four commercials for Chevrolet and another $75,000 from Marlboro (when cigarette advertising was banned from television, I took a real hit).

The Packers were so good that we beat the point spread all the time, so a lot of bettors started playing us in parlays with other teams. You win more if you hit a parlay, but it's generally a sucker bet because it's tough enough to pick the winner of one game, much less two or three or four. But with us as a virtual lock to cover the spread every week, it became easier for the bettors to win parlays. The bookmakers got tired of it, so sometimes they'd take us off the board, which raised a flag about gambling to the NFL and other authorities.

Until then, gambling had never been a big deal in the NFL, even though it was going on long before I came into the league. One of the legendary gamblers was Bobby Layne, the great quarterback with Detroit and Pittsburgh in the 1950s. Against the College All-Stars in 1958, Layne threw six interceptions and his backup another three in a suspicious 35–19 loss.

(LEFT) My mom, Loretta, and I on a Florida vacation.

(BELOW) My best friend, Sherrill Sipes, and I as Notre Dame sophomores— in the days before face masks. *(Courtesy of the University of Notre Dame Athletic Department)*

(RIGHT) I wore No. 5 in honor of my boyhood idol, Joe DiMaggio, the Yankee Clipper. I got to know him a bit after my playing days ended.

(BELOW) Sherrill (No. 12) and I were the only two boys from Louisville who ever started together in the same Notre Dame backfield. *(Courtesy of the University of Notre Dame Athletic Department)*

(LEFT) Me and my new best buddy, Mr. Heisman Trophy, 1956.

(BELOW) At the Walter Camp Award ceremony for Oklahoma's Jerry Tubbs in 1956. I don't know the guy on the left, but he must have been a campaign contributor, because then–Vice President Richard Nixon was paying more attention to him than to me or Tubbs. *(Reni Photos)*

(LEFT) Doing my part to keep the world safe for democracy at Fort Knox in 1957. (*AP/Wide World Photos*)

(BELOW) When Jackie Gleason threw a party, the guest list was strictly uptown.

(RIGHT) The famed "Packers sweep" was our bread-and-butter play throughout my career. After taking a handoff from Bart Starr (15), I followed the blocking of pulling guards Jerry Kramer (64) and Fuzzy Thurston (63) and fellow running back Jimmy Taylor (lower right).

(BELOW) The Baltimore Colts were so good that they always brought out the best in me. *(Photograph by John E. Biever)*

(RIGHT) PS: I lied.

(BELOW) Big smiles after another Packer win. The one on the far left with no teeth is Jimmy Taylor, with Lombardi, me, and Bart Starr.

(ABOVE) Lombardi always said I had a nose for pay dirt. *(Photograph by Vernon Biever)*

(BELOW) The form I used to kick 66 field goals and 190 extra points in my pro career. *(Photograph by Vernon Biever)*

(TOP) I had a terrific season in 1961, but so did these two fellows, Mickey Mantle (left) and Roger Maris.

(MIDDLE) To get to me, you've always had to go through my pal Ron Kramer.

(BOTTOM) Me with Jimmy Taylor, the toughest 215-pound SOB I've ever known.

(LEFT) Looking at this photo, you really wouldn't believe that I had just scored a touchdown against Cleveland, would you? *(Photograph by Vernon Biever)*

(BELOW) Lombardi and I both got a kick out of beating the Browns in the 1965 NFL championship game.

Just some of my endorsements: Marlboro cigarettes, Jantzen swimwear, Miller Lite beer, and Black & White scotch. Lombardi would never give me as big a raise as some of the other guys got because he figured I didn't need it with all my outside income.

What makes him the
football player's football player
makes us the
Scotch drinker's Scotch.

**Black & White.
The Scotch drinker's Scotch.**

In 188 countries around the world, Black & White is the Scotch drinker's Scotch.

(RIGHT) I'm not sure who the two guys flanking me and Frank Gifford are. Gifford is evidently telling me he'd never be caught dead wearing the sports jacket on the fellow next to him.

(BELOW) My buddy and longtime partner, sportscasting icon Lindsey Nelson, flanked by Bob Wussler (left) and yours truly. Lindsey and I worked for Bob at CBS and, later, at WTBS in Atlanta.

(LEFT) When I finally made it to the Pro Football Hall of Fame in Canton, Ohio, the "Golden Boy" felt very humble, indeed.

(BELOW) The 1986 class of inductees at the Pro Football Hall of Fame, left to right: Paul Hornung, halfback, Green Bay; Ken Houston, strong safety, Houston and Washington; Willie Lanier, linebacker, Kansas City; Fran Tarkenton, quarterback, Minnesota and New York Giants; and Doak Walker, halfback, Detroit. (*Photograph by Vernon Biever*)

(RIGHT) Max McGee, my fellow perpetrator, introduced me at the Hall of Fame induction ceremony. Thank God he didn't tell the good stories.

(BELOW) In 1988, Notre Dame made one of its Heisman winners the program cover boy at every one of its home games. Here I am, receiving a framed poster of my cover. (*Courtesy of the University of Notre Dame Athletic Department*)

(ABOVE) Our former Flaget High teammate, Howard Schnellenberger (center), pauses while telling Sherrill and me how he won
the 1983 national college championship at the University of Miami.

(BELOW) Frank Metts: my buddy, my partner, and the smartest man I ever knew.

(ABOVE) Angela and I at Churchill Downs on a Derby Day. Thank heavens I was lucky enough to meet her, the woman who makes me happy to this day.

(BELOW) Brett Favre, the best player in the history of the Green Bay Packers, shares a golden moment with Lombardi's No. 5.

Then, in the second game of the 1958 season, Layne did something peculiar against our team in Green Bay. The Lions were 3½-point favorites and, as Layne told me later, he had bet on them to cover the spread. With the score tied at 13 late in the fourth quarter, the Lions took over on their twenty and Layne marched them down to our seven, where they faced fourth down.

The field-goal team came on the field to win the game. But wait! Layne shushed them off. His coach, George Wilson, let Bobby call the plays on offense, which wasn't uncommon in those days. Layne then overthrew his receiver in the end zone and the game ended in a tie.

It was obvious he had bet on the game. Layne later told me that he was confident he could get a touchdown and win the game that way. Bobby gambled more than anybody who ever played football, period. How did the league go all those years without ever getting him?

After I confessed, Rozelle wanted me to go somewhere with some FBI guys and take a lie-detector test. I refused, because I knew what they wanted to do. They wanted to ask me what I knew about other players, including some of my teammates, whom they suspected of betting. Brodie, the 49ers' quarterback, and Len Dawson of the Kansas City Chiefs were suspects. I don't know about Brodie, but I'm confident Lenny never bet. I think they suspected him because of his friendship with Don Dawson, no relation, a big gambler whom I had met through Ron Kramer at the Red Run Country Club in Detroit.

I told Rozelle that he could ask me anything he wanted about my gambling, but I wasn't going to talk about anybody else and I wasn't going to take a lie-detector test. I remember saying,

"Pete, we both know that other guys are betting. I know who they are, and I'm not answering questions about anybody else. But if I go to Washington [where a Senate subcommittee was investigating gambling] and raise my right hand, this whole league is in trouble."

The meeting ended with Rozelle telling me that he'd call me when he had made his decision about what to do with me. He also told me not to say a word about our conversation to anybody. He wanted to keep a tight lid on it until he had made up his mind.

Over the next three months, I had plenty of time to think about the pickle I was in and how I got there. I grew up with gambling. As Ron Kramer once said, "There are three things you do in Louisville—you either bet, book bets, or do both." I can remember guys shooting craps on the street corners in my neighborhood of Portland, and, of course, I had begun sneaking into the racetrack at an early age.

During my career at Notre Dame and Green Bay, I was always in the hot nightclubs, so I got to meet all the sharpies. Take Manny Scar, the nightclub owner in Chicago that Abe Samuels had introduced me to. He knew everybody on Rush Street and he'd take me with him. He once asked me, "Don't you have any better clothes than that?" The next day he took me downtown and had four or five suits made for me.

The FBI once talked to me about Manny Scar and Sam Giancana. I knew Sam as a guy in the clubs, not the boss of the Chicago mob. I didn't really wise up about some of these characters until Manny was killed in a garage, shot at least twenty times.

Then there was Gil Beckley. I used to see him at Gulfstream Park all the time. He had a grandson whom he wanted to get into

Notre Dame, and asked me if I could help him. I'm not sure exactly how I learned he was one of the biggest bookmakers in the country. All I knew was that he was always nice to me.

I was hanging around in Miami when Floyd Patterson and Ingemar Johansson had their third heavyweight title fight on March 13, 1961, in Miami Beach. Johansson had knocked out Patterson to retain his title on June 26, 1959, in New York. Almost a year later to the day, they fought again at Madison Square Garden and this time Patterson won to regain the title.

One night, when Gil and I were at the Fontainebleau to hear Sinatra, Gil asked me who I liked in the fight. I told him Johansson. He smiled and said, "You want to bet on a winner or a loser?" Then he told me he was betting a thousand dollars for me on Patterson, besides giving me a ringside ticket to the fight.

"I don't want you sitting next to me," he said, "because you don't need the notoriety. I'll see you at the Eden Roc [nightclub] afterward."

At the fight, I sat next to a huge black man. I mean, when we shook hands, his hand just engulfed mine. It was Sonny Liston, sitting next to me in a seat that Gil had given him. That proved to me that Sonny was with the wiseguys.

Well, Patterson beat Johansson, just as Gil had promised, and I collected on the thousand-dollar bet he had made for me. Later I found out that Johansson really loved women, so Gil and his friends had made sure that hookers were following Johansson the whole week before the fight. In those days, boxing was where the wiseguys made the big money.

Liston later took Patterson's title with a first-round knockout, then defended it against Patterson with another first-round knockout. Patterson was scared to death of him, and I don't blame him. But then came Liston's 1964 title bout against Cassius Clay, my fellow athlete from Louisville. Sonny gave up the championship by not answering the bell for the seventh round. Then, in the rematch in Lewiston, Maine, Sonny went down in the first round to a "phantom punch" that nobody ever saw.

I once asked Gil, "When I played for Notre Dame, did you know when I was hurt?" And he said, "Paul, when you were at Notre Dame, I knew more about you than you did." He said that every year he followed five or six players around the country who had the ability to win, or lose, games.

I don't know what happened to Gil. He just vanished one day and nobody ever found him, as far as I know.

Gil wasn't a killer, but I may have met a few without knowing it. For example, I've always wondered about the mysterious disappearance of Carroll Rosenbloom, the Rams owner who vanished in 1979 and was presumed drowned. Like a lot of the men who have owned NFL teams over the years, Rosenbloom was a big gambler.

He was the Colts' owner in 1958 when they beat the Giants for the NFL title in that famous sudden-death overtime game. All the Colts needed to win was a nine-yard field goal by Steve Myra. That would have given them the victory but not the margin necessary to cover the point spread, which had them favored by 3½ points. So, on third down, Johnny Unitas handed off to Alan "The Horse" Ameche, who scored the TD that won the game by six and covered the spread.

Because Rosenbloom's gambling habits were well known, it has long been speculated that he ordered the Colts to go for the TD so he could win his bet. But that's a bunch of bullshit. Back then, you used all your downs. You didn't go for a field goal on third down. Plus, it was no cinch that Myra would make the kick from the angle of the hash mark.

Years later, after trading the Colts for the Rams, Rosenbloom was supposedly swimming at night off the pier behind his home on Golden Beach, Florida. There's no way he would have been doing that because those waters are vicious. I know, because after Carroll died, my friend Frank Metts bought Rosenbloom's house and I spent a lot of time there. That water is so rough you wouldn't swim in it in daytime, much less the night.

Was he murdered? Beats me.

Going back to my suspension, I'd hung around guys like Manny Scar and Gil Beckley without thinking much about it. They were always where the action was, and I loved the action. The concept of guilt-by-association never entered my mind.

Green Bay was like Louisville in that gambling was more or less a way of life. The parlay gambling cards were available in every bar, and there also was a popular game called "Ship, Captain, and Crew," in which you rolled dice for games or money. A lot of guys on the team played the parlay cards, and, of course, we had our games of poker and gin rummy.

So gambling to me was just another form of fun and entertainment, sort of like chasing girls and going out on the town. Hell, Lombardi himself loved the racetrack. His godfather, James "Sunny Jim" Fitzsimmons, was one of the great Thoroughbred trainers of all time. He trained Triple Crown winners Gallant Fox in 1930 and Omaha in 1935.

Rozelle finally called me on April 17, only a few weeks before the 1963 Kentucky Derby, to tell me he had reached a decision: he had decided to suspend me and another player, defensive tackle Alex Karras of Detroit, indefinitely for breaking the league's rule against gambling. He also suspended four other Lions players a couple of games for playing the parlay cards. Karras was stupid. Rozelle didn't have anything on him, but he had mentioned on a TV game show that he had played the parlay cards. Rozelle took that as a confession. Rozelle said he would watch our conduct for the next year, and reevaluate our status sometime early in 1964.

The hardest part about the suspension was telling my mom, but she responded better than I thought she might.

"We've gone through a lot of rough spots all our life," she said. "Growing up is pretty hard, Paul, and you've been fortunate all your life, and if the good Lord has handed you something like this, you need to accept it."

I called Lombardi to tell him, but apparently he already had talked to Rozelle. I went into seclusion at a Louisville motel, where Lombardi somehow found me. He told me he was disappointed that I hadn't come to him because maybe he could have done something. He was right. I should have gone to him. He also gave me some advice.

"I want you to keep your nose clean," he said. "Do not go to Churchill Downs, do not go to the Derby, do not go to Las Vegas."

I also called Jim Rathman at Jantzen to tell him about the suspension before I went out to play golf with my friend William H. King at the Audubon Country Club. I played badly because I was so distracted. When we were on the back nine, Chris Duvall, an attorney friend, came out to tell us that a mob of reporters and photographers were camped out in front of the club.

We went back to the clubhouse and I drafted a statement that Chris read. Early that evening, we had another press conference at Chris's house. A reporter from the Huntley-Brinkley show, NBC's nightly newscast, had come in, as had a couple of reporters from St. Louis. All the local guys were there.

After answering all their questions, I took a little blonde I knew out to dinner. We were interrupted by a phone call from Bill Quinlan, one of my teammates. When the people in Bill's hometown of Lawrence, Massachusetts, heard about the suspension, they chipped in to buy Bill a plane ticket so he could come to Louisville to be with me. He stayed for four days, and I showed him around town. By the time he left, I felt much better.

Of course, my teammate who had been my betting partner was scared shitless. I heard he was so scared he checked himself into a hospital because he didn't want anybody calling him for interviews. The doctor put him in quarantine for four days. He was worried to death something was going to happen to him. He asked me what I had told Rozelle. I told him, "I didn't mention a word about you." He got away with it. More power to him. He knows it's no big deal now. After all these years, what does it matter?

I had invited Ron Kramer, Fuzzy Thurston, and their wives to be my guests at the '63 Kentucky Derby, but I decided to take Lombardi's advice and not go. That is the only Derby I've missed in fifty years or so. The only time I saw the Packers play in person that year was when I attended a preseason exhibition game against the Giants on September 2 at Lambeau Field (which was still called City Stadium then). I didn't want anybody to recognize me, so I wore sunglasses and a hat as I sat next to Ron Kramer's wife, Nancy, and the Kramers' two children.

Nancy was a beautiful woman, so there was no chance we'd go unnoticed. Soon rumors were swirling around Green Bay that she was having an affair with the mystery man sitting next to her.

As the Packers tried to win their third straight title, but their first without me, I managed to stay surprisingly busy and I made more money than I would have playing football. I worked with Uncle Henry and Frank Metts in our Louisville real estate business, and I hosted a radio show on WHAS, a 50,000-watt station. I also continued doing commercials. Of more than twenty contracts to endorse commercial products, I kept about 85 percent of them.

William H. King, a longtime friend and a local promoter, and I formed Productions Unlimited. We promoted everything from appearances by me to Twister contests to fights involving Cassius Clay.

King usually had a shrewd eye for talent. However, he passed on a couple of kids who auditioned for him in the 1950s. He described one as a "greasy truck driver from Memphis," and the other as "a big-nosed Jewish broad from New York." Despite his rejection, Elvis Presley and Barbra Streisand went on to some pretty decent careers.

I caught the Packers on TV whenever I could. We opened the season with a 10–3 loss to the Bears in Green Bay. Then both teams won eight in a row to set up the rematch on November 17 in Wrigley Field. That was the game in which Ray Nitschke, our great linebacker, grabbed Chicago fullback Rick Casares's ankle, twisted it, and broke it, putting Casares out for the season. Nevertheless, with the Packers without me and Starr (who suffered a hairline fracture and was replaced by John Roach), the Bears won again, 26–7.

Rick and I had been friends for years and my mother loved

him, so he came down to spend a few weeks in Louisville with me. He was a cool guy, but if he ever got pissed at you, you were in deep trouble. He was the toughest SOB I've ever seen in my life and he could really fight. One night on Rush Street in Chicago, he hit a guy so hard that his face turned to mush. Then Casares jumped on him and began hitting him again. I pulled him off because I was afraid he was going to kill him.

While he was staying in Louisville, he told me he was going to get Nitschke for breaking his ankle. I knew he wasn't kidding.

On November 22, 1963, I had lunch in Philadelphia with Bill Quinlan, my former teammate, who had been traded to the Eagles. Then I headed back to Louisville with a stop at National Airport in Washington, D.C. I was getting ready to catch my plane home when I heard the news that President Kennedy had been shot in Dallas. I remember running into Jesse Jackson, and we were both stunned.

I had been invited to the Kennedy compound at Hyannisport, Massachusetts, two or three times, but I never could make it. I wished that I had, if for no other reason than to thank President Kennedy for getting me that leave to play in the '61 championship game.

Because of the national mourning, Rozelle was under pressure to cancel that Sunday's schedule, but he decided that the games should go on in order to maintain a sense of normalcy and continuity. The Packers defeated the 49ers, 28–10, before 45,905 in Milwaukee's County Stadium. The game marked Starr's return to action after missing four games because of that injury.

As it turned out, the losses to the Bears were our only two of the season, costing us the Western Division title and leading to a lot of speculation about what might have happened if I'd been playing. For some reason, I always played well against the Bears.

"Everything went well, except we didn't have Paul," Ron Kramer said. "There's just some sort of magic that certain people have in athletics and in life. He was that sort of guy with us. He was the guy everybody on the team—the black guys, the white guys, the tackles, the guards, the kickers—everybody loved this guy.

"Tom [Moore, my replacement] played well," said Kramer, "but he's no Hornung."

In the championship game, which Casares had to miss because of his injury, the Bears beat the Giants, 14–10. It rankled Lombardi that we had to give up the throne that he thought was rightfully ours, but he said that the team did about as well as it could under the circumstances.

"I have a soft spot for this team," Lombardi said. "It didn't win, but it always hung tight despite discouragements. Hornung's loss. Starr's injury. Other injuries. A bad start. We only had to beat the Bears once and we would have been champs. We didn't."

How much did the team miss me?

"Obviously, a lot," Lombardi said. "His blocking, his leadership, his 'devil may care' attitude, his field-goal kicking, his intelligence on the field."

From the moment the suspension was announced, there was a lot of speculation about whether the Packers would trade me. But Lombardi emphatically squelched that kind of thinking on January 30, 1964, at the annual NFL meeting in Miami Beach.

"Any trade talk is ridiculous," Lombardi told reporters. "I positively have no thought of trading him. If Hornung plays, he'll play for us. You know as much as I do about whether he'll be back. It is up to the commissioner. But we are including Paul in our plans if we get him. Whatever he is worth to another team, he is worth to us."

One of my first public appearances during my suspended year was at a banquet honoring Boston Celtics star Bob Cousy in Worcester, Massachusetts. He called me and invited me to come, even telling me that he wanted me to sit next to him. I'd met Bob when he and I were both doing photo shoots for Jantzen clothing. I really appreciated his loyalty, so I accepted.

Teddy Kennedy had turned down an invitation to appear at the banquet. But when he heard I was going to be there, he immediately reversed. He knew that my presence would attract a lot of media, which it did, and no politician ever turns down that kind of exposure.

The thing that bothered me most about my suspension was the word *indefinitely*. I had done everything that Vince had asked, keeping a low profile during the '63 season and staying away from gambling joints. Still, I didn't know if that would be good enough for Rozelle. My career was in his hands, and Rozelle would say only that he wouldn't look into the situation involving me and Karras until mid to late spring.

Early in February, this item ran in Walter Winchell's nationally syndicated gossip column: "Myrna Loy is being rushed by Paul Hornung, the football glamour boy. He long kisstances the one-time Hollywood star from his Old Kentucky Home." Oh, great, I thought. This was just what I needed.

At the time I was twenty-eight and Myrna Loy, a great actress from the silent days to the 1940s, was fifty-seven. I did have a date, and only one, with Myrna Ross, who was to be in Frank

Sinatra's next movie. I set the record straight when I got a call from Pat Harmon of the *Cincinnati Post & Times-Star.*

"I have never met Myrna Loy or talked with her on the phone," I said. "Winchell has had me married once, engaged twice, and attached to four or five different showgirls. I'm still single. Somebody probably told Winchell I had a date with a starlet named Myrna, and the only Myrna [that] Winchell could remember is Myrna Loy."

I also got a lot of media inquiries about whether I had stayed in shape, just in case Rozelle decided to reinstate me. I told them that I weighed 221, only a couple of pounds over my playing weight, and that I'd stayed in shape by working out at the YMCA and playing a lot of squash. Also, as Lombardi had advised me, I used every interview to express how sorry I was, how much I missed football, and how I had walked the straight and narrow since the suspension.

"This has been my first time away from the sport in seventeen years," I told Carl Craft of the Associated Press, "and I'm itching to get back into the league and to start practice at Green Bay. Football meant so much to me and I guess I let a lot of people down. I'm glad I told the truth. I feel more hurt because of my mother than myself."

Lombardi said repeatedly that he wasn't worried about my condition.

"He's usually not one to work by himself," Lombardi said. "But he's a great athlete, a great competitor, and he must understand what a year's layoff could mean. He has understood other things about his suspension so he kept well away from undesirable places and people, handled himself well with the press, and declared repeatedly that he wants to come back—that I think he understands the need for physical condition beyond what he would get in camp."

In March, Rozelle invited me to New York for a talk. I thought he was going to tell me his decision, but he just asked me a lot of stuff about my associations and what I had been doing.

I couldn't help but think that the NFL was being a little two-faced about gambling. The story goes that the Mara family, which owned the Giants, and the Rooney family, which owns the Steelers, had made a lot of money by gambling back in the '20s when bookmaking was legal. And, of course, everybody knew about Rosenbloom's gambling.

Hell, years later I even did some gambling with Edward J. DeBartolo Sr. after he bought the San Francisco 49ers for his son, Eddie Jr. I ran into Mr. D. at the 1979 Super Bowl between Dallas and Pittsburgh. I had known him through our mutual interest in horse racing (he owned three or four tracks) and Notre Dame. He loved Notre Dame so much that he and his son gave the university $33 million, which was, at the time, one of the largest single gifts given to any university.

On the occasion of the '79 Super Bowl, we talked about the point spread and finally, because of something I said, Mr. D. changed his mind and decided to bet the other way. I asked if he could bet a couple of dimes (thousands) for me because he had a bookie in Pittsburgh who was offering a more attractive point spread than the one I was getting in Louisville. We won our bets and Mr. D. said, "I saved a lot of money because of you." He called an attorney in Coral Gables, Florida, to have him write me a check. Mr. D. was my kind of guy.

But I had accepted the suspension as humbly as I could, with one exception. Rozelle told me I couldn't own 10 percent of Louisville Downs, the little harness-racing track that my friend William H. King was starting in Louisville. I said the hell with it and told King to count me in as a silent partner.

After my meeting with Rozelle, I went to Toots Shor's, where I told Toots and some others what had happened. Toots, Frank Gifford, and I left to go somewhere else for dinner because we knew the New York writers would figure they could find me at Toots's place. We spent the night drinking, and, oddly, it came to feel more like a celebration than a wake. On the way home, we walked down an alley throwing garbage cans at each other.

On April 17, 1964, I was in a beachfront hotel in Miami with Sandy Dietz, a little Italian girl from New York that Gifford had fixed me up with. At the time I met her, she was working at the Copacabana. Somebody called, I can't remember who, to tell me that Rozelle had announced in New York that he was lifting the suspensions of me and Karras.

It was a great relief. I called Coach Lombardi immediately. He told me he wanted me in Green Bay six weeks before training camp so he could get me back in shape. I immediately envisioned the sixty-four steps leading up and down the stands of City Stadium and I thought, *Oh, shit!*

16.

CALLING DR. LOMBARDI

As ordered, I arrived in Green Bay about six weeks before the 1964 camp began, and started working out with Boyd Dowler, who was living in Green Bay. Every day we'd do sprints against each other. Then we'd run up and down the steps at City Stadium, all sixty-four of them, about five times. By the beginning of camp, I was in the best shape of my life. If anything, I overdid it.

My best playing weight was about 215, but I was down to about 200 at the start of camp. I felt so good—my knees were coming around so well that I thought I might be able to kick again—that I even led the team when training camp started and it was time to run laps around the field. I was in front of everyone, which Max and some others thought was pretty funny.

But I was too light. I had to block a lot more than I ran, and, at 200 pounds, the blocking really wore me down. I hurt my shoulder and my knee, and that really set me back. In a way, I blamed Lombardi. We had a team doctor, but Lombardi was really our team doctor. There was no question about that. And if he thought you were OK to play, you were going to play.

Around the league, my return was the No. 1 topic of discussion.

"Mr. Lombardi will see to it that Mr. Hornung is in condition," said George Allen, the defensive coordinator of the Bears. "If he were a marginal player, it would be a different story, but he was too much the skillful artist to sacrifice everything he had. I felt Hornung was the best all-around back in the NFL."

Lions fullback Nick Pietrosante, who was a sophomore at Notre Dame when I was a senior, looked at it from a player's perspective.

"Will Paul come back strong? I hope not for our sake," he said, "because I think we've got a good shot this year. Seriously, the big thing is, he laid off two years. He really missed most of '62 with the bad knee."

While all this was going on, the thousand-yard rushers from the previous year were honored at Fuzzy Thurston's restaurant, The Left Guard, in Appleton. Rick Casares was there. Like me, he was trying to come back from an injury.

Well, Nitschke walked in and all Casares wanted was for Nitschke to say one thing to him. He was going to get him. So the first thing Nitschke said to Casares was, "Hey, Rick, congratulations. I heard you married that rich broad from Tampa." That was all Casares needed to hear. He asked Nitschke to repeat himself. Then he said, "You are a real asshole and I want you to come outside with me because I'm going to teach you a lesson."

Nitschke was one of the toughest guys in the league, but he wasn't in Rick's class. Hell, in Chicago, even Doug Atkins, the ferocious All-Pro defensive end and one of the meanest men in the league, wouldn't mess with Rick. I knew that if they went outside, he'd hurt Nitschke and hurt him bad.

So I stopped the fight before it started, even though Casares kept taunting and abusing Nitschke. He hurt him as badly with his mouth as he would have with his fists. He humiliated Nitschke, who took it without a peep. But as I told Nitschke later, not kidding, "What you don't understand is that I saved your life that day."

In those days, Nitschke could be a real asshole when he drank a lot, which was often. He once got pistol-whipped in Chicago. He would have been in the penitentiary had it not been for football.

I remember a time when we arrived in Los Angeles for a game against the Rams. In those days, the coaches and the players went to separate bars to drink. It was an unwritten rule that the two would always be separate. On this trip, Nitschke and some others went to a little place in Santa Monica where I knew the owner.

Nitschke was sitting at the bar by himself, which was a no-no. He was drinking in the daytime, which was another no-no. Then, damned if Lombardi and the coaches didn't come in, a violation of the unspoken agreement between coaches and players.

Instead of paying his check and sliding out of there, Nitschke, the dumb SOB, sent the coaches a beer. When Lombardi saw him, he went ballistic. "Get out, goddammit, you're suspended," yelled Lombardi. I thought he was going to kick Nitschke off the team then and there.

Once he cooled off, Lombardi realized we might not win the

game without the best linebacker in the NFL. So, cleverly, he put the Nitschke question up to the team, knowing we sure as hell wouldn't vote to kick him off.

"As far as I'm concerned, we'll do without him," Lombardi said. "It's not fair to you guys if I let him get away with this. I'm going to leave this room and let you guys vote."

When Lombardi was gone, I raised my hand and said, "I vote to kick him off the team and send his ass back to Chicago." Everybody laughed but Nitschke, who wasn't amused. "Goddammit, Hornung," he said, "I'm going to kick your ass." He was still mad when we voted to keep him on.

He got his revenge in practice. Every Tuesday, we'd have blitz-pickup drills. That meant the backs were supposed to pick up the linebackers and block them. I wasn't in helmet and pads, but every play, Nitschke would hit me hard with his forearm. I finally had enough. "You hit me with that forearm again," I said, "and I'm coming after that knee of yours."

Well, Lombardi blew the whistle and that stopped the drill. But the next Tuesday, I came out fully dressed in helmet and pads. When Lombardi asked me what was going on, I said, "I'm not gonna stand here and let him run over me like that. If he's going to hit me, I'm going to protect myself." And that was the end of that.

I always got on Nitschke's ass a little bit, but not too much because he'd have kicked the shit out of me. I remember the time that some group in Baltimore had a roast for me. It was real rough. Nitschke got up and ripped the shit out of me. He said I was the only guy he ever saw who could score more points in football than he could in basketball.

When I got up, I got Nitschke back. "Hell," I said, "he thinks he's the best all-time middle linebacker in the NFL, but he's not even the best to come out of Illinois." Butkus, of course, played at Illinois. Well, Nitschke was pissed. "What did you have to do that for?" he said. I had to explain to him that when you give a shot, you'd better be able to take one.

I was glad he was there, though. I ended my speech by saying, "I hate the fucking Colts." I figured if I needed any help getting out of there, at least Nitschke would be on my side.

Nitschke fell in love with Jackie, a girl who was working as a waitress at a Green Bay restaurant, and she told him she wouldn't have anything to do with him unless he stopped drinking and joined AA. He did, they got married, and Nitschke became "Mr. Packer," a really great guy. I've always said that football did more for Ray Nitschke than anybody I've known. I loved the guy.

We opened the 1964 season with a 23–12 home win over the Bears, the team that had defeated us twice the previous season. That day we sent two messages to the rest of the league: the Pack was back, and so was I. Besides carrying the ball fifteen times for 77 yards, I kicked three field goals and added two extra points.

One of the field goals was a unique 52-yarder near the end of the first half. After Elijah Pitts had made a fair catch at our fortyeight, Lombardi invoked an obscure rule that allows a team, after making a fair catch, to have a free kick without any interference from the defense. I drilled it.

After the game, Bears coach George Halas said, "Hornung is as good or better than ever. It doesn't look to me like the year off hurt him at all." But he was wrong. Because of my injuries, I had a horrible year kicking the ball. I was 41 for 43 on extra points, but the two misses were in one-point losses to the Colts (21–20) and the Vikings (24–23).

I also missed four field-goal attempts in a 24–14 loss to the Giants and five in a 24–21 loss to the Colts. I didn't make excuses, but it was obvious I couldn't lose a year like that at age twenty-seven or twenty-eight and at the top of my game. Some days I could kick the ball as far as ever, but then on the fourth or fifth try, my knee would lock up and I could barely kick it at all. Hurting my knee took a lot away from my game.

But Lombardi hated to see me in the training room, and he hated to see me limping. After one game, he noticed me limping in the locker room and yelled, "Hornung, stop that limping!" My mom and her friends were in town, and that night I took them to dinner at the Stratosphere Restaurant in Green Bay.

As I was limping through the restaurant to our table, I heard a voice out of nowhere roar, "Hornung, stop limping!" I turned around and there was Lombardi, at the other end of the restaurant, standing up with his napkin in his hand. He just lost it. I didn't pay any attention to him.

What Lombardi didn't know was that I was getting novocaine in my knee and cortisone in my back every week. I'd get shot up on Wednesday and feel great for a few days. By Monday morning, however, I'd wake up and could barely get out of bed. The truth was, I couldn't kick anymore and that's why the Packers got Don Chandler for the 1965 season.

During all those years, Lombardi was very lucky that somebody didn't suffer an injury that would cripple him for life. He scared a lot of guys into playing when they shouldn't have. He felt that the human spirit needed to be pushed to overcome pain. But sometimes he pushed too hard, and we let him get away with it.

The day before we played the Bears on December 5, 1964, Lombardi asked me for the name of a good restaurant in Chicago, so I gave him the Red Carpet. I knew Jerry Kovler, the owner. That night I met Pat West, a pretty little stewardess, at the Red Carpet at 7. We were to meet Ron Kramer, Pat Martin, and their wives, so I asked Pat if she wanted to have a drink in the lounge. But she said she'd prefer to wait in the bar.

Lombardi told us that he never wanted to catch us drinking in the daytime or sitting at a bar in a restaurant. But since nobody was there, I didn't think it would hurt to have a drink in the Red Carpet's bar before dinner.

"Honey," I said, "it would be terrible if Coach Lombardi walked in here."

"Don't worry about it," she said, laughing. "Chicago's a big city, Paul."

Then she glanced at the doorway and her jaw almost dropped.

"Oh, my God," she said. "There's Coach Lombardi."

When he saw me, he blew up.

"You're suspended, you're fined, see me when you get back to the hotel."

I figured we had better leave and go to another restaurant. I saw the head waiter on the way out and he apologized, saying he had sent Lombardi in my direction because he thought we were having dinner together.

Later, back at the hotel, I went to Lombardi's room and he said, "The fine stands. It's going to be $1,500. And you'd better have a good game tomorrow." I guess I played well enough in our 17–3 win. But when Lombardi cut the fine to $750, I said, "Either forgive it completely, which you should do, or keep it at $1,500."

He kept it at $1,500.

We finished the 1964 season with an 8–5–1 record, good enough only to tie Baltimore for second place in the Western Division and earn us a spot against St. Louis in the first Runner-Up Bowl, which Lombardi called the "Shit Bowl." We thought of ourselves as champions, so nobody wanted to play in this farce. We lost, 24–17, and, after one more season, the "Shit Bowl" died the merciful death it deserved.

I soon found myself in the doghouse again for missing a meeting due to a misunderstanding about the time, and Lombardi was pretty pissed at me. He chewed me out, but everything was fine the next day. Somehow the newspapers got hold of the story, and it got twisted around. The story came out that Lombardi was fed up with me and was going to put me on the trading block.

When I got back to Louisville, mom said Lombardi had been trying to reach me. When I got him, he said, "I just wanted to tell you my sentiments. I don't know where the stories started, but you're definitely not on the trading block. You had a rough year, and I think everything will be all right next year."

During the off-season, the AFL, which had been gradually gaining on us in popularity, dropped a bombshell. Sonny Werblin, the principal owner of the New York Jets, signed Alabama's Joe Namath, the nation's most ballyhooed college quarterback, for $400,000, an incredible sum in those days.

Besides being a great passer and leader, Namath had star

quality. He was a playboy, a ladies' man, who drew a lot of comparisons with me. He and the New York media were perfect for each other. It wasn't long before he became known as "Broadway Joe," the AFL's answer to the "Golden Boy."

Before the 1965 season, I returned to my old conditioning regimen, which was to play my way into shape. I always was in fairly good shape by the first game, but I didn't get into top football shape until the fifth or sixth game.

With everybody relatively healthy, we won our first six games. Then we hit a midseason slump where we lost three of five. I wasn't playing much because I'd hurt my knee again. After we squeaked past the Vikings, 24–19, in Green Bay, our next game was against the Colts, who were fighting us for the Western Division championship in Baltimore. That was the game where I scored five TDs after staying out all night.

Needing a win over the 49ers to win the Western Division title, we could manage only a 24–24 tie that gave us a final record of 10–3–1 and deadlocked us with the Colts for the division championship. In a classic playoff game for the right to meet Cleveland for the league championship, we beat the Colts again, but this time the teams fought through thirteen minutes of overtime before Chandler nailed a field goal to give us a 13–10 victory.

Well, to be honest, he didn't exactly nail it. In fact, the Colts were sure it had gone wide right. But the official standing under the goalpost called it good. That kick made Chandler's career.

The championship game was played on January 2, 1965, in Green Bay. By kickoff, the field was really sloppy because of the four inches of snow that had been shoveled off it. No doubt the playing conditions helped our defense stop the great Jim Brown, who had only 50 yards to show for 12 carries in what was to be his final NFL game. All day, Nitschke nailed Brown again and again.

Although Bart and Cleveland quarterback Frank Ryan each threw one touchdown pass in the first half, the game was pretty much a kicking duel between Chandler and Cleveland's veteran star, Lou "The Toe" Groza. Each kicked two field goals in the first half, which ended with us holding a 13–12 lead because a bad snap from center had cost the Browns an extra point.

In the third quarter, I scored what proved to be the winning points on a 13-yard touchdown run that was followed by Chandler's conversion. In the last quarter, we salted it away on Chandler's 29-yard field goal. We hadn't played as well as we had the previous year, but we still won, 23–12, for our fourth championship in six years.

I had a helluva game that day, gaining 105 yards on 18 carries. In fact, I thought I was in the hunt for another new car as MVP. But Jimmy Taylor, who had gained 96 yards on 27 carries, won it this time. I found out later that the deciding vote had been cast by Al Silverman, the editor in chief of *Sport* magazine and the writer with whom I had just finished doing a book called *Football and the Single Man.* Silverman told me he felt he might have a conflict of interest because of the book, so he voted for Taylor.

Now, looking back, that really pisses me off.

As soon as the game was over, I caught a plane for L.A. I got there in plenty of time to have dinner at one of my favorite spots, Mateo's. A couple of drunks walked past our table and one of them said, "There's Paul Hornung." And the other said,

"You're full of shit . . . I watched him play on TV this afternoon."
Even then, many Americans weren't used to the miracles of the
jet age.

The Pack was back, but I knew time was running out on my
career. My arm and knee injuries were beginning to take their
toll.

17.

WHEN THE SAINTS
COME MARCHING IN

By the spring of 1966, the AFL was really challenging our league, even though many of our officials didn't want to admit it. The leagues were engaged in open warfare over the top college stars, and the AFL owners seemed to have such deep pockets that our owners were getting worried. A young quarterback named Rick Norton, a kid from Louisville who had played at my old high school and Kentucky, got a far bigger signing bonus from the Miami Dolphins than what I was being paid by the Packers.

Our team signed a couple of running backs, Donny Anderson of Texas Tech and Jim Grabowski of Illinois, for a lot more than any of the veterans were making. Taylor was among those who were really pissed off about it, but Lombardi said it was necessary to keep the AFL from getting all the good young players.

But every time Lombardi would say that, Taylor would get furious. Several times Lombardi came to me and said, "Paul, get

Jimmy in the right frame of mind; he won't talk to me." But Tay-lor was right. There was no way those two guys should have been getting more than established stars.

The bidding war was getting so insane that the owners had to stop it. So, on June 8, the NFL and AFL announced a merger agreement under which there would be only one league, with twenty-eight teams, by 1970. The NFL would add one team for 1967, which turned out to be New Orleans, and the AFL would add one team for 1968 and two more by '70. Most importantly from our standpoint, the league champions would begin having a postseason playoff game, beginning with the 1966 season.

Known initially as the NFL-AFL World Championship of Football, it soon became widely known as the "Super Bowl," a name that many of us found to be childish and silly. The first to use the term apparently was Edwin Pope, the respected sports editor of the *Miami Herald*.

Although we didn't know it, the nucleus of the team that had won three of the previous five NFL titles was breaking apart. Ron Kramer had been traded to the Lions and Fuzzy Thurston was out for the season with an injury. Forrest Gregg had retired to be-come an assistant coach at Tennessee. We still had eight future Hall of Famers—me, Taylor, Starr, Davis, Jordan, Adderley, Nitschke, and Wood—but this would be the last year we played together.

Still bothered by injuries, I nevertheless was second on the team in scoring (48 points) and rushing (299 yards). I also was fourth in receptions (19) and even threw a couple of passes, completing one for nineteen yards. But no longer could Paul Hornung play like Paul Hornung.

In the last game of the 1966 regular season, we beat the

Rams, 27–23, in the Los Angeles Coliseum to finish with a 12–2 record and win the Western Division. Lombardi must have told Starr to run me a lot early in the game. I helped us get off to a 14–0 lead, but I was a beat SOB. Running ten times and getting hit takes far more out of you than working out for two or three hours.

I didn't play much in our 34–27 win over the Cowboys in the NFL title game on January 1, 1967. Bart threw four TD passes, including one to Max McGee, but the Cowboys and their quarterback, Don Meredith, gave us fits.

In fact, a poor punt by Chandler enabled the Cowboys to take over on our forty-eight late in the game. Meredith moved them to a first down inside the goal line, but then our defense held four straight times. The Cowboys' hopes ended when Tom Brown intercepted Meredith in the end zone.

Before we played the Kansas City Chiefs in the first NFL-AFL World Championship game, in Los Angeles, Lombardi took us to an out-of-the-way hotel in Santa Barbara, which was ridiculous. We hated it. It was horseshit. We didn't move back to the official team hotel on Wilshire Boulevard until the Friday before the game. That night, we went to Mateo's for dinner, and I brought Bob Rosburg, the pro golfer, with me.

Rossy was a big football fan, and he wanted to bet on the game. He was going to bet Jimmy Demaret, another pro and a huge AFL fan. But he was concerned that we were favored by ten points, a relatively big number for a championship game. Should he give Demaret the points?

"Bet on the Packers," I told him.

"But you aren't playing," Rossy said.

"They don't need me," I said.

That made me think: This is probably my last game. I loved us to win. Should I bet on the game or not? I hadn't made a bet since I had been reinstated. Then I figured the hell with it. I didn't bet, but I wanted to.

I didn't expect to play because of my injuries and Max figured he wouldn't get very much time, so Max wanted to go out and party. I didn't feel like it, so I went back to the hotel while Max stayed out and ran the streets. I'm not sure what time he got in, but the sun was up on the day of the game.

Although the game was broadcast by both NBC and CBS, it nevertheless drew more than 61,000 to the L.A. Coliseum. Most of them were curiosity seekers. The AFL had done such a good job of hyping itself, and signing the young players, that some misguided individuals actually thought the AFL could beat us.

On the third play of the game, the Chiefs injured Boyd Dowler and knocked him out of the game, so Lombardi called on McGee. He loved Max because Max could make plays. Plus, he liked Max's sense of humor. He once admitted to me, "It'd be very boring around here without you guys."

So Max grabbed Dave "Hog" Hanner's helmet—I don't know what had happened to his—and went into the game. And doggoned if he didn't catch a 37-yard touchdown pass from Starr that, along with Chandler's conversion, gave us a 7–0 lead. When he came back and sat next to me on the bench, he said, "If Bart throws me the football, I can win the car." He was talking about the new car that would be awarded to the game's most valuable player.

Well, the car went to Starr, who completed 16 of 24 passes in our 35–10 victory, but it just as easily could have gone to Max, who caught two TD passes and had seven receptions total. I'd never say this to Lombardi, but I swear Max and I had some of our best games after we had sneaked out the previous night.

Late in the game, Lombardi came up to me on the sideline and asked if I wanted to go in for a few plays. He wanted me to be able to say I had played in the first Super Bowl, but I said no. I was afraid that if I went in, I'd get clotheslined and never play again. So I didn't play in the game, but I did get a winner's ring. After the game, which we won by 37–10, I saw Bob Rosburg, and he was happy as hell.

I was scheduled to be married in L.A. the Wednesday after the Super Bowl to Pat Roeder, an aspiring actress that I had met at a party in Green Bay. I had started dating her in 1965, and it was a long-distance romance. We never spent as much as a whole month together. She lived in Los Angeles at the time, but she moved to Dallas and roomed with her friend Maureen, who was dating George Owen, a guy who lived in Dallas and had worked for the NFL's New Orleans Saints expansion team under minority owner Bedford Wynne.

George was a sort of "guy Friday" for Clint Murchison, the oilman who owned the Cowboys. He and Murchison ran around a lot with Wynne, a wealthy Dallas attorney. In fact, Murchison used his influence with the NFL to help get the New Orleans franchise for John W. Mecom Jr. and Wynne.

When Wynne came to New Orleans, George came with him. He was a character who knew a lot of girls. Just about every year, the Packers would spend a week in Dallas getting ready to play the Cowboys in a preseason exhibition known as the "Salesmanship Game." Murchison and Wynne told George to get Hornung and McGee each a broad, thinking they would wear us out before the game. It never worked, though. We always beat the Cowboys, and Max and I always had a great time in Dallas.

My family and Pat's were in town for the wedding, so on the Monday night after the Super Bowl, we had dinner at Chasen's, then one of the best restaurants in the country. Max, who was going to be my best man, said, "I'll pick up this check; this is mine." He was paying me back because when he got married to golfer Doug Sanders's ex-wife back in Green Bay, I had picked up the check for the food and booze at his rehearsal dinner. We had about eighty people at Max's deal and the bill for the whole thing was about $1,800 for food and drink.

Max also was grateful that I had been his best man even though the Catholic Church in Green Bay had threatened to have me excommunicated for participating in a Baptist wedding. I said the hell with that. Max was my best friend, and I was going to be in his wedding, period.

At my rehearsal dinner we drank expensive stuff. That's why our check for twelve people was more than $3,000. Max gave them a credit card, but they didn't take credit cards. They also didn't take checks, and Max didn't have $3,000 on him. So we called the manager over, and he finally agreed to take a check. I mean, this was Max McGee, the Super Bowl hero.

When we went outside, Max said, "That check's no good. I don't have $3,000 in my checking account, but the bank will cover it. I'll call them tomorrow." Fortunately for everybody, the bank took care of it.

Our wedding was held at a little church on Santa Monica Boulevard, off Rodeo Drive, and the reception was at the Beverly Hills Hotel. I was going to Honolulu for my honeymoon, but I also was supposed to play in the Bob Hope Classic golf tournament. I asked Max, "Why don't you take my place?" He did, and his streak of good luck kept going. He was paired with actor Donald O'Connor and they won the pro-am.

Meanwhile, Pat and I were getting to know each other in Honolulu.

Looking back, the marriage had failure written all over it. The first red flag for me was when I brought her home to Louisville right after our honeymoon, and she didn't like it one bit.

Even before the Super Bowl, the rumors were flying that Lombardi was going to put me on the list for the New Orleans expansion draft. Each NFL team was required to submit eleven names. After the Saints picked one player from each team, they returned the lists to the teams, who then could withdraw two names before resubmitting the list for the second round of the draft.

Some thought that Tom Fears, the Saints' first coach and general manager, would never take me because of my bad arm. Others thought that Lombardi would never give me up until I was ready to retire. But Lombardi also was a businessman, and he knew I might never be able to play football again.

Lombardi was sad and apologetic when he told me that he had put me on the list. I didn't say much of anything because I *wanted* to go to New Orleans for the money. In fact, I'd already worked it out secretly with Bedford Wynne. I'd get around $1 million for three years, including a radio deal. The most I'd ever been paid by Green Bay was about $80,000.

So when the expansion draft was held, I became the first Saint. I got the news in Louisville on Friday, February 10, when

Max and I were going to make an appearance for my friend William H. King at his annual Sport, Boat, and Vacation Show at the Kentucky State Fairgrounds.

When the story came over the Associated Press wire, I went downtown to make an appearance on WHAS radio with my old friend Milton Metz, the host of a popular call-in radio show. I also did a brief interview with the *Courier-Journal*, which was headquartered in the same building at Sixth and Broadway.

"It hasn't all sunk in yet," I said that night. "It's kind of hard to realize that I won't be in Green Bay next season. If my arm comes back and it's sound, I hope to do a good job for New Orleans. It feels pretty good right now."

The second round had yet to be conducted, so I was asked about the possibility that Taylor might join me in New Orleans. Although he had led the 1966 team in rushing with 705 yards, that was his lowest total since 1959. Plus, he was still angry with Lombardi about the money going to Anderson and Grabowski.

"We'll just have to wait and see about Jimmy," I said. "Naturally, I'd like to play in the same backfield with him."

Well, Taylor exercised an option clause in his contract and signed with the Saints instead of returning to Green Bay. It was a natural move for Jimmy, because he had played at LSU, was still wildly popular in Louisiana, and got more money than Vince was willing to pay. A part of our deal was that we would tour the state together, drumming up interest and selling tickets.

When I went down there to negotiate my first contract with Fears, owner Wynne, and minority owner Mecom, we even got to the point where we were talking about me getting 5 percent of the franchise. But I eventually signed for pretty much what I'd already negotiated with Fears.

"Hornung has a lot of good football left in him," Fears told the media. "It was worth the risk."

I befriended Mecom, a nice young guy who liked to have a good time. The team was really a toy with him, and I often wondered how he held his own in league meetings. But mostly I began working diligently to try to strengthen my left arm. I really thought I might be able to play one more season.

But when the arm didn't seem to improve, I finally went to the Houston Medical Center and had a spinal tap. I remember the doctor telling me that if I drank, I might want to go ahead and have a few that night because I was already going to have a headache from the spinal tap. He was right. But the good news was that he said I could play.

I reported for training camp early so I could start working out. It didn't hurt, of course, that the camp was in San Diego. That was Shangri-la for me, the exact opposite in every respect from Stevens Point, Wisconsin. I wish Ron Kramer could have been there. The weather was beautiful, sunny, and in the 80s every day, and our camp site was close to Del Mar, one of my favorite Thoroughbred racetracks. Mecom put me up in a suite on the top floor of the hotel, and, since my wife was in L.A., he and I ran the streets at night.

But my arms, especially the left one, were still bad, so I checked into the Scripps Medical Center in San Diego to get a second opinion. After looking at my X-rays, a doctor said to me, "You mean that a doctor in Houston actually cleared you to play?" He told me I'd have to retire immediately or take the risk of having one hit turn me into a paraplegic. I had something called a subluxation of the fifth and sixth cervical vertebrae.

I knew what decision I had to make. I told Mecom I was going to retire, and then I went to Hollywood to make the announcement on the Johnny Carson show. It was one of those nights when Johnny wasn't there. The guest host was Joey Bishop, a member of the Sinatra Rat Pack. I knew Joey and felt comfortable with him, but, for some reason, I was nervous as hell, and I never got nervous in front of a camera. Maybe I felt that way because it was finally dawning on me that for the first time since I was in grade school (not counting the suspension year), I wouldn't be playing football.

Now I had to figure out how I was going to get paid. The club was very generous, paying me a part of my contract and honoring my radio-TV deal, so I decided to stay in New Orleans. Pat came down there and didn't like it any better than she liked Louisville.

In Green Bay, Lombardi was answering questions about a two-part series of articles that he had written for *Look* magazine. He said Green Bay's board of directors hadn't been properly appreciative of him after we won the Super Bowl, and he even took a shot at the players' wives.

He said that after we had won the '61 title, he had given the wives mink stoles and they all wrote him thank-you notes. When we repeated in '62, he gave them color TV sets and most wrote thank-you notes. But when we won again in '66, he gave them silver tea sets and only a few sent notes.

I was too excited about being in New Orleans to pay much attention to what was happening in Green Bay.

On the first play of the New Orleans Saints' first game, rookie John Gilliam returned the kickoff 108 yards. The crowd in Tulane Stadium went so crazy that the game was delayed for twenty-five minutes. Even at Notre Dame and Green Bay, I'd never heard a stadium erupt like that.

Acting as a sort of unofficial assistant coach, in addition to my radio-TV duties, I went to all the games. I fell in love with the stewardess who was on all our flights to away games. I also started dating a nineteen-year-old Bourbon Street stripper known as "The Champagne Lady" because she could balance glasses of champagne on her boobs.

And then there was Chris Owens, who was performing on Bourbon Street when Max was in school at Tulane and, as far as I know, is still performing there. The actor Jeff Chandler had fallen head over heels in love with her, and I don't blame him. The term *statuesque* doesn't begin to describe her. Max and I both tried to get her to go out, but she wouldn't give us the time of day, although we became friends.

But the best woman I met in New Orleans was a nurse named Dell. She was a dark-complexioned, dark-eyed, dark-haired Cajun beauty. Years later, when a dear friend of mine was dying, she was his nurse. She was a beautiful person in every way.

One night before Mardi Gras, I was in the French Quarter, and Pat came down and caught me at a nightclub with Jimmy Moran, who owned a couple of restaurants, and four girls.

She went back to our apartment, gathered up all my clothes, and dumped them at Billy Kilmer's apartment. He was the Saints' quarterback and one of my running buddies. "Here," she said to him, "you take them; you spend more time with him than I do, anyway."

So after seven months in New Orleans, my marriage was on the rocks. I didn't want to divorce, just to get out as easily as possible, so we agreed to legally separate, with me paying her a certain amount every month for living expenses. We stayed legally married for thirteen years, which gave me protection from women who might want to get seriously involved. I could tell them I was married, and not lie about it.

I always got along with Pat, and still do. She wrote a book about our life together with Robin Moore, who had written *The French Connection* and *The Green Berets*, but it bombed because neither of them knew anything about football.

During the season, I had followed the Packers mainly through phone conversations with Max, who was playing his last season. He told me that at the start of preseason camp, Lombardi had talked emotionally about me and how much the team would miss me. All he said about Taylor was, "We'll replace the other guy."

Unsurprisingly, the Packers slipped a bit in 1967, going 9–4–1, but they still won the new NFL Central Division (the Saints were last in the Capitol Division with a 3–8 record). In the expanded playoffs, the Packers regained their old form and humiliated the Rams, 28–7, to earn the right to play the Cowboys, who had beaten the Browns 52–14 in their semifinal. The game turned out to be a classic forever known as the "Ice Bowl" because the temperature in Green Bay was minus 13 at kickoff.

Lombardi called me before the game and said, "I want you there." That's all I needed to hear. So I took a busman's holiday to attend the game, just so I could see my old teammates and let them know I was rooting for them. Here's how Jerry Kramer described it in *Instant Replay*, the best-selling diary of the season that he wrote with Dick Schaap:

"I was the first one out of the meeting, and the first thing I saw was a golden head on a pair of sloping shoulders—Paul Hornung. I thumped him hard on the head. I was really happy to see him, happy that he had decided to come up from New Orleans for the championship game.

"Even though I played on the same team with him for nine years, Paul's always been an idol of mine. I know that sounds a little ridiculous, especially since, as I told Paul, I did so much to make him as great as he was.

"Paul said hello to everyone and sat with us while we viewed the films, biting his fingernails the way he always did. Paul and Max sat together, and they got Gregg and Bob Skoronski giggling during the movies. The old man didn't get upset. He was practically giggling himself, he was so glad to see Paul.

"He's always had a weakness for Paul. I guess that's natural, the stern father being proud of the wild son."

I watched the game from the bench in a topcoat and suit. I sat with Max, who had played an extra year only because he had been a star in Super Bowl I. But he didn't even play against the Cowboys, so we sat together on the sidelines, huddled up near the heaters.

While I was sitting there keeping warm, Lombardi said, "Paul, come over here." There were three minutes left in the first half. He said, "You know the offense. If you see anything you think we ought to run, let me know." That was nice of him, to let me be a part of it, but I couldn't think of much except how cold I was.

Pat Summerall of CBS had asked me to be on his halftime show. I was happy to do it for Pat, except that when I tried to talk, I discovered that I couldn't move my jaw. It was frozen. We scratched the interview because, for the first time in my life, I was speechless.

How they completed that game, I'll never know. That's how cold it was. With thirteen seconds remaining and the Packers trailing 17–14, Starr followed Jerry's blocking on Jethro Pugh for a quarterback sneak that gave Green Bay a 21–17 victory. It was the team's third consecutive NFL title, fifth in seven years, and the first one I had missed.

After the game, I thawed out by getting drunk with Kramer and Max. I couldn't help but notice that Donny Anderson, who was trying to replace me in more ways than one, had a date with a former playmate of the month.

I went to Super Bowl II at the Orange Bowl in Miami, and Lombardi and I greeted each other warmly at practice. He asked if I wanted to sit on the bench, but I decided to watch from the stands. Once again, the Packers dominated the AFL champion, this time whipping the Oakland Raiders, 33–14.

On the Friday before the game, an emotional Lombardi had called the team together and said, "This may be the last time we are all together like this . . . Let's make the last game a good one."

I was happy for them, but I also sensed that Lombardi felt he had stolen one. This team simply wasn't as good as we had been. I think Vince knew the handwriting was on the wall, and he was already planning his exit.

18.

CHICAGO, MY KIND OF TOWN

I really wanted to be a color analyst for football, and I just wasn't getting the opportunity in New Orleans. So when I got a helluva job offer from WBBM in Chicago, the CBS television affiliate, to do sports on the 6 P.M. and 11 P.M. newscasts, I took it. In addition, I'd do the Bears' pregame shows with Bruce Roberts, and I got my own radio sports program.

My first day on the job in Chicago, I got a call in my office from Zygmont "Ziggy" Czarobski, who had played tackle for Notre Dame in 1942 and '43, took off two years to serve in World War II, and then came back and played in the '46 and '47 seasons. He was absolutely the funniest man I've ever met.

"No. 5," he said, "this is No. 76. I wanted to welcome you to Chicago and tell you we love you in Chicago. Come on down to the lobby 'cause I got a little present for you."

So I went down to the lobby and the "present" turned out to be a beautiful black girl. Ziggy said, "This is one of my secretaries." Of course, Ziggy called all his women his "secretaries." He was a real character.

Ziggy made so much money scalping tickets for the 1946 Notre Dame–Army game in Yankee Stadium that he bought a bar in Chicago. He had been picked by the Chicago Cardinals in the '45 NFL draft, but reported to camp about fifty pounds overweight. But because he was from Notre Dame and had a big name in Chicago's Polish community, the Cardinals would introduce him as a starter, and then take him out after one play.

Somehow George Connor, a former defensive tackle and linebacker who in my opinion was the best Notre Dame player ever, got Ziggy into the College Football Hall of Fame in 1977. At one time, Connor and I were the only two Notre Dame players who were in both the college and pro halls of fame. (Alan Page later joined us.) Joe Montana will never be in both because, believe it or not, you must have been an All-American to get into the College Football Hall of Fame.

At the time I went to Chicago, Ziggy ran the Aurora Hotel in Aurora, Illinois, and he had a big Notre Dame banquet every year. He was the emcee, the main speaker, and the entertainment. He had his "secretaries" all around. It was always a helluva time.

Ziggy would go into a night spot, and maybe Sophie Tucker would be singing. He would walk right up there on stage and take over the show, a habit I got into here or there. I especially liked a group called the Treniers, a black rock 'n' roll band. If we were playing in the same town where they were playing, I'd round up the guys and we'd go. I'd get Fuzzy on stage, and Jess Whittenton, one of our best defensive backs, would play the drums and Ron Kramer would carry one of the Treniers around on his shoulders. They called me their "white soul brother."

I got another call soon after I went to work in Chicago. This one came in early 1968 and it was from Lombardi. He knew that I was doing some radio and TV work, and he wanted to give me the "scoop" that he had decided to retire as coach of the Packers and move into the front office full-time. Right away I went on the air with my scoop, but since I wasn't surprised by it, I didn't really understand what a big story it was.

"We'll miss him," Ray Nitschke said. "He's an amazing man. Lombardi was up every day. He had extraordinary emotional drive. He yelled a lot, but that was part of an act for the benefit of the player he yelled at. He seldom yells at Jerry Kramer because Jerry doesn't respond to it. He yelled at me a lot in my early days because I was wild and needed it. It helped me, and it helped Jimmy Taylor and Paul Hornung and the other players he got on. He infected all of us with his demand for perfection and his dedication to it."

But by the time I had this scoop I already hated my job in Chicago. I just wasn't comfortable doing three-minute sportscasts. But those months in Chicago made me realize that I'd never again do anything I didn't like.

But as much as I hated the job, I loved Chicago and the nightlife. I was making about eighty thousand dollars a year but didn't save a quarter. I spent it all on Rush Street. The nightlife was my life. We drank hard and we played hard. I ate at the best restaurants and had my own "secretaries." At one time I was dating twenty-eight of them.

I had a beautiful apartment on Astor Avenue, but parking my Corvette was a problem. Even though I was paying two hundred dollars a month for a space at my apartment and another three hundred a month for a space at WBBM, I usually parked on the street. At one point I had two hundred outstanding parking tickets. It was a good thing that Ziggy was close to Mayor Daley.

Speaking of cars, I once was given one by Reggie Cornell, one of three men training for the storied Calumet Farm of Lexington, Kentucky, in the late 1960s. To this day, he's best known as the trainer of Silky Sullivan, the come-from-way-off-the-pace star who captivated the country in 1958. Through me, Reggie became great friends with Lombardi, and he named horses for me, Max, and Starr.

In 1971, Reggie was given a Buick for winning the Arlington Classic, a big race in those days, with Calumet's Son Ange. But Reggie didn't drive, so he gave the car to me during the victory party at the track. The problem was, when it was time to go, I didn't remember that I was supposed to take the car.

About eight weeks later, I got a call from Reggie. He asked me how I was enjoying the car. "What car?" I said. He reminded me about the Buick, so I hustled out to Arlington. Amazingly, it was still parked in the lot where Reggie had left it.

I was still dating Sandy Dietz, the little Italian girl from New York, and one day I bought her a $100 win ticket on a horse that won and paid about $60 for a $2 win bet. She left the track with about $2,000, and we celebrated until about 3:30 the next morning, when we stopped to get breakfast at an all-night diner.

We got into an argument and she finally got so mad at me that she picked up a ketchup bottle and threw it so hard at a window that the window shattered. I called over the manager and asked him how much it would cost to replace the window.

"About $400," he said.

I reached over, got $500 out of her purse, and gave it to him. Then I handed her another ketchup bottle.

"Here's another one," I said. "Want to go for another $500?"

Needless to say, we didn't date again for a while.

During this time I got a call from Toots Shor in New York. He told me he was coming to Chicago for a few days and was wondering if he could stay at my place. He had come to the Derby a few times, and I had taken him around Louisville. Once he got into a crap game before the Derby and got locked up. I had to bail him out. He might have been the king of the New York restaurateurs, but that didn't mean squat in Louisville.

So he came to Chicago and stayed with me. When we went out to dinner, I asked him what had brought him to town and he said, "I've got to see Jimmy Hoffa." Hoffa, the controversial boss of the Teamsters union, was on trial in Chicago on federal charges that he had misappropriated funds, or something like that. Naturally, it was in all the papers and security was extremely tight.

But Hoffa was a secret investor in Toots's restaurant in New York, and Toots needed some money, as he always did. The next day he went to the courthouse to see Hoffa. I didn't give him much chance under the circumstances. But that night he came back to the apartment and said, "I'm taking you out to dinner because I got something to be happy about."

At dinner, he showed me a check from Hoffa for $200,000. Somehow, Toots had gotten through security to see him. To tell you the truth, I thought that showed some class on Hoffa's part, helping out a friend when he was in trouble himself.

The greatest party I've ever attended was held in Chicago. I had a friend named Henry Norton, who owned a nightclub on Rush Street. When the controversial musical *Hair* came to Chicago, he and his brother rented out the theater and threw a huge costume party.

I came as a Roman emperor. I dyed my hair black, wore a toga (with nothing on underneath), and put my championship rings on my fingers. I looked like Caesar himself. I lost a couple of the rings on the dance floor, but my date, a girl named Suzie, found them. I don't know how she did it in that madhouse.

It was wild. One couple, dressed as Tarzan and Jane, came in on an elephant. Everybody from the play was stoned, and half of them were nude. The band was Wayne Cochran and the C.C. Riders. It was the best fun I've ever had in my life. We got smashed, sobered up, then got smashed again.

The way I had it figured, it must have been the marijuana. It was big back then, and, naturally, I had to try it. But I never drank anything but soft drinks or a glass of wine when I was smoking pot. And only once have I tried any coke that didn't come out of a soft-drink can.

During this time, I met and fell in love with a girl named Debbie Shelton. She had become Miss USA, competing as Miss Virginia, and then finished second in the Miss Universe contest. She was about 5-9 and weighed 130 pounds, and could play touch football better than any girl I ever knew. I mean, she'd knock you on your ass. She also had a beautiful young son.

My job in Chicago lasted a little more than a year. I was working there on January 12, 1969, when the New York Jets shocked the Baltimore Colts, 16–7, in Super Bowl III. The game turned Joe Willie Namath, the Jets' quarterback, into the hottest property in football. At a poolside press conference the week before the game, Namath had brashly predicted a Jets upset.

I was in Miami for CBS and staying at the Palm Bay Club. The Saturday before the game, I ran into my buddy Alex Hawkins, who had retired from the Colts after the 1968 season, and two Colts players, Jimmy Orr and Jerry Logan.

Hawk and I played Orr and Logan in a game of gin rummy and won $1,800 apiece. But they didn't have the money to pay up. I said, "Hawk, what is this deal? I don't know these guys. Are they good for it?" I told them I'd be on the field the next day and I wanted my money.

Thinking I was $1,800 to the good, I went ahead like a dumbass and bet a couple of dimes on the Colts, giving the Jets eighteen or nineteen points, whatever it was.

Almost everybody in the country thought Namath was just trying to promote himself. But when he backed up his boast, it made Super Bowl III the most important game in NFL history, in my opinion. It gave the AFL the credibility it needed and boosted interest in the merger, which would be finalized in the 1970 season.

And it cost me $3,800. Not only did I lose my $2,000 bet, but Orr and Logan never paid up. I told Alex Webster later, "Why do they gamble if they don't intend to pay?"

By the spring of 1969, I had quit my job in Chicago and gone home to Louisville. It was a good move for me. There was just too much in Chicago that I liked but shouldn't do. When I left, the station replaced me with a relatively new TV face, Brent Musburger.

For a while, it was fine in Louisville. I began working with Uncle Henry and Frank Metts in an office on Third Street. Uncle Henry had a partners desk that he and I shared. He was happy as a clam to have me and Frank, his two "boys," around to help him with his real estate deals. I wasn't much help, but Frank was the Donald Trump of Louisville.

But before I could settle comfortably into the Louisville business world, I got a call from Bob Wussler at CBS, who offered me a nice contract—I think it was about $7,500 per game, good money in those days—to do a schedule of nationally televised college games with Lindsey Nelson. At the same time, Lindsey and I took a job with C. D. Chesley, who owned the TV-radio rights to Notre Dame football, to do a condensed Sunday television wrap-up of every game.

That was the beginning of what turned out to be a twenty-year relationship with Lindsey. In the early years, we would do the Notre Dame game for rebroadcast on Sunday and then hop a plane to do an NFL game live for CBS.

I brought Debbie Shelton to Louisville a few times to introduce her to Mom and my friends. I also got her fixed up with Eileen Ford, who ran the biggest and best modeling agency in New York. I had met Eileen through her husband, Jerry, a Notre Dame grad. Eileen took on Debbie, but wanted her to lose about twenty pounds. It wasn't that she was overweight; it was just that Eileen liked her models to be super-thin. Even so, Debbie got a lot of work simply because of her beautiful face.

I set her up in an apartment on York Avenue in Manhattan and put her son into a Montessori school. Even then, which was around 1969 or '70, private school cost $7,500 a year for a second-grader. She was a great girl and a great mom, and we liked the same things.

After a while, however, my traveling for CBS and Chesley got in the way. When we were together, we were very happy, but we weren't together very much. The relationship became cumbersome and eventually ended.

In addition to my work with Lindsey, I did some TV work for the Minnesota Vikings during the years when they were annual Super Bowl contenders under Bud Grant. Fran Tarkenton was the scrambling quarterback, and they had a defensive front known as "The Purple People Eaters" that I was glad I never had to run against: Alan Page (an All-American at Notre Dame), Gary Larsen, Carl Eller, and Jim Marshall.

I got that job through my friendship with Jim Finks, the former Notre Dame assistant coach and Steelers quarterback, who moved into the front office and developed winners in Chicago, New Orleans, and Minnesota. Finks always called me "Meat," which I didn't understand. When I finally asked him, he said, "Because you're the best-looking piece of meat I've ever seen." So because of Finks, I did the Vikings games with Joe Mc-Connell for five seasons.

As fate would have it, the Minnesota job also enabled me to hook up again with Max McGee. When he retired from the Packers after the 1967 season, he didn't have any money. But even more than me, Max had a way of stepping into a shit hole and coming out smelling like a rose.

He got into the restaurant business through our old left guard, Fuzzy Thurston, who had a chain of Left Guard restaurants, mostly in Wisconsin. But Fuzzy and his partners were spending money as fast as they made it, which Max saw as a recipe for disaster, so he finally said he would give up his interest in all the other restaurants if they'd let him have the one in Minneapolis.

They agreed, but Max needed some help so he called upon

a guy named Marno McDermott, who had some experience with Mexican food. They changed the name of the restaurant to Chi-Chi's and it became the hottest restaurant in Minneapolis. It had a back room where Max and I would party whenever I was in Minneapolis doing a game.

For better or worse, it was just like old times. Don't ever let anybody tell you that Minneapolis is a dull town. Max and I smoked marijuana a few times in Minneapolis, and I even tried cocaine once. I hated it. I had broken my nose seven times and I sneezed for five days after I tried cocaine. I was so miserable that I told Max, "I don't see what's so great about this shit." So I stuck to the occasional joint and the usual amount of booze.

As the son of an alcoholic, I guess I should have been cautious about drinking, but I didn't really know my dad so I couldn't judge him. But I learned one thing about drinking when I was young: I'd never be an alcoholic because I never, ever wanted to drink in the morning. The day you start to drink in the morning, you know you're in trouble.

Eventually Max turned his Minneapolis restaurant into the Chi-Chi's chain of Mexican restaurants. When he took it public, I asked him if I should buy some stock in it. He said, "I have 100,000 shares and if I could sell it right now for four dollars a share, I would, so I could pay off my debts in Wisconsin." So I decided to take a pass.

A year later, Max asked me if I'd bought any Chi-Chi's stock. When I told him I hadn't, he said it had skyrocketed to eighteen dollars a share. So not buying that stock ended up costing me a lot of money. As for Max, he eventually got out of Chi Chi's with more than $10 million.

I wonder what Lombardi would have thought about that.

19

IT WAS HIS WAY OR
THE HIGHWAY

I learned a lot from Vince Lombardi about how stubborn Italian-Americans can be. They have a strict code about what's acceptable and what's not. I later found that same characteristic in my second wife, the former Angela DiBonaventura Cerelli and, much to my puzzlement, Frank Sinatra, my all-time favorite singer going back to my childhood days.

There's a bond of some kind between athletes and entertainers, and I've always enjoyed swapping stories with people like Dean Martin, Tony Bennett, and Sammy Davis Jr. One guy I always wanted to meet was Elvis Presley. I once had the chance and I blew it, which I regret to this day.

I happened to be in Vegas when he was staging his big comeback in 1969 at the International Hotel, which later became the Hilton. He hadn't performed in public for years, so, naturally, his first show became one of the hottest tickets Vegas had ever seen.

I knew a guy in the orchestra that would be backing up Elvis, so I told him I'd like to go. He went to Elvis, and it turned out that he was as big a fan of me as I was of him. Apparently Elvis loved to watch football on TV. So I got four front-row tickets for the show that any Elvis fan would have died to see.

Barney Shapiro and I got dates with a couple of showgirls. The only thing we didn't count on, however, was the traffic jam around the hotel. We couldn't get within six blocks of it, and even if we had gotten there, we had no place to park. So we turned around and went home.

I suppose I didn't think about it too much at the time because I figured that Elvis, who was about my age, would be around for a long time. I didn't look at him the same way, in other words, as I did Sinatra.

When Jon Arnett and I were running around together in L.A. in the '60s, we caught Sinatra's act a lot. I finally got to meet him one night in New York. We were introduced by Frank's good pal, Jilly Rizzo, at the popular Manhattan bar he owned called Jilly's.

The night I met Sinatra the word had gotten out that he was there, so there must have been a thousand people outside, trying to get in. The bouncer let me through, and Jilly made the introduction. We sat there talking until 3 or 4 in the morning, Sinatra drinking Jack Daniel's straight and continuously.

We got to be friends on a first-name basis. For some reason, he always called me "Pablo."

When the so-called Rat Pack (Sinatra, Sammy Davis Jr., Joey Bishop, Peter Lawford, and Dean Martin) made its very first appearance together at the Sands in Vegas, a pit boss at the hotel, whom I had gotten some football tickets for, got me a front-row table for the opening-night performance.

My mom was with me, and her date was Rick Casares. I had a date with some showgirl. When we were shown to our table, I couldn't help but notice that it was in front of Zsa Zsa Gabor and a lot of other big names.

Another time during my Packer days, when the Rat Pack played an outdoor nightclub in Chicago during the season, I got tickets for me and some of my teammates, including Max, Fuzzy, and Ron Kramer. We had sneaked out to the airport, where I had a private plane waiting to take us to Chicago.

We had seats right down in front, and we all really enjoyed it. On the way home, however, I was struck by an awful thought. Irv Kupcinet, the entertainment columnist for the *Chicago Tribune*, was there with a photographer. What if our picture showed up in the next day's paper? Lombardi would have us all for lunch.

We got back about 4 or 5 in the morning. One of the guys knew the restaurant where Lombardi had breakfast, so he hustled over there to buy all the papers before the coach could see them. Our worries were needless. The paper didn't run our photo and Lombardi never knew.

After the 1970 season, I took a sort of busman's holiday from my broadcasting and went to the Super Bowl in Miami with my mother, my friend Jimmy Lambert and his wife, and my date, the reigning Miss Teen-Age America. I had met her when I was a celebrity judge at the pageant, not that the fix was in or anything.

She was eighteen and I had just turned thirty-six. My mom never said much about my lifestyle, but this time she leaned over to me at the game and whispered, "Paul, don't you think this is a little ridiculous?"

Maybe, and it was about to get more so.

The morning of the game, Lambert was up and already drinking champagne. He had made a huge bet on the Colts, but I liked Dallas. We talked and argued for a while, and finally I came around to his way of thinking. We bet big on the Colts, who were slight favorites.

Heading into the final quarter, the Cowboys had a 13–6 lead. But then Dallas began coughing it up and throwing it away, with the result that Baltimore tied it. Finally, the Colts' Jim O'Brien kicked a 28-yard field goal on the last play to give Baltimore a 16–13 victory. We were so excited over winning our bets that we agreed to take off for Acapulco the next morning. I knew Sinatra was playing there.

I thought about backing out, but I was afraid that if I went back on my word, it would mean bad luck for me. Gamblers usually are very superstitious. So we went to Acapulco, not even thinking that it was the tourist season and there wouldn't be a room available in the whole place.

I tried to get us a room in the Villa Vera, where I'd stayed two or three times, but it was full. Then I tried to find comedian Alan King, who played tennis there in the winter, but I couldn't track him down. But just when we were about ready to give up, I heard somebody yell, "Paul!" and I turned around to see David Janssen, who had starred in the hit TV series *The Fugitive*.

He told me that his wife's father had become ill, so they were returning to L.A. immediately. I told him that we needed a couple of rooms, so he said, "Why not take ours?" They were staying at the Villa Vera.

The first night, we go to the bar and find John Wayne sitting there. I didn't know whether he knew me or not, but I went up and introduced myself. He had played football in college, so we had something to talk about. Finally, he invited us out to dinner, but I politely declined because we had another couple with us. So he invited us out to see his ship the next day. And I do mean *ship*. He had bought an old World War II destroyer and renovated it. It was the damnedest thing you ever saw.

When we came on board—you had to take a little boat from the pier out to the ship—he was playing cards with Ward Bond, the actor who had been in so many of his cowboy movies. I said to Bond, "You always play the SOB, right?" And Wayne said, "Yeah, Paul, he's an SOB, but he's my SOB." I thought that was a great way for one man to express affection for the other.

By now, I was as impressed as Miss Teen-Age America, but the fun wasn't over yet.

We barely missed Sinatra in Acapulco, so we moved on to L.A. and dropped into Chez Jay's, a bar owned by a friend, Jay Fiondella. He was girl crazy, and on this night he had a couple of beauties, one on each arm. He wanted to go to the Daisy in Beverly Hills, which then was just about the hottest spot in town. It was partly owned by Dominick Dunne, who now writes for *Vanity Fair*.

When we got there, somebody told me that Sinatra, who we'd just missed in Acapulco, was in the back room. We went back so I could say hi to Frank, and he invited us to his house. The only problem was, Jay had to ditch one of his girls because Frank said it had to be an even number of men and women. "We can't have an extra girl," he said.

So, minus a girl, we went to Frank's house. As the evening went on, I could tell he had a little eye for Miss Teen-Age America, who was a very healthy young lady. I finally told him that I had to leave the next morning on business, but that she was going to stay in L.A. for a screen test. So Frank told her she was welcome to spend the next night at his house.

I never knew what happened, but I guarantee you that Frank never would have been so generous if she hadn't been so pretty.

I really didn't think I'd get married again, and it didn't bother me. I liked my lifestyle and my independence. The girls came and went. The Italians call it "La Dolce Vita."

I met Angela at a party after the 1976 Kentucky Derby. She was with somebody else, but before she left Louisville to return home to Philadelphia, I took her out. She was drop-dead gorgeous and I had a great time, so I invited her to meet me in Baltimore for the Preakness.

The night before the race we had dinner with Sam Marilla, a good friend that I bet with, and his wife, and another old friend, Babe Waldman, who ran a popular Louisville bar named the Patio Lounge, and his wife. Naturally, I stuck Sam with the check since I was a customer. The next day, I had a good day at the track, beating Sam out of about nine thousand dollars, so I took them for dinner to the Pimlico Hotel, which used to be across the street from the track, and told everybody I was picking up the check.

That was all Sam needed to hear. "I'll get you, Hornung," he said. Before long, he was sending bottles of champagne to tables all over the place. He was going to stick me with the biggest tab he could run up. Unfortunately for Sam, the owner of Elocutionist, which had just won the Preakness, picked up the check for the whole restaurant, our table included. Sam was really pissed that I had gotten off the hook like that.

Since I had won all that money, I asked Angela if she was doing anything the next week. The Eagles had just fired Mike

McCormick and his entire coaching staff, including Angela, who was McCormick's assistant. So she said, "Sure, I don't have anything else to do." So I pulled the old Acapulco trick, asking her if she would like to join me there.

She said yes, but that she'd have to go home to Philadelphia to get some clothes. I told her that I was doing a commercial in New York on Monday, so maybe she could join me in Manhattan for dinner Monday night.

So that's how it came to be that we spent about eight or nine days in Acapulco. I was so crazy about her that I finally asked if she would come to Louisville and live with me. And she said yes.

After about a year and a half of living together, Angela gave me an ultimatum. If I didn't marry her before the 1979 Derby, she was going to leave and move back to Philadelphia. She had told her mother that she was living with me, but not her father because he wouldn't have approved.

I was in love with her and didn't want to lose her. I was forty-three, so I figured, "What the hell, it's time." The only problem was that, technically, I was still married to Pat Roeder. So I went to Florida and worked out a divorce with Pat, which cleared the way for Angela and me to be married.

When the word got out, three friends of mine from New Orleans—Louie Shushan and Tony and Jimmy Moran—said, "Why don't you come down here and have it?" So we did. All my family and friends came down from Louisville, and her family came from Philadelphia.

The night before, Shushan, an attorney and one of my best friends in New Orleans, threw a party for us and picked up the tab. I'd heard that his dad had been a close associate of the legendary former governor of Louisiana, Huey "Kingfish" Long.

We were married the next morning at the bar in Jimmy Moran's Riverside restaurant. When somebody asked me why we had it in the morning, I repeated a line from my first wedding: "Because if it doesn't work out, we've still got the rest of the day." Babe Waldman was my best man. To this day, he's one of my best friends.

As soon as the wedding was over, the party began. Jimmy could make fettucini alfredo like no other living human being. At the reception's peak, there must have been a hundred people there, and my friends Al Hirt and Pete Fountain both performed for us.

Let me tell you about Al Hirt. He owned about 9 percent of the New Orleans Saints, so he and I hit it off real well. He was an overly generous guy. When he was drinking, he would give you the shirt off his back. Literally.

Once I invited him to be my guest at a golf tournament in Louisville. We were out late on a boat on the Ohio River, and Al had drunk enough that he felt like he wanted to do something for me. So he took a ring off his right forefinger, the one he played the trumpet with, and said, "This is from me to you, I love you."

I didn't want to take it, but Al insisted. The ring appraised for twenty-five thousand dollars, and I knew I was going to give it back to him. I just waited until the right time. That turned out to be one of the Super Bowls in New Orleans.

Al was up on the stage, playing. After a number, I walked up, took the ring off my finger and said, "Now this is from me to you with love." He was almost in tears. Later his wife told me, "You're the only guy who gave anything back to him."

So now here he was, playing at my wedding party.

The bill had to be around fifteen thousand dollars considering that we kept the bar open for about seven or eight hours, but when I tried to settle up with Jimmy and his brother Tony, who owned the Old Absinthe House on Bourbon Street, they said it was all taken care of.

I've never been big on weddings, but I must say that ours was fun. After the reception, of course, we partied the night away on Bourbon Street.

Angela understood football and television, so she was a great partner for me. I remember that within the first three or four years of our marriage, *Oui* magazine came out with an issue that had the cover line, "See Mrs. Paul Hornung in the Nude." It was Pat, not Angela, but our friends sure had fun kidding us about it.

I was honest with Angela about having kids. I told her that if she wanted them, she would have to stay home and raise them because I was always going to be gone. Her other choice was to travel with me. She decided to travel with me, and it has been a lot of fun for both of us.

Because Angela knows football she puts up with all my friends. She also was my co-producer on *Paul Hornung's Sports Showcase*, my cable TV show from Louisville. She was responsible for arranging travel accommodations for the guests, making sure they knew how to get to the restaurant—first Chi-Chi's, then Damon's—and generally taking care of them.

She also has fallen in love with golf. When we got married, she didn't know how to swing a club. But in the last decade or so, she has become one of the best female golfers in the Louisville area, and she has the trophies to prove it.

As she got better, she and I would play even. Now she has to give me four shots a side. We bet, too, and I always have to pay up. On a good day, she'll beat me out of $250 or so. She has all her friends betting, too. They'll play a $5 Nassau, automatic presses, and all that.

Wonder where she got that from?

A couple of years after I married Angela, she and I were in Miami, having a 2 A.M. breakfast at the Jockey Club. We were on our way back to our room when a couple of limos pulled up to the front of the hotel. Sinatra got out of one.

"Hey, Pablo," he said, "come on in and have a drink with us."

"Frank," I said, "give me a rain check. We've got to catch a plane at 8 in the morning."

And that's the last time I ever spoke to him. After that he would barely acknowledge me, even when we were in the same place. I finally asked Jilly Rizzo about it and he said, "I don't know, but it must go back to that night in Miami when you wouldn't have a drink with him. With Frank, that's a no-no."

20

GOOD-BYE, VINCE; HELLO, HOWARD

On September 3, 1970, I was staying in a motel outside Laurel, Maryland, where I was to attend the opening of an Arthur Treacher's seafood restaurant. I owned part of about four of them in partnership with my friend John Y. Brown Jr., who had made a fortune in the 1960s with Kentucky Fried Chicken. But early in the morning, I bolted upright in bed and said to myself, "We've lost the coach." Sure enough, that was the day Lombardi died. He was only fifty-seven years old.

After Lombardi had given me the scoop on his retirement as the Packers' head coach early in 1968, he and I didn't talk very often, but I figured he wasn't too happy in his role as general manager, especially since the '68 team got off to a 2–3–1 start under Phil Bengtson, who had been defensive coach under Lombardi. Naturally, this didn't sit well with Vince, who visited practice every day for a half hour or so.

"I stand on the sidelines and watch, just to let the boys know I still have my eye on them," he told Tex Maule of *Sports Illustrated*. "I see them cutting their eyes at me, and I know what they're thinking, but I don't say anything."

Lombardi told me how much he missed coaching. He couldn't stay away from the practice field, and he became frustrated by Bengtson's nice-guy approach. He watched games in a soundproof booth in the press box so nobody could hear him yelling.

Bengtson never got the hang of it and the team finished the season with a 6–7–1 record. Lombardi couldn't stand to watch his dynasty come unraveled, so when his buddy Edward Bennett Williams approached him about coaching the Washington Redskins, Lombardi was more than willing to listen. As it turned out, Williams made him an offer he couldn't refuse: the highest coaching salary in the league, total control over all football operations, and an ownership percentage in the club.

Although Lombardi had a five-year contract with Green Bay, the board of directors released him when he told them he wanted to take Williams's offer. Had they refused, Lombardi said, he would have stayed in Green Bay. What he really meant was that he would have stayed until he could find another way to get back into coaching. "Getting out was the biggest mistake I ever made," Lombardi said.

When Lombardi took the Washington job, I immediately got a call from Sonny Jurgensen, the talented Redskins quarterback, who loved the nightlife as much as I. Naturally, he wanted to know how I had managed to get along with Lombardi.

"Sonny, don't worry about a thing," I told him. "Forget everything else you've ever heard. You'll *love* Vince Lombardi. He'll be fair, and it'll be a whole new deal for you. Look, *I* played for him, didn't I?"

Jurgensen understood what I was talking about when he met with Lombardi in February 1969. Looking back on that meeting, Jurgensen said in *Sports Illustrated* during the season that Lombardi had told him his playboy reputation didn't matter—the same thing Lombardi told me when he came to Green Bay.

"I can't tell you how good I felt," Sonny said. "I know now I've always wanted to play for a coach like him. I wish it had happened long ago, when I had my career in front of me. I loved talking about football with him. Such knowledge. I'm a student of the game and I can tell you right now, he's the best."

In Jurgensen, Lombardi saw the same yearning for success that he had seen in many of us when he came to Green Bay.

"The thing about Jurgensen is that he always wanted to win so fiercely," Lombardi said at the time. "All the great ones have that. Sonny Jurgensen can throw a football as well or better than anyone, but he has not won. He has missed out on all that glory, and that is something all the great ones have: the hunger for glory. Hornung had it. Inside the twenty, Paul Hornung was the greatest player around."

Just as all the Green Bay guys expected, Lombardi turned the Redskins around immediately. He became the toast of the nation's capital, far bigger than any U.S. senator or Supreme Court justice. He was so excited about his team, especially Jurgensen, that he invited Max and me to be his guests at the Redskins' final home game against New Orleans on December 14, 1969, in RFK Stadium. The team had a 6–4–2 record and needed a win to keep intact Lombardi's record of never having a record of .500 or less in the NFL.

Lombardi had a limo pick us up at the airport and take us to the Redskins offices, where he announced that he wanted Max and me to spend the night at his home in Virginia. "No way, Coach," I said. "I've had enough bed checks from you." The way Max and I had it planned, we wanted to get rid of Lombardi at about 10:30 P.M. and hit the streets. He probably figured as much. So he put us up in two suites at one of the downtown luxury hotels.

That night he took us to his favorite Italian restaurant, and as we were heading to our table, everybody in the place got up and gave him a standing ovation. He owned the city, and he knew everybody worth knowing from President Nixon on down. After dinner, he invited us back to his house to have a couple of after-dinner drinks, but we respectfully declined. We couldn't wait to hit the streets.

The next day, naturally, the Redskins beat the Saints, 17–14, to assure Lombardi of a winning season, and we went over to his house after the game to join Vince and what seemed to be about half of Washington. Earl Warren, the chief justice of the U.S. Supreme Court, dropped by for a drink. Lombardi had someone who helped him whom everybody knew as "the Colonel." When the Colonel finally went home, Lombardi got behind the bar, so Max and I asked him to fix us a drink.

He refused. "I'm never going to fix you two a drink," he said, "so get your asses back here and do it yourself." We begged him to do it as a gesture of goodwill, but no way he was going to do it. That was just his way of showing us he was still the boss.

Sometime in the spring of 1970, I got a call from Lombardi's wife, Marie. I knew he had gotten sick since Max and I had visited him, but I had no idea it had gotten as bad as it was. She told me that I might want to come to Washington because he wasn't doing too well.

I was shocked when I saw him. He was down from 210 pounds to about 130. He looked horrible, but his mind was still sharp. I stayed for a half hour and we talked mostly about how he was looking forward to coaching Jurgensen and the rest of his team in the coming season. He said that in his system he wouldn't be surprised to see Jurgensen complete 80 percent of his passes. "I've never seen a guy throw the ball like he does," Lombardi said.

When I left, I told Marie to keep me posted. But I also had an odd feeling that I might never see him again. Sadly, I was right.

The funeral was held at St. Patrick's Cathedral in New York, and, judging by the size of the crowd, which was estimated at 3,500, you would have thought a head of state had passed away. The police had midtown traffic blocked all the way to New Jersey, where Lombardi was to be buried. I was an honorary pallbearer, and the reality that he was gone really took a lot out of me.

On the way to Mount Olivet Cemetery in Middletown, New Jersey, I rode in the same limo with Colonel Earl "Red" Blaik, the former great Army coach of the 1940s and '50s. I'd never had the opportunity to meet Colonel Blaik, so I told him that I thought Coach Lombardi had predicated his whole life after what he had learned under him at West Point. Colonel Blaik then told me a story about Lombardi and General Douglas MacArthur.

It seems that after President Harry S. Truman had fired MacArthur as supreme commander of the U.S. forces in the Far East during the Korean War, MacArthur established his residence in the Waldorf-Astoria towers in mid-Manhattan. MacArthur was a huge fan of Blaik's team, but in those days the Army games weren't available on TV. So after practice every Sunday, Lombardi would take the game films to MacArthur's penthouse and tell him about Blaik's game plan and decision making.

I would have loved to have been a fly on the wall at one of those sessions.

Lombardi's death left a big hole in my life. Everybody he touched as a personal friend went on to do something great in life. I wish I'd called him about the gambling situation. I know he would have tried to help me, just as he did with President Kennedy in 1961. He might not have been able to do anything, but he would have tried.

After Lombardi's funeral, I returned to broadcasting. Like everyone else in the football world, I was curious about how the new show *Monday Night Football* would do.

Riding the unprecedented wave of interest in the NFL that Namath and Super Bowl III had generated, Commissioner Pete Rozelle had come up with a novel idea for the 1970 season, the one in which the leagues were officially merged. Why not extend the weekend, and the fans' need for action, by having an NFL regular-season game on Monday night?

He first dangled the idea in front of CBS and NBC, but neither was interested. Can you imagine the idiots turning down *Monday Night Football?* The same bunch at CBS sold the Yankees to George Steinbrenner for $10 million not long after this, if you can believe that. So, in those days before the cable networks, that left ABC, which had a sports division that was No. 3 but rising swiftly, under the inspired leadership of Roone Arledge.

Arledge had turned ABC's *Wide World of Sports*, hosted by Jim McKay, into a ratings bonanza. He also had won much critical acclaim for ABC's broadcast of the Olympic Games. But he knew that if ABC was ever to seriously challenge NBC and CBS, it would have to get involved with the traditional bread-and-butter professional sports, most notably Major League Baseball and the NFL.

So Arledge quickly bought into Rozelle's new idea, a meeting of fertile minds if there ever was one. The next item of business was to come up with an announcing team that would be colorful enough to draw fans from the traditional lineup of sitcoms on NBC and CBS.

For play-by-play man, Arledge picked my old buddy Frank Gifford, who was bland but solid. But instead of going with one color analyst, Arledge surprised everyone by picking an odd couple, Howard Cosell and Don Meredith, to join Gifford on the first three-man announcing team in sports history.

Cosell, abrasive but intelligent, had made a name for himself in the 1960s by defending Cassius Clay after he joined the Black Muslims, changed his name to Muhammad Ali, and refused on religious grounds to be drafted by the U.S. Army. The exchange of verbal jabs between Cosell, the Jewish lawyer from New York, and Ali, the black fighter and rights activist from Louisville, provided television that was both entertaining and enlightening.

Meredith was pretty much a TV novice—hell, he didn't

have nearly as much experience as me—but he was a charming, down-home sort of guy who had a great Texas drawl and quarterback's knowledge of the game. I liked and respected Don, who had almost beaten us as the Cowboys' quarterback in the "Ice Bowl" game of 1967. But I wasn't interested in Meredith's job, and ABC wasn't interested in me.

From its first game in the fall of 1970, the novel show was a huge ratings success. Gifford performed well in his role as referee between Cosell and Meredith. Cosell liked to needle Meredith by calling him "Dandy Don" or "Dan-de-roo" in that grating, nasal voice of his, and Meredith loved to put down Cosell with his down-home wit and Texas drawl.

I'd known Cosell since my early days with the Packers. He was a radio reporter then, and every time he would hear that I was at Toots Shor's in New York, he'd show up with a tape recorder he always had with him. He was full of braggadocio, even then, but I always liked Howard. You may not have liked his style or tone, but you had to give him credit for being honest.

When Meredith abruptly left the announcing team in 1974, Cosell suggested several replacements to Arledge. I was one of them, along with Namath and Dick Butkus, because Howard was aware of my work with Notre Dame and CBS, along with a sideline reporter's job at a couple of Super Bowls. But the job finally went to Fred "The Hammer" Williamson, the former defensive back for the Oakland Raiders, who had gotten hammered by the Packers in Super Bowl II.

The next spring, I ran into Arledge at a party before the Kentucky Derby—ABC also owned the rights to the Triple Crown races—and asked him point-blank why I didn't get the job. He told me it was because he thought I was too much like Gifford.

We both were known as good-looking playboys, we had played the same position in college and the pros, and we both had played for Lombardi (Frank as a New York Giant from 1954 to '58). I'm not sure that I agreed, but I wasn't disappointed or upset because I had so much else going on in my life as a broadcaster and businessman. (By the way, "The Hammer" lasted only a year before being replaced by Alex Karras.)

So I remained with CBS while *Monday Night Football* became the sports broadcasting phenomenon of the 1970s. I covered a lot of college bowl games, including the Cotton Bowl, the Sun Bowl, the Fiesta Bowl, and the Peach Bowl, largely doing color commentary.

I made my first $5,000 bet while covering the 1978 Peach Bowl between Georgia Tech and Purdue. One afternoon the week before the game, I noticed that Georgia Tech was running the wishbone offense instead of the option attack that coach Pepper Rodgers had used during the season.

When I asked Pepper what was going on, he told me that his great runner Eddie Lee Ivory was injured and wouldn't be nearly at full speed for the game. So he had gone back to the wishbone, the offense that his seniors had played before he took the Tech job. But the thing that got my attention was that he hadn't yet announced Ivory's condition to the media.

The next day I saw in the paper that Tech was a two- or three-point favorite. But there was still no news about Ivory's injury. So I asked Pepper when he planned on announcing it, and he told me he didn't plan to say anything until his press conference at 4:30 that afternoon.

I called Barney Shapiro in Vegas and told him I wanted to bet five thousand dollars on Purdue. He was shocked because he knew I had never bet that much. But when I told him what I knew, he got me down on Purdue and he also bet on the Boilermakers.

When the news of Ivory's injury broke, the gambling line changed dramatically until Purdue went off as a seven-point favorite. But it didn't make any difference. The Boilermakers rolled to a 41–21 victory and I won the biggest bet of my life.

That was the most enjoyable game I ever called. It was what gamblers call a "popcorn game," meaning that you can just relax and eat your popcorn because you know you are going to win. I've never been more loose, relaxed, or funny on the air than I was that day.

I was still with CBS in 1980 when the Rams and Steelers played in Super Bowl XIV on January 20 in the Rose Bowl. The network had rented actor Carroll O'Connor's restaurant, Hamburger Hamlet in Beverly Hills, so that Phyllis George and I could watch the game with celebrities and do a show from there. Phyllis had married my old friend John Y. Brown Jr., the former Kentucky Fried Chicken magnate, and he had used her star quality to help him get elected governor of Kentucky in November of '79.

I give Phyllis a lot of credit. A former Miss America from Denton, Texas, she had the guts to enter the all-male domain of football broadcasting. At first, she had to put up with a lot of criticism and snide comments from chauvinistic players and writers. But she did such a good job, especially with Musburger, Irv Cross, and Jimmy "The Greek" Snyder on the NFL Today show, that she paved the way for all the female analysts and interviewers that you see on TV today.

That year the network had a luncheon for its affiliates, and all the on-the-air people were there. We were asked to pick the Super Bowl winner and explain why. Almost everyone had picked the Rams until they got to me. I picked the Steelers, reasoning that "most teams who play in the Super Bowl for the first time don't win." Hell, the Steelers already had won three rings in the 1970s. I lambasted everyone who had picked the Rams, including John Madden.

Madden had retired from coaching after winning the 1977 Super Bowl with the Raiders, and now he was beginning his career as a TV commentator. He gave a talk about the intricacies of the game. You know the stuff he does. If the quarterback scratches his nose two times instead of three, it means such-and-such. That sort of thing. But that speech got him in with the affiliates, and from then on he was the fair-haired boy at CBS.

Only two years later, in fact, Madden was alongside Summerall in the booth for Super Bowl XVI, the 49ers' 26–21 win over the Bengals in Pontiac, Michigan. That was the third Super Bowl played in a domed stadium, and it was a damned good thing. It was so cold in Pontiac that day that it would have been almost impossible to play an outdoor game.

I left CBS in 1982, at about the same time my friend and patron saint, executive director Bob Wussler, decided to move on. I had seen what the network had done to Johnny Unitas and Tom Brookshier. The new guys just coming out of the NFL were replacing the old guys as analysts. It was a slow death, however. They kept cutting back your games until one day they didn't call anymore. Plus, I didn't like the fact that CBS was trying to make me cover some schlock sports—I specifically remember some kind of figure-8 car race in Oregon—that I refused to do.

Wussler went from CBS to Ted Turner's cable empire in At-

lanta, and he quickly signed up Lindsey Nelson and me to do
college football on WTBS. I also got to do a weekly show on
TNT, another Turner station, with Norm Van Brocklin, Alex
Hawkins, and sportscaster Bob Neal called *Saturday Football
Live.* We'd fly in on Friday night, get together for dinner, and
then do the show on Saturday.

We were irreverent as hell, and I loved it. I'd get the gambling lines from Vegas, and Hawkins and I would discuss them,
which was unheard of in those days. We pushed the envelope as
far as we could, but our most animated discussions took place
over dinner.

Hawkins was the first guy to use the line "That's my story and
I'm sticking to it." In fact, I think he did a book and a song with
that for the title. We ripped the NFL all the time, and the fans
loved it. But we could get away with a lot because we were on
cable, which was a lot looser than the regular networks.

I remember that during one show, Hawkins was bragging
about South Carolina. George Rogers, who won the Heisman in
1980, had gone there. Van Brocklin finally had heard enough.
"Don't give me that crap about South Carolina," he said. "You
can get [enrolled] in South Carolina with an expired driver's license."

Well, the shit really hit the fan. We got all sorts of mail from
South Carolina, including a threat from a state cop, telling us
what would happen if he ever caught Van Brocklin in South
Carolina. They were beside themselves.

Still, our show became the hottest one in Atlanta. It might
not have been *Monday Night Football.* Hell, it might have been
better.

When Marie Lombardi died in 1982, I went to New York

alone for her funeral. I checked into the St. Regis Hotel and met Duncan MacCalman for dinner. He owned his own bar, Duncan's, which was popular at the time. Tucker Frederickson, the former Giants running star, owned a piece of it, and Phyllis George Brown hung out there with her pals whenever she was in New York.

After a Chinese dinner and a few drinks, Duncan and I went to P. J. Clarke's at about midnight. I remember legendary Chicago White Sox announcer Harry Caray coming in and saying, "Let's have a beer." But that's about all I remember. At some point, Duncan left. The next thing I knew, I was in Bellevue Hospital. I didn't remember a thing from Harry Caray on.

In trying to piece it together, the cops figured that somebody had doctored my drink with scopolamine, a "truth serum" used in World War II. When you're under its effects, you'll do or say anything you're told to. Whoever drugged me must have recognized me and anonymously called the cops to tell them that somebody was in trouble in a room on the third floor of a fleabag hotel at the corner of Eighteenth Street and Tenth Avenue, which is where the cops had found me. I had no idea how I got there.

The cops told me that when they tried to get me up, I went after one of them and they had to restrain me. By that, they meant that one of them knocked me out with a billy club.

I woke up in the hospital about eight hours later, looking up at Governor Brown and Frank Metts. The cops had called them and they found me lying on a gurney. The NFL and the hospital had tried to keep it quiet, but the word had leaked out and a lot of press showed up.

I finally got released and went out a back door, where I was taken directly to an airport and put on a plane to Louisville. I had only one shoe on. No telling where I'd lost the other. Whoever drugged me took my Rolex watch and about fifteen hundred dollars in cash, but didn't get my Super Bowl ring, which was in a repair shop getting fixed.

The cops told me I was lucky I had the money and the Rolex on me. "If they hadn't gotten something," said one of the officers, "they'd have killed your ass right there."

21.

HALLS OF SHAME
AND FAME

At the time Lindsey Nelson and I agreed to work for Bob Wussler at WTBS, the cable station was negotiating with the NCAA to get the rights to a new package of college football games. The two sides finally agreed that the station would pay the NCAA $17 million for the rights to do nineteen games on Thursday nights in 1982 and '83. As part of the deal, WTBS agreed to give the NCAA final approval over any announcer or color analyst.

Wussler told me that he wanted to submit my name for the NCAA Television Committee's approval because he wanted Lindsey and me to be his announcing team, just as we had been for CBS and Notre Dame. I certainly had no problem with that.

Lindsey was approved for play-by-play, and on March 29, 1982, the NCAA committee met at the Final Four basketball tournament in New Orleans, the city where Angela and I had been married almost three years earlier. Wussler and Terry Hanson, TBS's executive producer of sports, gave the nineteen-person committee a list of four color announcers it wanted to use on the new series. One of them was me.

After a brief discussion, the committee approved Tim Foley and Alan Page, but rejected me and former Georgia Tech coach Pepper Rodgers. Rodgers's sin was that he had filed a lawsuit against the Georgia Tech Athletic Association.

During a recess, two members of the committee approached Wussler and Hanson to lobby for Eddie Crowder, the Colorado athletics director and former Oklahoma quarterback, who was a committee member. Crowder's name had not been submitted by WTBS, nor had it been discussed prior to the committee's rejection of me.

About three weeks after the meeting, a reporter from Atlanta called Wiles Hallock, the chairman of the NCAA Television Committee. During the conversation, Hallock was asked why I hadn't been approved, and he said "The committee objected to Paul Hornung because ever since Paul graduated from Notre Dame, he has been associated with pro football and does not represent college football."

What the hell did he think Alan Page had done with his life since he graduated from Notre Dame? That lame reason was as transparent as cellophane. The real reason came in a letter that Hanson had requested from the NCAA so he would have verification that WTBS had no part in this decision. The letter said:

> Paul Hornung was not approved for 1982. The Committee believes he is closely identified with professional football,

that he had at least one undesirable public situation while a professional player, and that the image which he projects or is projected for him does not personify college football.

Naturally, they were talking about my 1963 suspension for gambling, and the playboy image that I projected in—among other things—the "Practice, practice, practice" commercial for Miller Lite. What hypocrites! Did they really think that college coaches and players were choirboys? And did they really believe that a Heisman Trophy winner from Notre Dame, who had been doing Notre Dame games on TV for almost fifteen years, didn't fit the image of college football? To me and a lot of others, their position reflected their phoniness rather than my character.

For years, I had been blackballed by the College Football Hall of Fame near Cincinnati and the Pro Football Hall of Fame in Canton, Ohio. The pro hall already had inducted Lombardi and six of my Packers teammates—Starr, Taylor, Gregg, Davis, Adderley, and Wood. The NCAA decision was the final straw.

I felt the time had finally come for me to take action. So on July 30, 1982, I sued the NCAA in Jefferson County (Kentucky) Circuit Court for $3 million because of "intentional interference with prospective contractual relations."

In an interview with the *Louisville Courier-Journal*, my attorney, Bill Boone, said, "I don't think anybody's ever challenged the NCAA like this. Paul really has been seriously damaged. This is not just a funny suit to salvage Paul's ego."

No, it wasn't funny at all. If the NCAA was so concerned about my Miller Lite commercials, it shouldn't take sponsorship or advertising money from beer companies, and if it was concerned about gambling, as it should be, it had far bigger fish to fry than Paul Hornung.

Gambling on college football and basketball increased steadily during my playing days at Notre Dame. For years, newspapers have been printing the Las Vegas point spread on games. Since 1952, when the first major college basketball point-shaving scandal broke, college football, too, has been plagued by various gambling scandals.

In 1982, at about the same time I was filing my suit against the NCAA, the U.S. Supreme Court ruled that the NCAA no longer could monopolize college football, so WTBS was able to hire me to broadcast college football, anyway, taking some of the sting out of my lawsuit.

Then early in '85, while I was waiting for my suit against the NCAA to go to trial, I learned that I had been elected to the College Football Hall of Fame. My mother was really tickled to death, and I think it helped my lawsuit. How could the NCAA say a Hall of Famer didn't represent college football?

My suit finally went to trial in August of that year, and, after hearing several witnesses, the jury left the courtroom, deliberated only an hour or so, and then awarded me $100,000 in compensatory damages and $1 million in punitive damages. I was elated. As I told the media, "I've had some wins and I've had some losses, but this is a big win. It's been a long two or three years, and I really think this decision vindicates me." Naturally, the NCAA wasn't about to give up. It petitioned the Kentucky Court of Appeals to overturn the lower court's verdict.

At the 1985 Heisman Trophy banquet in New York, Don Criqui, the network sports announcer, told me he'd heard that I was going to be voted into the pro Hall of Fame in January. I didn't pay much attention to that. I'd been passed over for so many years that I figured they'd forgotten about me.

But Criqui's source was a good one. On January 27, 1986, I was informed that I had finally been elected to the Pro Football Hall of Fame.

For years, the guy mainly responsible for keeping me out was John Steadman, a veteran columnist from Baltimore who died in 2001. I don't know why he had it in for me. Maybe he didn't like it that I always played well against the Colts, but, more likely, he was a morally conservative person who held the gambling suspension against me.

It wasn't so bad that he voted against me—that was his right—but he also campaigned to have others vote against me. I didn't think that was right, and neither did Cooper Rollow, then the sports editor of the *Chicago Tribune*. He finally went to Steadman and told Steadman that if he didn't stop soliciting votes against me, he was going to expose his campaign against me in the *Tribune*. Maybe it was only a coincidence, but I was voted in the next time around.

The induction ceremony took place on Saturday, August 2, and I took a busload of my family and friends to Canton. The night before the ceremony, I was drinking with a bunch of my buddies at the hotel bar when a woman walked up, exposed her breasts, and asked me to sign them. Thank God my mother and my wife were upstairs, sleeping.

My fellow inductees on a swelteringly hot morning were Fran Tarkenton, Doak Walker, Willie Lanier, and Ken Houston. Bobby Layne, who was to introduce Walker, said he was nervous, and that made Max McGee, who was to introduce me,

nervous. When it was finally time for the ceremony, both Max
and I were as nervous as we had ever seen each other. But Max
was fine once he started talking.

"Paul was what they call an 'impact player' nowadays," Max
said. "He was an impact player on the Green Bay Packers, but
also an impact player on half the females in the United States."

He closed by saying, "I wouldn't be doing this today if Vince
were still alive. He and Paul had a great personal relationship as
well as a great football relationship. And now I present 'The
Golden Boy,' Paul Hornung."

Early in my speech, I looked out at Fuzzy Thurston, who was
sitting near the stage. He had a patch on his throat and his voice
had become a whisper because of throat cancer. But he had
made the trip for me, and it meant a lot. He always told me that
if I stuck close to him, I'd get to Canton. So I said, "Well, Fuzzy,
we're here. And I'm just so happy you're here with me."

Ron Kramer also was in the crowd that day. Up on the dais
were Bart Starr, Ray Nitschke and Herb Adderley, all of whom
already had been inducted.

Ordinarily, I'm not a very sentimental person. But on that
day, I had to fight off tears when I thanked my mother, my wife,
my teammates, and, of course, Vince Lombardi. "Gregg and
Adderley were the only Packers who had the ability to make the
Hall of Fame no matter where they played," I said. "The rest of
us are here only because of Lombardi and what he stood for.
This is the greatest day of my life. I've waited a long time to get
here, but now I can take this weekend with me and keep it forever."

Almost a year later, on July 17, 1987, the Kentucky Court of
Appeals unanimously rejected the NCAA's appeal of my victory

in court. Still, the NCAA wouldn't give up. They took their appeal to the Kentucky Supreme Court, and this is where my luck ran out.

I was disappointed—about $1 million of the money that had been awarded me was tax-free—but I also realized that circumstances had changed considerably since I had filed the suit in 1982. I had been inducted into both the college and pro halls of fame, and I was again broadcasting college games for WTBS.

So even though I lost, I still felt vindicated.

22.

WHERE HAVE YOU GONE, LINDSEY NELSON?

When I was playing, the media were a lot different than they are now. For one thing, today there's a lot more media. We never had to face the batteries of notepads, microphones, and cameras that today's coaches and players deal with on a daily basis. Television was still in its infancy in the 1950s and early '60s, so the guys with most of the clout were the big-city newspaper columnists and magazine writers.

I had a great rapport with the press, mainly because I didn't mind doing interviews or getting called at home. The only problem with giving out my home number on a confidential basis was that the writer would give it to a friend of his on a confidential basis. Before you knew it, everybody had it.

In those days, there was a feeling of mutual trust, but that ceased to exist when the players started making the big bucks and everyone in the media seemed to want to become the next Woodward and Bernstein. Back then the press would protect us.

Like us, they observed the sign we had in our locker room: "What's said here and done here stays here when you leave here."

The press always gathered around my locker because I had the reputation of being a good interview. They liked guys like Bart Starr and Forrest Gregg, but they didn't interview them as much because they weren't controversial. Then, as now, the writers like somebody who will say something they can build a story around.

I can't remember ever having an altercation with a writer, and I can't remember any writer that the team shunned. Of course, you don't get pissed off at the media when you're winning, only when you're losing. And we didn't lose very often in those days.

Few of today's players understand what an ally the media can be to them. They're making so much money they don't care. In our day, we all needed jobs in the off-season to make ends meet, so it paid to get as much good press as we could.

Now there's nothing but animosity, mean-spiritedness, and contempt on both sides. The players and the coaches see the media people as nuisances and pests who are only interested in ripping them or prying into their personal lives. The media people, on the other hand, see the players and coaches as egomaniacs who are spoiled, overpaid, rude, and crude.

Max and I, along with a lot of others, are lucky we played when we did. In those days, the writers and broadcasters who covered the Packers were interested only in football. Of all the times that Lombardi fined Max and me, very few made the papers.

Can you imagine some of the headlines and cable TV stories if Max and I played today? It makes me shudder to think about it. But I know this: Lombardi wouldn't let the media coach his team or discipline his players. Even when he was angry with us, he was protective of us.

After practices, Lombardi liked to take his coaches out and have a beer. He called it the "Five O'Clock Club." On the road, he'd invite the writers. He didn't like the press, and the press didn't particularly like him, except for the favorites that Lombardi played whenever he needed something. It was another example of how shrewd he was.

During my years at Notre Dame, I grew accustomed to dealing with the national media. I got to know the great sports columnists of the time — Red Smith, Jim Murray, Jimmy Breslin, Jimmy Cannon, Arthur Daley, and many others. My favorite among the New York writers was Dick Schaap. He wasn't a real drinker, unlike most of the others. He was more of a thinker. He liked to look to the future and figure out what he was going to do with his career.

My first two years in Green Bay, we got very little coverage because we were so bad. The only columns about me concerned how much of a disappointment I'd been. There was a lot of talk about the Golden Boy being a bust in the NFL. They had no idea how hard it was to play in the losing environment that Lisle Blackbourn had created and Ray McLean had perpetuated.

But after Lombardi arrived and had immediate success, we began to see the national media more frequently. One of our favorites was Tex Maule, the pro football writer for *Sports Illustrated*. Tex loved to cover us, at least partly because he liked to drink with us. We'd even fix him up with dates. We gave him a lot of good stuff, too, because we knew he would keep our little secrets.

Hell, the writers were on the streets just as much as we were. The writers in those days were heavy drinkers, and very few would pass up a free drink. The same was true for broadcasters, as I learned when I got into radio and TV after I retired.

Even when I was suspended for gambling in 1963, the media were generally kind to me. I made my second appearance on the cover of *SI*, but the story was more about the moral crisis in athletics than just me. Because I admitted my guilt and asked forgiveness, most of the press and the public were willing to give me a second chance. Had Pete Rose done something similar, I think baseball would have reinstated him after only a few years.

When I came back in 1964, it was a big story. How much had I lost during the year off? Would my teammates accept me? Could I pick up where I had left off? But nobody in the media argued that Rozelle had let me off too lightly, nor did they question my character. Bygones were bygones, and everyone seemed happy to see me again wearing No. 5 in the green and gold.

It was common knowledge that I'd refused to blow the whistle on any of my fellow players when I got caught gambling, and that helped me when I went into broadcasting. The coaches and players knew they could tell me anything without worrying about it getting on the air.

You can't buy that kind of credibility, and it enabled me to get some background information and insights that really helped me as a broadcaster. I have always tried to treat the coaches and players the same way I wanted to be treated as a player.

Speaking of credibility, a funny thing happened not too long after I was inducted into the Pro Football Hall of Fame. Pete Rozelle announced his retirement as commissioner of the NFL, and on April 22, 1989, I wrote him a letter congratulating him on all his accomplishments. I wrote:

Dear Pete,

No one in the history of professional football has ever given more or been more responsible for the popularity of the game than Pete Rozelle. Long after we're gone, your name will stand beside the few who really made a difference . . . Halas, Rooney, Mara, Lombardi, Lambeau . . . and not take a back seat. You can rest knowing that there never was a better commissioner of any sport and that, during your stay, professional football became the most popular sport in America. I am proud to have known you.

Sincerely,
Paul Hornung

Somehow a newspaper sports columnist got hold of that letter and wrote that he thought mine was the most significant message Rozelle received on his retirement. He wrote, "To Hornung's everlasting credit, there is no grudge, resentment or acrimony" because of my one-year suspension by Rozelle. And the columnist quoted Rozelle as saying, "I'm overwhelmed, but knowing Paul like I do, I can't say I'm entirely surprised. He has always been a gentleman." The sportswriter went on to say that Rozelle and I went our separate ways with regret over what had happened but also with the utmost respect for each other, and he concluded, "It would seem that this is what being a man is all about."

That sports columnist was none other than John Steadman of the *Baltimore Sun*, the same writer who until three years earlier had so opposed my entry to the Hall of Fame.

As a broadcaster I was lucky to have Lindsey Nelson as a mentor for more than twenty years. He taught me as much about broadcasting as any coach ever taught me about football. He loved the game and he loved announcing, and he conveyed that to his audiences. Some of today's announcers would do themselves a favor by studying some of Lindsey's old films and tapes.

A native of Tennessee, Lindsey had served as a graduate assistant coach to General Robert Neyland in Knoxville before starting the Volunteers' radio network in 1949 and becoming the sports information director in 1951. He became nationally known after he joined the Liberty Broadcasting Network in the mid-1950s. From there he moved to CBS, where he quickly established himself as the premier football announcer in the country.

Lindsey's style and delivery reminded people of Red Barber, the great baseball announcer. Lindsey was the radio voice of the New York Mets from 1962 through 1979, and the San Francisco Giants for three years after that. When somebody would hit a homer, he'd say something like "Bye, bye, Dolly Cray." Nobody knew what that meant, but, coming out of Lindsey's mouth, it sounded just right.

Lindsey was one of the finest human beings, and one of the most talented announcers, I've ever known. He had such a great voice. Whenever you'd hear him say, "Hello, everybody, this is Lindsey Nelson," you knew it was time for football. He was the lead announcer at the Cotton Bowl from 1970 through his retirement in 1986, and I did about six of those broadcasts with him.

Lindsey's trademark was a wardrobe of loud plaid sport coats that he bought at Marsh's in Huntington Village, New York. They were wasted on audiences in the black-and-white era. But when color TV became popular, the public finally could appreciate how truly loud and garish they were. I sent him one every Christmas for years.

Lindsey was a great partner and a great guy to travel with. We talked a lot about football, naturally, but also about a lot of stuff in our personal lives. Like me, Lindsey was a bachelor. But where I had a little black book with the names of women in every city who would be available on a moment's notice, he never had a date nor talked about women when I was around. I'd say, "Damn, Lindsey, where are your women?" I mean, he was handsome, intelligent, charming, rich, and famous. But he always was very coy about women.

He also was naïve about gambling. The first time I told him that much of the NFL's popularity was because of the combination of TV and gambling, he was shocked. He couldn't believe that gambling had anything to do with it. Poor Lindsey had bought the NFL party line.

The thing a lot of people didn't know about Lindsey was that he was a closet drinker. One year I had to give up doing the Notre Dame games on Saturdays because CBS wanted one of us, Lindsey or me, to be at the NFL site a day before the game, and I was the one who went. That year I always prepared myself to do both play-by-play and color just in case Lindsey had too much to drink the night before.

Sure enough, after doing a Notre Dame game at Miami on Saturday, Lindsey showed up half smashed for a Tampa Bay game the next day. His cab pulled up at the hotel at about 9:30 A.M., and they almost had to pour him out. He told me all he needed was to get some coffee and sleep it off for an hour or so.

I loved Lindsey so much that I didn't want him to embarrass himself. So I went to Tom O'Neil, who was producing the game for CBS, and told him that I didn't think Lindsey was in any shape to go on the air, but that I was ready to do both play-by-play and color.

During our pregame rehearsal, Lindsey was still thick-tongued. But he insisted that if he had some more coffee, he'd be fine. When it was time to go on the air, however, it was the same thing. After Lindsey had slurred his way through the opening, Bob Wussler, who was watching all the games in New York, called O'Neil and said, "Get Lindsey off the fucking air now."

So I did the rest of the game by myself. That experience really had a profound effect on Lindsey. I don't think he ever touched another drink after that. I used to kid him about that game. "I'd have bet five hundred dollars that I would have been in that spot before you," I said.

Luckily for me, I'd learned early in my career that I couldn't drink hard the night before I had to go on the air. Unlike Pat Summerall, who could drink a lot of martinis before a game and never miss a call, my tongue was too thick and my brain too foggy to withstand serious drinking.

Even after we went to WTBS, Lindsey and I continued to do some work for CBS. When Lindsey retired from broadcasting after the 1986 Cotton Bowl, the network paired me up with Vin Scully, the great Dodgers baseball announcer. Pee Wee Reese, the captain of Brooklyn's "Boys of Summer" teams of the 1940s and '50s, lived in Louisville and, like me, belonged to the Audubon Country Club. He told me that Scully was a wonderful guy and fun to be around, which I found to be true. The only problem was, he didn't know a damned thing about football.

Once, when Vin and I were doing an exhibition between the 49ers and Rams, the game got so boring that Robert Stenner, the best producer CBS ever had, decided to fill some of the time by having us interview some of the college All-Americans who were in the crowd.

They were in San Diego to play in an all-star game, and they'd been given tickets to the pro game. That was fine with me, but Scully didn't want to do it, mainly because he had no idea who the kids were. So I did most of the interviewing with little help from Vin.

Scully watched a game through binoculars and scripted everything, including his jokes. He ran such a tight ship, unlike Lindsey, that I never knew when to jump in. He tried to get by on his reputation and his voice, but it didn't work.

After a couple of years, he returned to doing baseball full-time. This was good for both baseball and football.

23.

MY UNBUCKLE SPECIALS

lthough I continued to do the Notre Dame games on the radio after Lindsey retired, I figured it was time to put the knowledge and experience that I had accumulated in TV to work for myself. So in 1988, I began doing my own cable show, *Paul Hornung's Sports Showcase*, from Louisville.

For thirteen years, I sold the ads, lined up the guests, served as the host, and promoted the show until I was in cable markets all over the country. I've never had so much fun in broadcasting, nor did I make as much money as I did the last few years of the show.

We first did the show from a Chi-Chi's restaurant in Louisville—not because of Max McGee, who had gotten out of Chi-Chi's by this time, but because the local manager wanted to generate some business and publicity. We always taped the show before a live audience, and it was completely ad-libbed.

The format was always the same. I'd use my contacts in the

sports world to bring in a guest. The guest and I would banter most of the show, interrupted only by a segment in which I picked the top college and pro games against the point spread. When I had a game I really liked, I'd call it an "unbuckle special." That means unbuckle the money belt and bet it all.

It was such a different format, and I was able to get such interesting guests, that we eventually outgrew Chi Chi's and moved to Damon's, a larger, sports bar–type restaurant. After a few years there, I worked out a deal with Caesar's to originate the show from their casino boat on the Indiana side of the Ohio River, only about five miles from downtown Louisville.

By then I was making a fortune on the show. I charged Caesar's an arm and a leg, and I oversold the ad time. Instead of twelve minutes of commercials in an hour, I had about sixteen. So I was able to pay guests five thousand dollars or so to come in from out of town instead of just giving them free coupons for Chi-Chi's.

My guest list was better than that of any show on ESPN or any network. Because they knew me and trusted me, people like Gale Sayers, Dick Butkus, Lou Holtz, Oscar Robertson, Denny Crum, Rick Pitino, Fuzzy Zoeller, D. Wayne Lukas, Jim Harbaugh, Anthony Muñoz, Tom Jackson, and Ken Anderson did the show. Naturally, I also brought in former Packer teammates such as McGee, Taylor, Starr, Ron and Jerry Kramer, and Bill Curry.

Pitino told me that once when he was coaching at Kentucky, he was recruiting a player from Boston. The kid told him that he had seen him on the Paul Hornung show. That impressed Rick, and it pleased me tremendously.

One of the most popular guests was Art Donovan, the Colts'

Hall of Fame tackle from the 1950s and one of the funniest men alive. His grandfather, Mike, had fought in the Civil War at age fifteen and later became the middleweight boxing champion. His dad, known as "Big Arthur" in the Bronx, where Artie grew up, was a boxing referee who officiated eighteen of Joe Louis's fights.

Donovan played for the Colts from 1950 through '62. His experience was like mine in the sense that, when he arrived in Baltimore out of Baltimore College, the team was horrible. It had a 1–11 record in Art's first season, and didn't have a winning season until the Colts went 7–5 in 1957.

As a player, Art was one of those guys who was so huge that nobody could move him. After his playing days, Art did an interview with NFL Films about the golden era of pro football. Somebody from *Late Night with David Letterman* saw it, and Art got a guest spot on the show. An agent from Atlanta saw Donovan on the show, signed him up, and put him on the banquet circuit.

This led to a TV commercial for the Maryland state lottery that featured Art diving into a huge pile of hot dogs. And that led to some commercials for Schlitz, his favorite beer, and the ownership of a Baltimore liquor store.

Art used some of his football earnings to buy some land outside of Baltimore, where he built a swimming and tennis club. As Baltimore spread outward, the land and his club became more and more valuable. Once while painting the pool, Art slipped and fell twenty-three feet to the concrete bottom. He lay there in agony for an hour before somebody found him.

"They had to call the fire truck to pull me out," Art said. "The guy says, 'You think you can go up the ladder?' And I say, 'I just came down on it.' They took my kneecap out. I broke all my ribs. I broke my wrist and my elbow. They got me to the hospital and they put me on the table and the table's too small. I fell off the table."

During one of his trips to Louisville for the TV show, I took Art to a little place named Ginny's Diner, which advertised that it sold the biggest cheeseburgers in the country. Art didn't believe it. On his first visit, he finished the cheeseburger, but it was a struggle. Before he left, he got another one to take back home to Baltimore. Before he had his heart attack in 1991, it was nothing for Art to eat 18 hot dogs at a sitting, and drink 18 to 20 beers a night.

When George Steinbrenner came on, he just took over for the first six minutes. When he was done, I thanked him for dominating my show. "Paul," he said, "that's why they call me 'The Boss.' "

The New York writers love to rip George, but there's a side of him that only a few know. Ask Warren DeSantis, who was basketball coach Pat Riley's best high school buddy in Schenectady, New York. When Warren's dad was seriously ill with liver disease, doctors told Warren that he needed to get his father into the Yale Liver Treatment Center as soon as possible.

When Warren called the center, however, he found out that the next patient opening would be at least two months in the future. His dad didn't have that kind of time to wait. At his wit's end, Warren remembered that Steinbrenner, who had been a neighbor when he lived in Florida, was good friends with Bart Giamatti, the commissioner of baseball and former president of Yale. So he called Steinbrenner and begged for help.

"I'll get back to you in an hour," Steinbrenner said.

Forty-five minutes later, the phone rang.

"Have your dad at Yale at 9 A.M. tomorrow," Steinbrenner said. "And don't worry. The cost is all taken care of."

That's "The Boss" that you never read about.

I wish I had been able to do a show with Lindsey Nelson before he died of Parkinson's disease on June 10, 1995. One of the last times I saw him was on February 23, 1993, when Tennessee dedicated its new $2.2 million baseball stadium and named it for Lindsey. He was such a nice man that in all the years I knew him, I saw him get upset with only one person, Lombardi, and there was no doubt in my mind who was at fault there. It wasn't Lindsey.

For eight straight years, I had Pete Rose on the show annually and for eight straight years Rose told me he had never bet on baseball while managing the Cincinnati Reds in the late 1980s. Well, as the saying goes, you can't bullshit an old bullshitter. I told Pete that if he had bet on baseball, he should come clean and apologize, as I had done.

But Pete not only wouldn't admit to gambling on baseball, he refused to quit gambling and hustling. There were a lot of Rose sightings at racetracks, casinos, and memorabilia shows. This was hardly the smartest way of getting back in baseball's good graces. It was more like arrogantly defying the powers that be and acting bigger than the game.

I'm not judging Pete. Hell, I'm the last person in the world who's qualified to do that. I just tried to tell him that I thought a little humility and an apology would have gone a long way toward getting his lifetime ban lifted and putting him in line to be voted into the Hall of Fame. He should be in there, regardless, simply because of what he did between the lines.

Anybody who went on my show knew that gambling would

be mentioned sooner or later. Maybe that's why Bobby Knight, who's morally opposed to gambling, never answered my calls when I wanted him to be a guest.

My favorite guests, of course, were the football guys, especially Brett Favre. Considering our age difference, we get along great. He likes to tell people that he wrote a paper about me in high school. Thanks, Brett.

I first became interested in him in 1989, his senior season at Southern Miss. They were playing Louisville in our old stadium at the Kentucky State Fairgrounds. On the last play of the game, with the score tied at 10, Favre unleashed a Hail Mary that hit a Louisville defender right on the helmet and bounced into a Southern Miss receiver's hands to give them a 16–10 win.

It was the weirdest play I've ever seen.

On the TV show, Favre was a good guest for me because he was loose and liked to kid around as much as I did. One time, after I had plugged the bottled-water brand that was one of my sponsors, I poured Brett a glass and we toasted each other. "You know, Paul," he said with a grin, "I never thought I'd come here to do a show, and you and me would be drinking water."

Although Favre has led the Packers to only one Super Bowl championship, I think he's the best player in the team's history. He's as tough as he is talented. Hell, he has started more than two hundred games in a row. He's just a great athlete. He knocks the golf ball out of sight and probably plays to a seven or eight handicap.

I ended the show after its 2001 season because I was tired of doing everything myself. The sponsors and Caesar's wanted me to do another year, but I just couldn't. The only broadcasting I wanted to do was for the Notre Dame radio network.

For years, I had made the drive from Louisville to South Bend every Friday. I was really getting tired of that when Angela said, "Why don't you charter a private plane? You can afford it." So I did, and that saved me. At my age, believe me, flying is the only way to go.

24.

ONCE A NOTRE DAME MAN, ALWAYS A NOTRE DAME MAN

I really love Notre Dame, but sometimes the administration there drives me nuts with the decisions they make. I completely agree with my old friend Jim Morse, the captain of our senior team in 1956, who said this in June 2004 while accepting the Ed "Moose" Krause award from the Monogram Club.

"Like it or not, athletics have been a huge part of the history and tradition of the university, yet there are only two Monogram winners on the board of trustees. I think that had we had more representation on the board, perhaps some of the mistakes we have made over the past years would not have occurred."

What mistakes? Well, let's examine the coaches they've hired since they made the mistake of firing Terry Brennan after the 1958 season.

All Brennan did was go 32–18 in five seasons. Take away our horrible 2–8 season in 1956, and he's 30–10. The season after I left, Notre Dame upset Oklahoma, 7–0, in Norman to end the

Sooners' 47-game winning streak, still the longest in college football history.

Brennan was replaced by Joe Kuharich. I'm sorry to say this, but he was not too smart, which makes me wonder how he conned the Philadelphia Eagles into giving him the first long-term contract in NFL history. In four years at Notre Dame, he went 5–5, 2–8, 5–5, and 5–5.

He was replaced in 1963 by Hugh Devore, who was making his second appearance as an interim coach. In 1945, he had filled in when Frank Leahy was serving in the Navy, and coached Notre Dame to a 7–2–1 record. But his second one-year stint resulted in a disastrous 2–7.

Then came Ara Parseghian, whom I consider Leahy's equal. I know that's heresy to a lot of Notre Dame's "subway alumni." But Parseghian took over the program when it hadn't had a winning season in five years and returned it to past glory. In his first season, Notre Dame went from 2–7 to 9–1, one of the great turn-arounds in college history.

When poor health forced him to retire in 1974 after eleven seasons, Parseghian had a 95–17–4 record and had won two national championships. It was on his watch that the university finally began accepting bowl invitations, and he coached us to victories in the Orange, Sugar, and Cotton bowls.

I couldn't stand Ara's successor, Dan Devine. I knew his act from Green Bay, where he almost ruined the franchise by trading some first-round draft picks for Dan Fouts. He knew that I knew what a phony he was, so we never got along. In four seasons with the Packers, Devine had three losing seasons and only one playoff team, which got beat by the Redskins in the first round.

He got the Notre Dame job by kissing a lot of asses at the university and in the media. He was publicity-conscious and vain. I think he had "Head Coach" stenciled in his shorts. I really got upset when Parseghian told me that Devine had moved his locker out of the stadium locker room. Ara still lived in South Bend, and he liked to come to campus to play handball.

I know what I'm talking about because, at the time, I was doing the Notre Dame games on delayed TV with Lindsey. Devine liked to brag that he wanted the game films immediately after a game so he could study them at home on Saturday night. But this was baloney, as we found out when I told George Kelly, an assistant athletic director and longtime Notre Dame man, to seal the film cans with a small bit of paper. If the paper hadn't moved when Devine brought them back on Sunday, we would know that he hadn't even opened the cans.

Guess what? Week after week, the paper never moved.

Devine almost messed up Joe Montana. During his career at Notre Dame, Montana was always in a quarterback controversy with somebody. When he was a sophomore and junior, he came off the bench to save Devine's butt several times. As a junior in 1978, he was benched in favor of Rusty Lisch before the opening game at Pitt. But when Notre Dame fell behind, he came off the bench again to save a victory—and Devine.

At the end of his senior year, Montana added to Notre Dame folklore in a 35–34 win over Houston in the Cotton Bowl. After throwing four interceptions, he had to leave the game in the third quarter because of below-normal body temperature. But after warming up with some chicken soup, he came back to lead a miraculous 23-point comeback in the final quarter.

Toward the end of the 1980 season, Devine announced that he would resign after the season for unexplained "personal reasons." That suited me fine, but then Notre Dame gave the job once held by Rockne, Leahy, and Parseghian to Gerry Faust, who had built a dynasty at Moeller High in Cincinnati.

Gerry was a devout Catholic and the biggest Notre Dame fan in the world. He was so religious that he might have discouraged some non-Catholic recruits from coming to Notre Dame. Heck, we'd always had non-Catholics on the football team. When I was playing, we even had a Jewish kid.

Inevitably, the good Catholic got devoured in the lion's den. After five seasons, Gerry had only a 30–26–1 record, so he resigned, much to the delight of all the fans who had adopted "Oust Faust" as their motto.

This time the program's savior turned out to be Lou Holtz, a good coach and a great storyteller. Although I often felt that he was too conservative, especially considering the talent he had at his disposal, I loved to be around the guy. He was really funny.

Holtz took Notre Dame to the 1988 national championship, its first since 1977, and should have had another in 1993 if the writers who voted in the Associated Press poll hadn't screwed him. Both Florida State and Notre Dame had one loss, but Florida State's loss was to us in South Bend. I still can't understand how the writers gave them the trophy over us.

When Holtz was forced out after 1996, he was only five wins shy of tying Rockne as Notre Dame's winningest coach. I swear, I don't think some of the powers that be wanted him to beat Rockne's record, so they ran him off before he got the chance.

Bob Davie, who succeeded Holtz in 1997, looked like he came straight out of central casting. He was articulate, handsome, and he knew how to coach. But poor recruiting did him in. After he went 35–25 over five years, Notre Dame didn't

renew his contract and offered the job to George O'Leary, a jour-
neyman coach who had enjoyed a couple of successful seasons
at Georgia Tech. But then he quickly had to step down because
he admitted having falsified some information on his resume.

I was surprised that Notre Dame even considered O'Leary. I
was hoping and praying they would hire Jon Gruden, then the
young head coach of the Oakland Raiders. His dad, Jim, had
been a Notre Dame assistant from 1978 to '80, so Jon had a real
interest in coming back to South Bend. He would have been the
perfect name for Notre Dame to go after and he finally would
have installed the pro-style "West Coast" passing game as our
basic attack. But the university couldn't wait until after the
Raiders had finished their season, so we ended up with O'Leary.

I was excited when Notre Dame hired Ty Willingham, because he, too, uses the West Coast offense that the best players,
the pro prospects, love to play. They don't want to play in an option offense because the NFL doesn't use it.

After two seasons, the jury is still out on Ty, but it didn't look
good to the national media in the fall of 2003 when Brian Brohm
of Trinity High in Louisville, the nation's top-rated high school
quarterback and winner of the Paul Hornung Award for best
player in the state, picked Louisville over Notre Dame.

In case you were wondering, it was against the NCAA rules
for me to recruit Brohm for Notre Dame. I think that's a crock.
Who knows better about a university or its football program than
somebody who has played there?

I got a lot of heat in 1996 when I spoke at Tim Couch's senior banquet. A lot of Kentucky fans were convinced I was trying
to recruit him for Notre Dame, but, really, I was trying to help
Bill Curry, then the Kentucky coach. Bill played center for us at

Green Bay my last two seasons, and I've always been interested in the welfare of my former teammates.

For whatever reasons, it's not as easy to recruit for Notre Dame today as it was when I played. The university no longer has its pick of the best Catholic players, and the entrance requirements and academic standards are higher than those of most of Notre Dame's competitors for the national championship.

Still, win or lose, there's something special about Notre Dame. The spirit is always there. It's the only university with its own national TV contract. And, of course, when you're a Notre Dame football hero, you become a living legend. Whenever I go to Europe, I have far more people who come up to me because of Notre Dame than the Packers.

A Heisman Trophy winner from Notre Dame is never forgotten. I've sold or given away a lot of my trophies. In fact, after I won the Heisman, I gave it to my mom. I told her she had earned it for pointing me to Notre Dame and supporting me all these years. Well, a few years later, I got a call from Notre Dame telling me they were establishing a special room to display the Heismans won by Notre Dame players.

So I borrowed the one I gave mom and sent it to them, which didn't please her at all. In fact, she raised so much hell about it that I finally called Rudy Riska, who's in charge of the Heismans for the Downtown Athletic Club in New York, and asked him to authorize the making of an exact duplicate for me.

But then Notre Dame had its own replicas made, and sent back the originals. So now I have two Heismans and I only need one. After mom died, I gave the replica to the Packers to put outside the room that they named after me when they did their $400 million renovation a few years ago. There are six such rooms, and they're named after Lombardi, Starr, Lambeau, Willie Davis, Johnny Blood, and me.

Then I got an offer from restaurateur Joe Walsh, who owns The Stadium in Garrison, New York. At the time, a couple of Heismans already had been sold. The estate of Yale's Larry Kelley, the 1936 winner, had sold his for $328,110 so his nieces and nephews could have an inheritance. O. J. Simpson sold the 1968 Heisman he had won at Southern Cal for $230,000 to help pay the legal fees he had incurred in his double-murder trial.

Walsh paid me $250,000 for my original, and I used the money to establish an annual scholarship at Notre Dame for a good student from the Louisville area.

That left me with no Heisman Trophy. Because almost everybody who comes to the house wants to see it, I called Riska again and asked if he would authorize the making of a second replica for me. That's another $7,000. But at least I have it to display at Derby time and any other appropriate occasion.

Every year, I try my damnedest to make the Heisman dinner in New York. A lot of ex-winners don't, and that really pisses me off. This is the highest award a college player can get. We all should be grateful that we won it, because there's nothing else in sports quite like it.

In the past few years, I've been lobbying the Downtown Athletic Club to make a change in the voting procedures. Instead of voting at the end of the regular season, the ballots should be returned after all the bowl games. Sometimes, if two or three candidates are very close in the voters' minds, how they play in the bowls could make a difference one way or another. So far I've had no success, but I'll keep trying.

25.

TO ERR IS HUMAN . . .

I've been accused of many things in my life, but being a racist was not one of them—not until March 30, 2004, that is. Because of some stupid remarks I made before a dinner in Detroit, I suddenly found myself the topic of discussion on virtually every cable TV network and radio talk show in the nation. It was the worst thing to happen to me since the gambling suspension in 1963.

It began, innocently enough, when I flew from Louisville to Detroit to see my longtime friend Mike Lucci inducted into the University of Michigan Hall of Fame. I was picked up at the airport by Ron Kramer, a longtime member of the Wolverine Hall of Fame, and taken to the Renaissance Center downtown, where the banquet was to be held.

At a reception before the banquet, a reporter from a Detroit radio station asked me about a variety of football topics, most concerning Notre Dame and the Packers.

In trying to explain why Notre Dame hadn't been competitive for the national championship in recent years, I said:

"As far as Notre Dame is concerned, we're going to have to ease it up a little bit. We can't stay as strict as we are as far as the academic structure is concerned because we've got to get the black athlete. We must get the black athlete to compete. We open with Michigan, then go to Michigan State and Purdue— those are the first three games, you know, and you can't play a schedule like this unless you have the black athlete today."

I didn't think anymore about it until I got to my Louisville office the next day. I had more than thirty requests for interviews from both the national and local media. My wife, Angela, told me that because of my remarks the previous night in Detroit, I was accused of being a racist for saying that Notre Dame had to lower its academic standards in order to recruit black athletes.

At first I was angry. But the more I thought about it and listened to replays of my remarks, I could understand why many African-Americans were offended. My point was that Notre Dame's academic standards were too high to recruit most of the top one hundred prospects in the nation, the large majority of whom are black, the future pros who these days are going to Florida State, Miami, Tennessee, and many of our other competitors for the national title.

From a recruiting standpoint, Notre Dame had been playing on an unlevel field. The university had to either forget about competing for the national title or do something to its entrance requirements to recruit some of those kids.

Once, when I was in Lou Holtz's office, he pulled out a sheet that he had just gotten back from the registrar's office. It was a list of the top fifty high school football seniors in America. Beside the name of all but four or five, somebody had written "No," meaning don't even bother contacting them. But I never should have mentioned race in my comments. I should have simply said that Notre Dame had a hard time recruiting the top athletes in football, both black *and* white. For example, at Notre Dame many students are required to take calculus as freshmen. That's too demanding for many kids, including most athletes, black or white, who often come from a weak academic background.

Unfortunately, my argument about academic requirements was overwhelmed by the question of whether I was a racist. I was forced to defend myself, which is difficult for any white man of my age and background to do. The longer and louder you proclaim you're not a racist, the more some people assume that you are.

I well remember the days when Louisville was segregated, when blacks had separate restrooms and water fountains. They couldn't swim in the public pools; they had to sit in the back of the bus and in the "colored only" section of public lunch counters.

I remember when I was at St. Patrick's, playing basketball against a team from St. Augustine's, a black parish school. They beat us, 66–4. A couple of their players invited me to come to their neighborhood to play playground ball. I did, not to make any kind of social statement but because I knew the black kids were the best basketball players and playing against them could only make me better.

At Flaget High, I didn't have black teammates and we rarely played against them. Meanwhile the all-black high school in Louisville, Central, was producing great African-American athletes such as Cassius Clay (Muhammad Ali) and Lenny Lyles.

In 1954, after I had gone to Notre Dame, Lenny was one of a handful of blacks who integrated the football team at the University of Louisville, the first predominantly white institution south of the Mason-Dixon Line to recruit blacks. Sad to say, but I really didn't know Lenny until we both were in the NFL, me with the Packers and him with the Colts.

In my senior year at Notre Dame, after I had won the Heisman Trophy, I learned that a certain downtown restaurant had refused to serve Tom Hawkins, a black sophomore basketball star, because of his race. That bothered me. I felt that, black or white, the athletes at Notre Dame had to stick together. So I rounded up about six other football players and went down to the restaurant. I had a little clout because of my status at ND. I got up in the owner's face and told him that if he didn't serve Hawkins, we were going to rip the place apart, then and there. He backed down in a hurry. He didn't need any publicity about Paul Hornung leading a protest against his discriminatory policies.

Hawkins, who later played pro ball with the L.A. Lakers, never forgot that. Years later, he'd tell the story about how I was the ringleader of the group that stood up for him.

When I arrived in Green Bay, there weren't many black players in the NFL. So the first thing Lombardi did after he got Willie Davis was to assign him to room with a white guy in preseason camp. That was unheard of in those days, but Lombardi wanted to send the message that we were all in this together and that color didn't matter. Still, when we won the 1962 NFL championship, we had only four black players on our 37-man team: Herb Adderley, Willie Davis, Elijah Pitts, and Willie Wood. All but Pitts made the Hall of Fame.

In those days, after we broke camp in some years, we'd spend a week in Winston-Salem, North Carolina. The white players stayed at the Oaks Hotel, but the blacks were forced to stay on the campus of Winston-Salem State, the black college in town where the great Earl "The Pearl" Monroe played basketball from 1963 to '67. Whenever they would complain about discrimination, I'd tease them.

"You guys aren't fooling me," I said. "Over there you don't have any coaches to check on you, so you guys are out running the streets at night, chasing coeds. Hell, I'll change places with you."

After Lenny Lyles and I retired from the NFL and came home to Louisville, Frank Metts brokered a deal that made us partners in a shopping center that we still own together. When reporters called Lenny to ask him about my remarks in Detroit, he said they were regrettable, but that he knew for sure that I wasn't a racist. I appreciated that.

By early afternoon on the day following my trip to Detroit, the furor was so intense that I wasn't sure what to do. Somebody at Notre Dame issued a press release deploring my comments and saying they didn't represent the university's point of view. But the release indicated that the university had missed my point. It pointed out that 55.2 percent of the current players are black, but I never talked about the *quantity* of Notre Dame's black players. I was referring to the *quality*, the number of the top one hundred prospects who come to Notre Dame.

The university also said that it hadn't changed its admission standards over the years. In other words, they were basically the same when Notre Dame had great teams as when they had mediocre ones. That may be true, but many of our rivals *have* changed their standards, lowering them in order to recruit the quality prospects.

Well, I certainly didn't want to say anything that would make matters worse. So at my request, Bob Stallings, my Louisville attorney, called a public-relations man who recommended that I not say anything and duck the media. But Angela pointed out that hiding wasn't my style. She urged me to be the same sort of stand-up guy I'd always been and use the media to apologize to anyone whom I might have offended and ask their forgiveness.

I took her advice. I wrote a statement and read it on Terry Meiners' popular afternoon show on WHAS radio. "It was not my intention to insult African-Americans or to imply that any university should compromise its academic standards to accommodate athletes," I said. "As a Notre Dame graduate, I'm as proud of the university's academic reputation as I am of its football tradition, and I'm equally proud of the university's long-standing progressive policies toward minorities. I apologize if my remarks offended anyone."

That night we drove to each of Louisville's four television stations and did live interviews. We responded to calls from the Associated Press, ESPN, and Fox's *The Best Damned Sports Show Period*. I talked to reporters from Green Bay, Milwaukee, Detroit, New York, Los Angeles, New Orleans, Miami, and, of course, Louisville. We couldn't do them all—I especially regret that we couldn't work out something with Paula Zahn of CNN—but we did the best we could.

Some commentators bashed me completely, but others took the position that while what I said and the way I said it was dumb, I had made a point worth considering. I especially liked a column by Michael Wilbon, an African-American sports columnist for the *Washington Post* and co-host with Tony Kornheiser on ESPN's popular *Pardon the Interruption.*

He pointed out that he and I had eaten dinner together several times with our mutual friend the late Dick Schaap, and that he knew from those meetings that I wasn't a racist. He also said that Notre Dame hadn't been winning not only because of the tough academic requirements, but because we played a boring offense that turned off the top prospects. I couldn't agree more.

The only thing I didn't like, in fact, was when he said, "It would be easy to dismiss a 68-year-old white guy from Kentucky, and someone who unfairly was awarded the 1956 Heisman over the more deserving Jim Brown, as being a product of a certain time and place." To me, that sounded suspiciously like the same kind of slur and broad generalization that I was being accused of. But I let it pass. The last thing I needed was more media exposure.

After doing as many interviews as I could on Wednesday, I spent most of Thursday talking to the people with whom I do business. Much to my relief and gratitude, they hung with me. They weren't happy with me, of course, but they were willing to give me the benefit of the doubt. I appreciated that. I would have hated to see all those years of happiness and goodwill ended by some stupid remarks on my part.

I was especially pleased that my former Packer teammates, black and white, stood up for me. Consider Marv Fleming, for example. When we were teammates from 1963 to '66, he was the only one who took my advice about investing in Kentucky Fried Chicken stock. During the firestorm, Marv sent me an e-mail saying, "I love you and know what you were trying to get across. People are always looking for issues these days. I still have my wonderful investment money you got me into. God bless good people like you."

Marv, of course, is an African-American. After all these years, my teammates were still throwing blocks so I could run to daylight.

In mid-May, however, things took a turn for the worse. I got a letter from Kevin White, Notre Dame's athletic director, that read as if it had been written by an attorney. Notre Dame didn't want me to do any more broadcasts of Irish football games. Reading between the lines, I could tell that Notre Dame—or, rather, some members of the board of trustees—had decided it was more important to curry favor with the politically correct crowd than to stand up for me. I'm sure White was caught in the middle. But the thing that galled me was that instead of accepting responsibility for the decision, Notre Dame tried to blame it on Westwood One. Well, that was a lie. I know, because I'd talked to Larry Michael at Westwood One.

I think Notre Dame was afraid I might sue the university for defamation of character or something—which, of course, I'd never do—or that my friends at Ford might pull out of their sponsorship deals at Notre Dame in support of me. The university wanted me to go quietly and act as if I had made the decision to stop doing Notre Dame broadcasts on my own. But that's not my style. I'm not going to lie, and I'm not going to let them lie. I'm going to tell the truth. That's something I learned at an early age, something that was reinforced constantly during my years at Notre Dame.

When my friends heard that Notre Dame wouldn't forgive one of its family who had repeatedly apologized, they were very angry. Jim Morse even had the guts to stick up for me when, as

I've mentioned, he accepted the Ed "Moose" Krause award from the Monogram Club.

"I've known Paul since 1953 and played with him for four years here at Notre Dame," Morse said, "and I can tell you there's not a prejudiced bone in his body. Did he say something dumb? Did he make a mistake? Sure, he did. But I think it provides Notre Dame a great opportunity to stand up and be the classy university it is by simply saying, 'Paul Hornung made a mistake, but he's one of our own. He acknowledged his mistake and he has apologized. We accept his apology and hope he continues on the Notre Dame broadcasts.' End of story.

"So let me give you a positive to think about. How many of you here have read or heard or seen stories about Angela Butcher? Who has ever heard of her? Let me tell you who she is. Angela is a Notre Dame graduate. She also is an African-American. Her education here at Notre Dame was made possible by a scholarship endowed by Paul Hornung. So I submit to you that Paul has done far more good things for Notre Dame— things that aren't reported—than this one mistake that has been widely reported."

When I heard about Jimmy's remarks, I got a little choked up. What a friend! What a stand-up guy! It made me feel a lot better about giving up something that has been a big part of my life for more than three decades.

26

THE END ZONE

'm not going to be doing the Notre Dame games anymore because I don't want to be somewhere I'm not wanted. I'm sad and disappointed that certain people in the university's hierarchy wouldn't forgive me. But I'll always pull for Notre Dame, and I'll continue to support the university through my scholarships. Notre Dame is bigger and more important than any one person or group of people.

How can I possibly be bitter about anything? I really have enjoyed a golden life. The Notre Dame years were awesome. It was a privilege to be a football player at a special place where history, tradition, and academics are revered. I met some wonderful people at Notre Dame, many of whom are still friends. Whenever I go back, I'm always recognized, which is nice when you haven't played a down of football in thirty-eight years.

At Green Bay, I played for the greatest football coach ever, in my opinion. I'm not at all surprised that Lombardi is still quoted and admired. I'm sure he would have been every bit as success- ful in the military or in business as he was in football. He just had a burning desire for excellence and the talent to transfer it to each of his players.

He was the most influential man in my life. Under him, a Green Bay Packer had three responsibilities: family, religion, and the team, in that order. He was tough and he always meant business, certainly, but he also talked about love in the context of being successful by observing the old values. "You can't have success unless there is love," he said. "Love for your teammates and for the game."

I've always tried to keep football in perspective. Hell, nobody wanted to win more than I did and nobody tried harder. But when the game was over, win or lose, I was going to be me and have some fun. I guess I should feel guilty about that, because I was different from many of my teammates.

I remember one year when I fumbled five times in a close loss to the Bears. I very seldom fumbled, but that day I just couldn't hold on to the damned ball. After the game, Bart was sobbing as he sat in front of his locker. Despite my fumbles, he had almost pulled it out for us. I thought, "What the hell is he crying for? I should be the one who's crying." I've been disap- pointed after losses, but I don't think I've ever cried. I don't know why.

My life in television and radio has been rewarding in a differ- ent way. For one thing, I've made more money from it than I ever did from football. For another, it was great fun, not to men- tion a privilege, to work with Lindsey Nelson all those years.

But I'm hardly the only former Packer who has prospered. In fact, I'm sure Lombardi would be pleased to know that most of his "boys" had a life after football, mostly because of what they had learned from him about discipline and hard work and doing things right.

Center Jim Ringo was a successful coach at various places. Unfortunately, he's currently suffering the effects of dementia. Guards Fuzzy Thurston and Jerry Kramer live in Green Bay and Idaho, respectively. Fuzzy, who survived his throat cancer, owns Fuzzy's, a successful restaurant in Green Bay. Kramer is in demand as a motivational speaker.

Hall of Fame tackle Forrest Gregg, who went into coaching and took the Cincinnati Bengals to the Super Bowl in the 1981 season, lives in Dallas with his family—and the first nickel he ever earned. The "other" tackle, Bob Skoronski, is the CEO of his own company in Green Bay and enjoys his friendship with Bobby Knight, the renowned basketball coach.

Tight end Ron Kramer owns a sales company in Detroit and has been involved with more charities than anyone I've ever known. He has been my guest at the Kentucky Derby for more than forty-five years. Another tight end, Marv Fleming, made a small fortune on KFC, as mentioned. He also earned seven Super Bowl rings with the Packers, Dolphins, and Redskins.

Max McGee, my old running buddy, used some of the money he earned as the founder of the Chi-Chi's restaurant chain to start a juvenile diabetes center in Minneapolis. Flanker Boyd Dowler is still an NFL scout.

Bart Starr owns a successful real estate holding company in Birmingham, Alabama. He also speaks at a lot of banquets. After a few divorces, fullback Jimmy Taylor is now happily married to a veteran Delta stewardess, who helps him in various business ventures.

Four of our defensive stars—Ray Nitschke, Leroy Caffey, Ron Kostelnik, and Henry Jordan—have died.

Defensive end Willie Davis owns five radio stations in Los Angeles and Milwaukee. Before that, he made a lot of money from a Schlitz distributorship in the Watts section of Los Angeles. Safety Willie Wood and cornerback Herb Adderley live in Washington, D.C., and Philadelphia, respectively. Both do a lot of PR work in their home cities, as well as Wisconsin.

Cornerback Jesse Whittenton is involved with golf enterprises and has had some pretty good success. In fact, at one of his golf courses he had a young pro he thought very highly of. Jesse and his cousin Don staked the course pro $5,000 to try to make it on the pro tour, telling him that if he ran out of money, he could always come back to the club and get his old job back. That pro was Lee Trevino, and Jesse and Don became his agents for a number of years.

Linebacker Dan Currie does security work for the Stardust hotel in Las Vegas. Defensive end Bill Quinlan saved his own life when he quit drinking seventeen years ago.

In the first chapter, I lied about having no regrets. I have a few, as Sinatra sang it, but they're probably not the kind you might expect.

I regret that Sherrill Sipes got injured during our sophomore year at Notre Dame and never got to show the world the kind of football player he was. Had he stayed healthy, he might have won the 1956 Heisman instead of me.

I regret that Notre Dame forced out Frank Leahy before I had a chance to play for him, then failed to recognize Terry Brennan for doing a great job under very difficult circumstances.

I regret that I didn't get to have dinner with Kim Novak in New York after my junior season.

I regret that Joe Montana will never enter the College Football Hall of Fame until they change the stupid rule that says only All-Americans are eligible.

I regret that Jerry Kramer and Fuzzy Thurston aren't in the Pro Football Hall of Fame. I'm prejudiced, of course, but I hardly think I'm the only one who would say they were the best pair of offensive guards ever.

I regret that I got Cosell into a gin rummy game with Max when Humble Howard came to Green Bay to do a documentary about us and got clipped for about eight hundred dollars. (Well, on second thought, maybe I don't regret that so much.)

I regret that I didn't get to play — and I mean *play*, not just make a cameo appearance — in at least one Super Bowl.

I regret that the NFL hasn't done better by the former players in its pension plan. Ron Kramer, for example, has undergone replacement surgery in the shoulders, hips, and knees. All his physical problems were the result of football injuries, but the NFL didn't pay a nickel for his surgeries. His personal insurance paid for them. That's simply not right. Hell, today's players wouldn't be nearly as well off if it hadn't been for us.

I regret that I didn't give the movies a serious shot. I did play a bit part in a movie called *Devil's Brigade*. I played a cowboy who started a fight in a bar. It was no Academy Award performance, I guarantee you that, but I still get a check for twelve dollars every time the movie is shown somewhere.

I regret that I didn't get to tell Lombardi how much I loved him just before he died. He is the greatest man I've ever known,

and I've met more than my share of U.S. presidents, Army gen-
erals, movie stars, and multimillionaires.

I regret that I couldn't have spent more time with Max's sons,
Dallas and Maxwell. Dallas is a juvenile diabetic and Maxwell
has Down syndrome. When he says, "I love you, Paul," it makes
my heart break.

And, sure, I regret that I got caught gambling and had to sit
out the 1963 season, but I don't regret being a gambler. Ever
since I was a kid sneaking into Churchill Downs and Miles Park,
I've enjoyed gambling. To me, the stock market is just a legal
way for the "Golden Boy" to gamble.

Besides gambling and football, the other constant in my life
has been women. Looking back, I realize I never played a down
of football while I was married. I retired soon after I met Pat, and
I was ten years out of the league when I met Angela. But I was
close four or five other times. There were Janie and Doness and
Donna and Della and Sandy and Debbie. They were all great
ladies and I toyed with the idea of marrying them, but none of
them worked out.

But the best women in my life were my mom, who passed
away in 1990, and Angela, the perfect girl for me. When Max
married Denise, his current wife, he told her, "Honey, anything
I did before we met doesn't count." And she came up with the
perfect reply: "Surely you don't think that Angela and I were just
sitting around, waiting for you two SOBs, do you?"

I'm sure that during my playing days I wasn't considered a
good role model for the nation's youth. But the way times have
changed, I'd look like an altar boy if I played today. I never beat
up a woman, carried a gun or a knife, shot somebody, or got ar-

rested for disturbing the peace. I never even experimented with drugs during the season.

On a lesser level, I never taunted an opponent after scoring a touchdown. Had any of us done that, we would have been on the first plane out of Green Bay, gone as quickly as Jim Ringo when Lombardi found out that he had hired an agent.

All I did, really, was seek out fun wherever I could find it. Everything was all tied in together—the drinking, the womanizing, the partying, the traveling, the gambling. And, of course, football made it all possible.

I won almost everything I could win playing the game. I was all-state in high school, a Heisman winner in college, and an MVP in the NFL. And I think I'm the only player who ever won the top college honor while playing quarterback, and then won the NFL's top honor at a different position, halfback.

I was far from being as good a player as Jim Brown or Forrest Gregg or Dick Butkus, but I guarantee that no football star ever got more out of the available opportunities, both fun and money, than I did. Mostly, I'm gratified by the thought that a lot of my contemporaries felt I was the most versatile player of my time, and one of the best in the big games.

I'm on life's back nine, and I have no idea what's ahead for me. I want to stay active in something because my energy level is still high. But I'm also going to try to relax and smell the roses more than I have. I love to play golf with Angela, who's one of the top woman golfers in the Louisville area, and I enjoy Louie, the pet French bulldog that we bought several months ago.

Angela is Louie's disciplinarian, the Lombardi. When he's trying to bite somebody or chew up a pillow, she scolds him. I'm more inclined to let him go. I guess it's a good thing I was never a coach or a parent.

I don't know why, but I never really wanted to have kids. I loved my teammates' kids and my friends' kids, but I just never saw myself as anything more than "Uncle Paul." I suppose my kids are the ones who are on a Paul Hornung scholarship at Notre Dame, or the ones who benefit from the money I give and raise for charities. You wouldn't believe some of the letters I get from those kids at Notre Dame. They're just beautiful.

Since I didn't play in a Super Bowl, I'm not qualified to discuss how thrilling it must be to win one. But I've always thought that there could be no bigger thrill for a Kentuckian than to have a horse run in the Derby. Not even win it, just be in the starting gate when it springs open on the first Saturday in May.

I've owned all or part of four or five horses, but none of them was nearly good enough to be a Derby horse. I've also never been asked to do any Derby stuff on TV. So every year I watch from the stands with my buddies. You might think it would be old hat for me after all these years, but every Derby is just as fresh and exciting to me as the first one I saw, back in the early '50s. If you're a Kentuckian, you'll understand my feelings. If you're not, there's no way I can make you understand.

As the years have gone by, the knowledge that I was loved and respected by Lombardi and my teammates has been far more important to me than any trophy or award or contract.

After I was inducted into the pro Hall of Fame, Herb Adderley grabbed me in a bear hug and said, "We're on the same team again, man, except now it's forever. Forget about everything else. This team is forever."

So are the friendships I've been fortunate enough to make.

When he was interviewed by *Sports Illustrated* for an article about me in 2002, Ron Kramer said, "People always thought he was a playboy because women loved him. That's true, they did. But his friends loved him, too. And their wives and kids, too. And anybody else who was lucky enough to meet him. He's charming and generous and just a beautiful guy to know."

To me, that's more precious than gold.

Appendix

PAUL HORNUNG'S CAREER STATISTICS

NOTRE DAME

YEAR	ATT	COMP	INT	YDS	TD	TC	YDS	AVG
1954	19	5	1	36	0	23	59	6.9
1955	103	46	10	743	9	92	472	5.1
1956	111	59	13	917	3	94	420	4.5
TOTALS	233	110	24	1696	12	209	1051	5.0

YEAR	REC	YDS	AVG	P RET	YDS	KO RET	YDS	INT	YDS
1954	0	0	0.0	1	6	1	58	3	94
1955	0	0	0.0	0	0	6	109	5	59
1956	3	26	8.7	4	63	16	496	2	59
TOTALS	3	26	8.7	5	69	23	663	10	212

YEAR	TD	PAT	FG	PTS
1954	2	6	0	18
1955	6	5	2	47
1956	7	14	0	56
TOTALS	15	25	2	121

Green Bay

RUSHING

YEAR	G	ATT	YDS	AVG	TD
1957	12	60	319	5.3	3
1958	12	69	310	4.5	2
1959	12	152	681	4.5	7
1960	12	160	671	4.2	13
1961	12	127	597	4.7	8
1962	9	57	219	3.8	5
1964	14	103	415	4.0	5
1965	12	89	299	3.4	5
1966	9	76	200	2.6	2
TOTALS	104	893	3,711	4.2	50

RECEIVING

REC	YDS	AVG	TD
6	34	5.7	0
15	137	9.1	0
15	113	7.5	0
28	257	9.2	2
15	145	9.7	2
9	168	18.7	2
9	98	10.9	0
19	336	17.7	3
14	192	13.7	3
130	1,480	11.4	12

PASSING

YEAR	ATT	COMP	%	YDS	YPA	TD	INT	RATING
1957	6	1	16.7	-1	-0.17	0	0	39.6
1958	1	0	0.0	0	0.00	0	0	39.6
1959	8	5	62.5	95	11.88	2	0	143.2
1960	16	6	37.5	118	7.38	2	0	103.6
1961	5	3	60.0	42	8.40	1	0	126.7
1962	6	4	66.7	80	13.33	0	2	70.1
1964	10	3	30.0	25	2.50	0	1	0.0
1965	2	1	50.0	19	9.50	0	1	43.8
1966	1	1	100.0	5	5.00	0	0	87.5
TOTALS	55	24	43.6	383	6.96	5	4	67.5

SCORING

YEAR	PTS	FG	FGA	%	PAT	PAT	%	FUM	TOT. TD
1957	18	0	4	0.0	0	0	—	2	3
1958	67	11	21	52.4	22	23	95.7	1	2
1959	94	7	17	41.2	31	32	96.9	7	7
1960	176	15	28	53.6	41	41	100.0	3	15

1961	146	15	22	68.2	41	41	100.0	1	10
1962	74	6	10	60.0	14	14	100.0	1	7
1964	107	12	38	31.6	41	43	95.3	4	5
1965	0	0	0	—	0	0	—	2	8
1966	0	0	0	—	0	0	—	1	5
TOTALS	760	66	140	47.1	190	194	97.9	22	62

Index

278   INDEX